DEVELOPMENT DIALOGUES OF GROWING ECONOMIES

DEVELOPMENT DIALOGUES OF GROWING ECONOMIES

V. B. Jugale

SERIALS PUBLICATIONS
New Delhi (India)

First Published - 2008

ISBN: 978-81-8387-151-8

Published by

SERIALS PUBLICATIONS
4830/24, Prahlad Street, Ansari Road
Darya Ganj, New Delhi-110002 (India)
Phone : +91-11-23245225. Fax : +91-11-23272135
E-mail: serials@satyam.net.in
www.serialspublications.com

CONTENTS

PREFACE

The Sectoral growth experiences in developing economies since the World War-II have various dimensions. The paradoxical but practical growth paradigms have been locally and domestically demonstrated as a replica of wide-range of experiences in the growing economies. Backwardness in fact, provides ample opportunities development. Development is a discontinuous spontaneous overflow of socio-economic change in the institutional outlooks. In a democratic set up, the perception and percolation of such ideologies among the common public remains much slower, if the abilities and capabilities of the people are imperfect. Imperfection is an obstacle in the process of development. Removal of such imperfections is one of the institutional efforts of the states.

This book introduces such growth experiences empirically identified by the experts. Fadzlan Sufian has identified the efficient management of non-banking financial intermediaries by using non-stochastic frontier analysis with non-discretionary input variables. An access of credit to the poors in South Africa has been explored by Francis Nathan Okurut. An exhaustive household data from 1995-2000 has been used to register the change. Rudra Prakash Pradhan exhibited the present Scenario and future course of action for reasonable social infrastructure in India. Joachin Myemeck Binam and *et, al.* have introduced the role of credit access for improving the Cocoa production in West African countries.

Kishor Sharma demonstrated the intra-industry linkages and trading activities in respect of Australia. Fisheries policies and Southern Blue Fin Tuna Fishery in Australia has been evaluated by R. Sathiendra Kumar. The Smithian Classical dilemma and the Sen's Public Action has been comparatively introduced by Ratan Lal Basu.

An effort of G-8 for growing the economies has been symbolically narrated by Ismail Shariff and *et al.* Drs. Mazhar Islam and others have linked their analysis to FDI, R&D, experts and growth of Brazil and Chile. An empirical evidences of growth and unemployment have been noticed by Raja Nazrin and Eu Chye Tan.

There are two experiences of Bangladesh. The comparative analysis of domestic and foreign banks operations in Bangladesh has been accounted by Abdus Samad. While Hedayet Chowdhury has compared the technical efficiencies in formal and informal manufacturing industries in Bangladesh.

The challenges of govt. expenditure in Botswana is an area of interest to Christopher Mupimpila. Fotis Ch atzitheodoridis and others have compared the issues of sheep & goat farming in respect of environment concerns in typical Greek Island. A doubt on under valuation for promoting the exports has been expressed by Saadiah Mohammad and Mahendhiran Nair. The institutional factors of sharing the burden of adjustments for emerging economies has been explored by Hiller Neumann and John Meyer.

This volume contains some scattered views on various dimensions of development. The efforts made by the selected countries and the experiences sought by the paper writers are the insights to the potential countries of the globe. The readers will enjoy these articles.

The Editor express his sincere thanks to the Serials and its family for encouragement and inspiration to mediate between the writers and the readers. The Editor feel indebted for the contributions made by the paper writers of this volume.

THE EFFICIENCY OF NON-BANK FINANCIAL INTERMEDIARIES: A Non-Stochastic Frontier Analysis with Non-Discretionary Input Variable

FADZLAN SUFIAN
Bumiputra-Commerce Bank Berhad (BCB)
University of Malaya (UM)

This paper investigates the performance of Malaysian non-bank financial institutions during the period of 2000-2004. Several efficiency estimates of individual NBFIs are evaluated using the non-parametric Data Envelopment Analysis (DEA) method. To examine the impact of risk factor on NBFIs efficiency, we have incorporated provisions for defaulted loans as a non-discretionary input variable in the analysis. The findings suggest that during the period of study, scale inefficiency dominates pure technical inefficiency in the Malaysian NBFI sector. We have found that the merchant banks have exhibited higher technical efficiency compared to its finance companies peers. The empirical findings suggest that scale efficiency tends to be more sensitive to the exclusion of risk factor, implying that potential economies of scale may be overestimated when risk factors are excluded. As the actual potential economies of scale may significantly be lower than initially expected, policy makers should be more cautious in promoting mergers as a mean to achieve greater financial institutions' efficiency by attaining better economies of scale.

JEL Classification: *G21; G28.*

Keywords: *Non-Bank Financial Institutions, Data Envelopment Analysis (DEA), Risk.*

1. INTRODUCTION

Non-Bank Financial Institutions (NBFIs) play an important dual role in a financial system. Traditionally NBFIs comprise of a mixed bag of institutions that includes all financial institutions, which are not classified as commercial banks. They complement the role of commercial banks, filling in financial intermediation gaps by offering a range of products and services that they offered. Nevertheless, they also compete with commercial banks, forcing the latter to be more efficient and responsive to their customers needs. Most NBFIs are also actively involved in the securities markets and in the mobilization and allocation of long-term financial resources. The state of development of NBFIs is usually a good indicator to the state of development of a country's financial system as a whole.

Corresponding Author: *E-mail: fadzlan.sufian@cimb.com; fadzlan14@gmail.com*

The importance to investigate the efficiency and productivity of Malaysian NBFIs could be best justified by the fact that in Malaysia, the NBFIs play important roles in complementing the facilities offered by the commercial banks and are the key players in the development of the capital markets in Malaysia. The existence of Banking Financial Institutions (BFIs) and NBFIs, supported by efficient money and capital markets, keeps the financial sector complete, while enhancing the overall growth of the economy. Although Malaysia is moving towards a full market based economy, its capital markets are still at its infancy. As a sophisticated and well-developed capital markets are considered as the hallmark for a market-based economy worldwide, study of this nature is particularly important as the health and development of the capital market rely largely on the performance of the NBFIs. Hence, efficient and productive NBFIs are expected to enhance the Malaysian capital markets in its pursuit to move towards a full market based economy.

The main motivation for this study is the Malaysia's Financial Sector Master Plan (FSMP), a long-term development plan charting the future direction of the financial services industry in Malaysia to achieve a more competitive, resilient and efficient financial system (see BNM Financial Sector Master Plan, 2001). Among the measures outlined in the plan is further liberalization of the banking sector, ahead of the opening of the financial sector to foreign competitions in 2007. Despite the progress in financial liberalization that was pursued during the 1990, which saw the banking sector expanding at a rapid pace, earlier findings have suggested that the management of Malaysian commercial banks were inefficient (Okuda and Hashimoto, 2004). The study attempts to highlight the effectiveness of microeconomic reforms introduced by the Malaysian government to enhance the competitiveness of the Malaysian financial services industry.

The study will also be the first to investigate the sources of productivity of NBFI in a developing economy. Despite the significance of the NBFI sector towards economic developments, studies that attempt to investigate this issue are relatively scarce. Over the years, while there have been extensive literature examining the productivity and efficiency of banking industries in various countries, empirical works on NBFIs productivity and efficiency are still in its infancy. To the best of our knowledge, there has been no microeconomic study performed in this area of research with respect to the NBFIs.

Since its introduction by Charnes *et al.* (1978), researchers have welcomed Data Envelopment Analysis (DEA) as a methodology for performance evaluation (Gregoriou and Zhou, 2005). DEA has many advantages over traditional parametric techniques such as regression techniques. While regression analysis approximates the efficiency of banks under investigation relative to the average performance, DEA in contrast, focuses on the yearly observations of individual banks and optimizes the performance measure of each bank. Constructing a separate frontier for each of the years under study is a critical issue in a dynamic business environment because a financial institution may be the most efficient in one year but may not be in the following year. In the Malaysian context, it becomes more important, as there is an ongoing liberalization in the banking sector over the estimation period. A separate frontier will highlight any significant changes taking place in the sector that are induced by Bank Negara Malaysia's (BNM) supervisory policies.

By applying the non-parametric Data Envelopment Analysis (DEA) methodology, we attempt to investigate the efficiency of Malaysian non-bank financial institutions during the period of 2000-2004. The preferred non-parametric Data Envelopment Analysis (DEA) methodology has allowed us to distinguish between three different types of efficiency, such as technical, pure technical and scale efficiencies. Additionally we have performed a series of parametric and non-parametric tests to examine whether the merchant banks and finance companies were drawn from the same population.

During the period of study, the empirical findings suggest that, the Malaysian merchant banks have exhibited mean overall or technical efficiency of 69.6 per cent while the finance companies have exhibited lower mean technical efficiency of 44.7 per cent. Overall, the results suggest that scale inefficiency dominates pure technical inefficiency effects in determining Malaysian NBFIs overall or technical inefficiency. The findings also seem to suggest that scale efficiency tend to be much more sensitive to the exclusion of risk factors, implying that potential economies of scale may be overestimated when risk factors are excluded.

This paper is set out as follows: The second section will provide a brief overview of the Malaysian financial system. Section 3 reviews the related studies. Section 4 outlines the approaches to the measurement and estimation of efficiency change. Section 5 discusses the results and finally Section 6 concludes.

2. BRIEF OVERVIEW OF THE MALAYSIAN FINANCIAL SYSTEM

The Malaysian financial system can broadly be divided into the banking system and the non-bank financial intermediaries. These two banking institutions are different with respect to their activities. For a well functioning financial market along with the BFIs, NBFIs have an important role to uplift the economic activity. These two financial sectors can simultaneously build up and strengthen the financial system of the country. The banking system is the largest component, accounting for approximately 70 per cent of the total assets of the financial system. The banking system can be further divided into three main groups namely the commercial banks, finance companies and the merchant banks.

The commercial banks are the main players in the banking system. They are the largest and most significant providers of funds in the banking system. As at end-2004, there were 10 domestically incorporated and 13 locally incorporated foreign commercial banks in Malaysia. Legally, Malaysian commercial banks enjoy the widest scope of permissible activities and are able to engage in a full range of banking services. Traditionally, Malaysian commercial banks main functions include retail-banking services, trade financing facilities, treasury services, cross border payment services and custody services. Apart from the more traditional activities, Malaysian commercial banks are also allowed to engage in foreign exchange activities i.e. to buy, sell, and lend foreign currencies and the only financial institutions allowed to provide current account facilities.

Finance companies formed the second largest group of deposit taking institutions in Malaysia. There were 10 domestically incorporated finance companies in Malaysia as at end-2004. Traditionally, finance companies specialize in consumption credit, comprising mainly of hire purchase financing, leasing, housing loans, block discounting, and secured personal loans. The finance companies are allowed to accept savings and fixed deposits from the public, but are prohibited from providing current account facilities. They are also not allowed to engage in foreign exchange transactions compared to their commercial banks counterparts. During the later part of the last decade, the finance companies began to expand its traditional role in retail financing to include wholesale banking as well.

Merchant banks emerged in the Malaysian banking scene in the late 1970s, marking an important milestone in the development of the financial system alongside of the corporate development of the country. As the country's small businesses prospered and grew into large corporations, the banking needs of the nation became larger and more sophisticated, requiring more bulk financing and complex banking services.

Merchant banks filled the need for such services by complementing the facilities offered by commercial banks, which were at times more focused on providing short-term credit for working capital and trade financing. They play a role in the short-term money market and capital raising activities such as financing, syndicating, corporate financing, providing management advisory services, arranging for the issue and listing of shares as well as managing investment portfolio. As at end-2004, there were 10 merchant banks in Malaysia and all were domestically controlled institutions.

Table 1
Assets of the Financial System–1960–2004

Year	*Commercial Banks*		*Finance Companies*		*Merchant Banks*	
	RM million	*As a Ratio of GDP*	*RM million*	*As a Ratio of GDP*	*RM million*	*As a Ratio of GDP*
1960	1,231.9	0.21	n.a.	n.a.	n.a.	n.a.
1970	4,460.2	0.38	531.0	0.05	19.6*	0.002
1980	32,186.1	0.63	5,635.4	0.13	2,228.7	0.05
1990	129,284.9	1.23	39,448.0	0.50	11,063.2	0.14
1995	295,460.0	1.77	91,892.0	0.55	27,062.0	0.16
1996	360,126.8	1.98	119,768.8	0.65	34,072.8	0.19
1997	480,248.1	2.46	152,386.8	0.77	44,300.0	0.23
1998	453,492.0	2.52	123,596.9	0.68	39,227.8	0.22
1999	482,738.3	2.50	116,438.0	0.60	39,184.0	0.20
2000	512,714.7	2.44	109,409.8	0.52	36,876.0	0.18
2001	529,735.5	2.51	121,811.1	0.58	41,025.2	0.19
2002	563,254.1	2.56	130,520.0	0.59	41,415.5	0.19
2003	629,975.3	2.71	141,911.0	0.61	44,103.6	0.19
2004	761,254.8	3.05	68,421.1	0.27	42,691.0	0.17

Source: Bank Negara Malaysia
*as at end 1971

The Malaysian financial system's assets and liabilities continued to be highly concentrated at the commercial banking sector with total assets and liabilities amounting to RM761,254.8 billion or 3.05 times the national GDP as at end 2004. Prior to the Asian financial crisis in 1997/98, the finance companies' assets and liabilities were seen increasing from only RM531 million or 0.05 times of the national GDP in 1970 to reach a high of RM152.4 billion or 0.77 times in 1997. The ratio however has gradually declined to RM123.6 billion or 0.60 times in 1998 to RM109,409.8 billion or 0.52 times GDP in 2000, before increasing again in year 2001, to reach a post crisis high of RM141,911.0 billion or 0.61 times of the national GDP in 2003.

Due to further consolidation in the Malaysian financial sector, the finance companies assets as a ratio of the national GDP declined again to reach a low of 0.27 times in 2004. As for the merchant banks, a similar trend is observed where its assets and liabilities as a ratio of the national GDP have been increasing since 1971 to reach a peak of RM44.3 billion or 0.23 times GDP in 1997 i.e. before the Asian financial crisis. During the post crisis period, the merchant banks' assets and liabilities continued to remain stable at 0.17 to 0.22 times of the national GDP. A combination of both the finance companies and merchant banks total assets reveal that, the non-bank financial sector command approximately 22.8 per cent of the banking system's total assets and liabilities[1].

3. RELATED STUDIES

In the past few years, DEA have frequently been applied to banking industry studies. Berger and Humphrey (1997) made a wide survey of efficiency studies of financial institutions from 21 different countries around the world. They identified 130 studies that estimate frontiers of efficiency for different type of institutions and used different methodologies. Despite these differences, the studies reviewed have exhibited surprisingly similar results; X-inefficiencies tend to be large and amount of to approximately 20 per cent of the total costs of the banking industry. Additionally, X-inefficiency was in most cases more important than scale and scope inefficiencies. There is not, however, a clear understanding of the reasons for the differences observed in those studies. Berger and Mester (1997) explored the sources of the differences in measured efficiency issue in more detail. Their findings indicate that the use of different methods, functional forms and variables usually make very little difference in the ranking of individual firms or the average industry efficiency.

Despite substantial studies performed on the developed economies banking industry with regard to the efficiency and productivity of financial institutions, there were only a handful of studies performed on the Malaysian financial industry partly due to the lack of available data sources and the small sample of institutions. As pointed out by Kwan (2003), the lack of research on the efficiency of Asian banks was due to the lack of publicly available data for non-publicly traded Asian financial institutions.

Among the notable microeconomic research performed on Malaysian banks' efficiency was by Katib and Mathews (2000), which studied the characteristics of the management structure and technical efficiency of the banking industry in Malaysia by DEA from 1989 to 1995. They found that on the average, Malaysian banks do not efficiently combine their inputs. They suggest that over the period of observation, average technical efficiency of Malaysian banks range from 68.0 per cent to 80.0 per cent. They also suggest that most of the Malaysian commercial banks do not operate at constant returns to scale and that the technical inefficiency of Malaysian banks were attributed to scale inefficiency.

Okuda and Hashimoto (2004) conducted a research on the production technology of Malaysian domestic commercial banks with Stochastic Cost Functions approach adjusted to non-performing loans from the year 1991 to 1997. They found that fixed costs were higher for the large banks compared to its small and medium sized peers. Despite that, they found economies of scale do exist for the large banks while economies of scale were not evident for the small and medium sized banks.

These studies have arrived at similarities and differences. Katib and Mathews (2000) concluded that most commercial banks in Malaysia do not operate at constant returns to scale with technical efficiency ranged from 68 per cent to 80 per cent. They also found that technical inefficiency is mainly due to scale inefficiency adding that scale inefficiency is relatively large in the Malaysian commercial banks. Supporting to the view, Okuda and Hashimoto (2004) have also concluded that the estimated total elasticity of scale is greater than unity and that economies of scale were not observed. Okuda and Hashimoto (2004) also found that there was a tendency that the operational cost of Malaysian commercial banks increases over time and negative technological progress was observed. Correspondingly, Katib and Mathews (2000) suggests the deterioration of technical efficiency of Malaysian commercial banks during 1989 and 1994.

With regard to the efficiency of banks in different forms, Okuda and Hashimoto (2004) arrived at a different conclusion to that of Katib and Mathews (2000). Okuda and Hashimoto (2004) found that small sized banks are more cost efficient than the large size counterparts, while Katib and Mathews (2000) suggests that the best practice is provided by the medium sized banks. They found that banks of smaller size have constant or increasing returns to scale, which implies that they are too small to realize scale merit. On the other hand, scale inefficiency exists in large banks implying that they are too large to operate business efficiently.

Okuda and Hashimoto (2004) suggest that the management of Malaysian domestic banks was not efficient in spite of the progress in financial liberalization that was pursued during the 1990s, which sees the banking sector grew rapidly. They also suggested that there are possibilities that the Malaysian banking sector was under various forms of government influence until the 1980s and that banks are required to provide loans for specific policy purposes. Furthermore, the government was a major stockholder in many banks, which may impede independent management to pursuit managerial efficiency.

4. METHODOLOGY

A non-parametric Data Envelopment Analysis (DEA) is employed with variable return to scale assumption to measure input-oriented technical efficiency of the

Malaysian NBFI. DEA involves constructing a non-parametric production frontier based on the actual input-output observations in the sample relative to which efficiency of each firm in the sample is measured (Coelli, 1996). Let us give a short description of the Data Envelopment Analysis[2]. Assume that there is data on K inputs and M outputs for each N bank. For ith bank, these are represented by the vectors x_i and y_i respectively. Let us call the K x N input matrix – X and the M x N output matrix–Y. To measure the efficiency for each bank we calculate a ratio of all inputs, such as $(u'y_i/v'x_i)$ where u is an M x 1 vector of output weights and v is a K x 1 vector of input weights. To select optimal weights we specify the following mathematical programming problem:

$$\min_{u,v} (u'y_i/v'x_i),$$

$$u'y_i/v'x_i \text{ d} \leq 1, \qquad j = 1, 2,\ldots, N,$$
$$u,v \geq 0 \qquad (1)$$

The above formulation has a problem of infinite solutions and therefore we impose the constraint $v'x_i = 1$, which leads to:

$$\min_{\mu,\varphi} (\mu'y_i),$$

$$\varphi'x_i = 1$$
$$\mu'y_i - \varphi'x_j \leq 0 \qquad j = 1, 2,\ldots, N,$$
$$\mu,\varphi \geq 0 \qquad (2)$$

where we change notation from u and v to ì and ö, respectively, in order to reflect transformations. Using the duality in linear programming, an equivalent envelopment form of this problem can be derived:

$$\min_{\theta,\lambda} \theta,$$

$$y_i + Y\lambda \geq 0$$
$$\theta x_i - X\lambda \geq 0$$
$$\lambda \geq 0 \qquad (3)$$

where θ is a scalar representing the value of the efficiency score for the ith decision-making unit which will range between 0 and 1. λ is a vector of N x 1 constants. The linear programming has to be solved N times, once for each decision-making unit in the sample. In order to calculate efficiency under the assumption of variable returns to scale, the convexity constraint ($N1'\lambda = 1$) will be added to ensure that an inefficient firm is only compared against firms of similar size, and therefore provides the basis for measuring economies of scale within the DEA concept. The convexity constraint determines how closely the production frontier envelops the observed input-output combinations and is not imposed in the constant returns to scale case. The variable returns to scale technique therefore forms a convex hull which envelops the data more tightly than the constant returns to scale, and thus provides efficiency scores that are greater than or equal to those obtained from the constant returns to scale model.

Amongst the strengths of the DEA is that, DEA is less data demanding as it works fine with small sample size (Canhoto and Dermine, 2003). The small sample size is among other reasons, which leads us to DEA as the tool of choice for evaluating Malaysian NBFIs X-efficiency. Furthermore, DEA does not require a preconceived structure or specific functional form to be imposed on the data in identifying and determining the efficient frontier, error, and inefficiency structures of the DMUs[3] (Bauer *et al.*, 1998; Evanoff and Israelvich, 1991; Grifell-Tatje and Lovell, 1997). Hababou (2006) adds that it is better to adopt the DEA technique when it have been shown that a commonly agreed functional form relating inputs to outputs is difficult to prove or find. Such specific functional form is truly difficult to show for financial services entities. Avkiran (1999) acknowledges the edge of the DEA by stating that this technique allows the researchers to choose any kind of input and output of managerial interest, regardless of different measurement units. There is no need for standardization.

Three useful features of DEA are first, each DMU is assigned a single efficiency score, hence allowing ranking amongst the DMUs in the sample. Second, it highlights the areas of improvement for each single DMU. For example, since a DMU is compared to a set of efficient DMUs with similar input-output configurations, the DMU in question is able to identify whether it has used input excessively or its output has been under-produced. Finally, there is possibility of making inferences on the DMUs general profile. We should be aware that the technique used here is a comparison between the production performances of each DMU to a set of efficient DMUs. The set of efficient DMUs is called the reference set. The owners of the DMUs may be interested to know which DMU frequently appears in this set. A DMU that appears more than others in this set is called the global leader. Clearly, this information gives huge benefits to the DMU owner, especially in positioning its entity in the market.

The main weakness of DEA is that it assumes data are free from measurement errors. Furthermore, since efficiency is measured in a relative way, its analysis is confined to the sample set used. This means that an efficient DMU found in the analysis cannot be compared with other DMUs outside of the sample. The reason is simple. Each sample, separated, let us say, by year, represents a single frontier, which is constructed on the assumption of the same technology.

DEA can be use to derive measures of scale efficiency by using the variable returns to scale (VRS), or the BCC model, alongside the constant returns to scale (CRS), or the CCR model. Coelli *et al.* (1998) noted that the BCC model has been the most commonly used since the beginning of the 1990s. A DEA model can be constructed either to minimize inputs or to maximize outputs. An input orientation aims at reducing the input amounts as much as possible while keeping at least the present output levels, while an output orientation aims at maximizing output levels without increasing use of inputs (Cooper *et al.*, 2000). The focus on costs in banking and the fact that outputs are inclined to be demand determined means that input-oriented models are most commonly used (Kumbhakar and Lozano Vivas, 2005).

As we are looking at relative efficiency, it is important that the DMUs to be sufficiently similar, so that comparisons are meaningful. This is particularly the case with DEA, where Dyson *et al.* (2001) have developed what they describe as a series of homogeneity assumptions. The first of these is that the DMUs the performance of which is being compared should be undertaking similar activities and producing comparable products and services so that a common set of outputs can be defined. The second homogeneity assumption is that a similar range of resources is available to all DMUs, and they are operating in a similar environment.

4.1 Data Sample, Inputs-Outputs Definition, and the Choice of Variables

For the empirical analysis, all Malaysian NBFIs would be incorporated in the study. The annual balance sheets and income statements used to construct the variables for the empirical analysis are sourced from published balance sheet information in annual reports of each individual NBFI. Due to the unavailability of data resulting from mergers and acquisitions, the final sample comprised of an unbalanced panel sample of 92 NBFI year observations.

The definition and measurement of inputs and outputs in the banking function remains a contentious issue among researchers. To determine what constitutes inputs and outputs of banks, one should first decide on the nature of banking technology. In the banking theory literature, there are two main approaches competing with each other in this regard: the production and intermediation approaches (Sealey and Lindley, 1977).

Under the production approach, pioneered by Benston (1965), a financial institution is defined as a producer of services for account holders, that is, they perform transactions on deposit accounts and process documents such as loans. Hence, according to this approach, the number of accounts or its related transactions is the best measures for output, while the number of employees and physical capital is considered as inputs. Previous studies that adopted this approach are among others Ferrier and Lovell (1990), Fried *et al.* (1993), and Sherman and Gold (1985).

The intermediation approach on the other hand assumes that financial firms act as an intermediary between savers and borrowers and posits total loans and securities as outputs, whereas deposits along with labour and physical capital are defined as inputs. Previous banking efficiency studies research that adopted this approach are among others Bhattacharyya *et al.* (1997), Charnes *et al.* (1990), and Sathye (2001).

For the purpose of this study, a variation of the intermediation approach or asset approach originally developed by Sealey and Lindley (1977) will be adopted in the definition of inputs and outputs used[4]. According to Berger and Humphrey (1997), the production approach might be more suitable for branch efficiency studies, as at most times bank branches process customer documents and bank funding, while investment decisions are mostly not under the control of branches.

The aim in the choice of variables for this study is to provide a parsimonious model and to avoid the use of unnecessary variables that may reduce the degree of freedom[5]. All variables are measured in millions of Malaysian Ringgit (RM).

Given the sensitivity of efficiency estimates to the specification of outputs and inputs, we have estimated two alternative models. In DEA Model A, we model Malaysian NBFIs as multi-product firms, producing two outputs by employing two inputs. Accordingly, *Total Deposits* (*x1*), which include deposits from customers and other banks and *Fixed Assets* (*x2*), are used as an input vectors to produce *Total Loans* (*y1*), which include loans to customers and other banks and *Investments* (*y2*), which include investment securities held for trading, investment securities available for sale (AFS) and investment securities held to maturity. To assess the importance of risk and lending quality problems in explaining the efficiency of Malaysian NBFIs, following the approach by among others Drake and Hall (2003) and Charnes *et al.* (1990), *Loan Loss Provisions* (*x3*) is incorporated as an input variable in DEA Model B.

Table 2 presents the summary statistics of the input and output variables used to construct the efficiency frontier. During the period of study, it is apparent that the finance companies were almost three times larger (in terms of asset size), and command higher market share in terms of loans and deposits relative to its merchant banks peers. On the other hand, although the merchant banks were smaller, they seem to have produced higher amount of investments and have lower amount of defaulted loans. The differences are further confirmed by a series of parametric (*t*-test) and non-parametric (Kruskal-Wallis and Mann-Whitney [Wilcoxon Rank-Sum] tests), which suggest that the differences in the mean are significant for all variables at the 1 per cent level of significance[6].

5. RESULTS

In this section, we will discuss the technical efficiency change (TE) of the Malaysian NBFI sector, measured by the Data Envelopment Analysis (DEA) method and its decomposition into pure technical efficiency (PTE) and scale efficiency (SE) components. In the event of the existence of scale inefficiency, we will attempt to provide evidence on the nature of returns to scale of the Malaysian NBFI. The efficiency of Malaysian NBFIs was first examined by applying the DEA method for each year under investigation by employing the traditional input-output variables. We extend the analysis to examine the merchant banks and finance companies efficiency results derived from an alternative model, which incorporates a non-discretionary input variable.

5.1 Efficiency of the Malaysian NBFI Sector

Table 3 presents the mean efficiency scores of Malaysian NBFIs for the years 2000 (Panel A), 2001 (Panel B), 2002 (Panel C), 2003 (Panel D), 2004 (Panel E), Merchant Banks (Panel F), and Finance Companies (Panel G). The results from DEA Model A seems to suggest that Malaysian NBFIs mean technical efficiency has been on a declining trend during the earlier part of the studies, before increasing again during the latter years. The decomposition of overall efficiency into its pure technical and scale efficiency components suggest that while scale inefficiency dominates pure technical inefficiency of the finance companies during all years, the merchant banks on the other hand have exhibited higher scale efficiency during 2000 and 2002. Overall, the results imply that during the period

Table 2
Descriptive Statistics for Inputs and Outputs

The table presents summary statistics of the variables used to construct the efficiency frontier for both DEA Model A and DEA Model B over the period 2000-2004. The sample is divided into peer groups i.e. merchant banks and finance companies. MB denotes merchant banks and FC denotes finance companies.

		2000 (RMb)		2001 (RMb)		2002 (RMb)		2003 (RMb)		2004 (RMb)	
Outputs		*MB*	*FC*	*MB*	*FC*	*MB*	*FC*	*MB*	*FC*	*MB*	*FC*
Total Loans	Min	172.05	1,927.44	135.04	887.41	136.73	1,116.10	89.77	1,363.46	136.55	1408.4
	Mean	1,784.70	6,832.02	1,549.44	6,904.33	1,336.28	7,383.17	1,173.53	9,773.36	1,045.39	9,454.49
	Max	7,677.01	15,743.03	7,571.63	15,765.02	6,906.83	16,732.43	5,582.32	25,160.44	5,274.91	26,048.86
	S.D	2,426.46	4,537.73	2,192.84	4,929.12	2,014.58	5,095.30	1,706.99	7,690.041	1,628.510	8,241.46
Investments	Min	61.79	180.97	74.8	40.55	57.82	41.69	99.51	75.77	98.67	69.91
	Mean	1,710.31	1,473.56	1,530.41	1,116.91	1,655.44	818.38	2,085.44	966.80	2,058.65	797.97
	Max	5,525.08	3,416.52	4,985.66	2,800.68	5,999.55	1,730.22	8,023.00	2,454.12	6,558.26	2,317.31
	S.D	1,945.90	1,220.12	1,858.97	1,063.46	2,035.57	599.90	2,503.18	991.46	1,974.16	910.38
Inputs											
Fixed Assets	Min	0.84	21.68	0.25	5.31	0.32	6.71	0.10	6.54	0.06	2.02
	Mean	4.46	55.66	7.90	49.63	11.51	88.86	16.21	87.12	14.56	95.84
	Max	11.71	186.94	39.69	205.86	45.00	425.22	53.69	439.35	54.17	424.60
	S.D	4.07	54.42	12.45	58.76	16.62	130.90	19.61	134.07	19.93	141.93
Total Deposits	Min	58.30	1,480.76	88.86	913.12	20.23	1,164.16	63.78	1,226.55	74.62	1,084.00
	Mean	2,331.99	7,145.82	1,906.52	6,514.09	1,555.06	7,445.49	1,660.76	8,306.54	2,003.80	7,903.50
	Max	8,110.02	14,546.27	8,853.50	13,928.60	5,356.46	16,025.89	5,302.27	19,609.19	5,929.86	20,411.79
	S.D	2,543.59	4,183.57	2,596.72	4,757.44	1,676.94	5,590.04	1,676.48	6,506.15	1,796.95	7,057.08
Loan Loss Provisions	Min	1.18	0.60	10.00	35.18	0.08	17.78	7.47	33.79	17.70	59.72
	Mean	55.7925	136.40	71.09	119.96	32.78	107.03	47.45	108.10	58.43	155.74
	Max	160.28	519.78	229.44	384.38	154.35	311.64	253.24	378.73	159.31	347.76
	S.D	58.02	168.09	68.35	106.56	47.14	84.65	79.14	101.04	40.40	96.39

of study, the Malaysian NBFIs have been operating at the wrong scale of operations.

Table 3
Summary Statistics of Efficiency Measures (DEA Model A)

The table presents mean, minimum, maximum, and standard deviation of Malaysian NBFIs technical efficiency (TE), and its mutually exhaustive pure technical efficiency (PTE) and scale efficiency (SE) components derived from DEA Model A (Excluding the risk factor). Panel A, B, C, D, and E shows the mean, minimum, maximum and standard deviation of TE, PTE, and SE of the merchant banks and finance companies for the years 2000, 2001, 2002, 2003, and 2004 respectively. Panel F and G presents the merchant banks and finance companies mean, minimum, maximum and standard deviation of TE, PTE and SE scores, respectively. The TE, PTE, and SE scores are bounded between a minimum of 0 and a maximum of 1. MB denotes merchant banks. FC denotes finance companies

Efficiency Measures	*Mean*		*Minimum*		*Maximum*		*Std. Dev.*	
	MB	*FC*	*MB*	*FC*	*MB*	*FC*	*MB*	*FC*
Panel A: 2000								
Technical Efficiency	0.908	0.538	0.443	0.350	1.000	1.000	0.193	0.216
Pure Technical Efficiency	0.925	0.811	0.527	0.466	1.000	1.000	0.167	0.197
Scale Efficiency	0.974	0.679	0.841	0.399	1.000	1.000	0.056	0.228
Panel B: 2001								
Technical Efficiency	0.745	0.389	0.342	0.266	1.000	0.693	0.271	0.142
Pure Technical Efficiency	0.897	0.807	0.547	0.491	1.000	1.000	0.180	0.219
Scale Efficiency	0.822	0.489	0.372	0.342	1.000	0.693	0.218	0.124
Panel C: 2002								
Technical Efficiency	0.750	0.248	0.216	0.058	1.000	0.589	0.327	0.149
Pure Technical Efficiency	0.851	0.828	0.266	0.530	1.000	1.000	0.266	0.186
Scale Efficiency	0.861	0.300	0.438	0.092	1.000	0.589	0.222	0.155
Panel D: 2003								
Technical Efficiency	0.506	0.490	0.188	0.243	1.000	0.769	0.320	0.140
Pure Technical Efficiency	0.894	0.822	0.429	0.440	1.000	1.000	0.201	0.199
Scale Efficiency	0.562	0.599	0.188	0.446	1.000	0.769	0.298	0.104
Panel E: 2004								
Technical Efficiency	0.582	0.625	0.331	0.296	1.000	0.974	0.209	0.188
Pure Technical Efficiency	0.924	0.835	0.685	0.428	1.000	1.000	0.133	0.209
Scale Efficiency	0.636	0.758	0.386	0.540	1.000	0.974	0.226	0.169
Panel F: Merchant Banks All Years								
Technical Efficiency	0.696		0.188		1.000		0.295	
Pure Technical Efficiency	0.897		0.266		1.000		0.190	
Scale Efficiency	0.770		0.188		1.000		0.258	
Panel G: Finance Companies All Years								
Technical Efficiency	0.447		0.058		1.000		0.205	
Pure Technical Efficiency	0.820		0.428		1.000		0.193	
Scale Efficiency	0.552		0.092		1.000		0.220	

During the period of study, the results seem to suggest that the merchant banks (Panel F) have exhibited mean technical efficiency of 69.6 per cent, suggesting mean input waste of 30.4 per cent. In other words, the merchant banks could have produced the same amount of outputs by only using 69.6 per cent of the amount of inputs it uses. From Table 3 (Panel F) it is also clear that scale inefficiency dominates pure technical inefficiency of the merchant banks. On the other hand, the results from Table 3 (Panel G) suggest that the finance companies have exhibited lower mean technical efficiency of 44.7 per cent compared to its merchant banks counterparts. Likewise, the results also suggest that the finance companies inefficiency were mainly due to scale rather than pure technical albeit at a higher degree of 44.8 per cent (merchant banks – 23.0 per cent). The finance companies also seem to have exhibited lower pure technical efficiency of 82.0 per cent (merchant banks–89.7 per cent). Overall, the results suggest that, compared to their finance companies counterparts, the merchant banks were relatively managerially efficient in controlling their operating costs and have been operating at a relatively more optimal scale of operations.

Table 4
Composition of Production Frontiers (DEA Model A)

Bank	*Type*	*2000*	*2001*	*2002*	*2003*	*2004*	*Count*
Affin Merchant Bank	MB	IRS	DRS	DRS	DRS	DRS	0
Affin-ACF Finance	FC	DRS	DRS	DRS	DRS	DRS	0
Alliance Finance	FC		DRS	DRS	DRS	DRS	0
Alliance Merchant Bank	MB		DRS	DRS	DRS	DRS	0
Arab-Malaysian Finance	FC	CRS	DRS	DRS	DRS	DRS	1
Arab-Malaysian Merchant Bank	MB	CRS	DRS	DRS	DRS	DRS	1
Aseambankers	MB	CRS	DRS	CRS	DRS	DRS	1
Bumiputra-Commerce Finance	FC	DRS	DRS	DRS	DRS	DRS	0
Commerce International Merchant Bankers	MB	CRS	CRS	DRS	DRS	DRS	2
EON Finance	FC	DRS	DRS	DRS	DRS		0
Hong Leong Finance	FC	DRS	DRS	DRS	DRS	DRS	0
Malaysian International Merchant Bankers	MB	IRS	CRS	CRS			2
Mayban Finance	FC	DRS	DRS	DRS	DRS	DRS	0
Public Finance	FC	DRS	DRS	DRS	DRS		0
Public Merchant Bank	MB		CRS	CRS	DRS	DRS	2
RHB Delta Finance	FC		DRS	DRS	DRS	DRS	0
RHB Sakura Merchant Bankers	MB	CRS	CRS	CRS	DRS	DRS	3
Southern Finance	FC	DRS	DRS	DRS	DRS	DRS	0
Southern Investment Bank	MB	CRS	IRS	DRS	CRS	IRS	2
Utama Merchant Bank	MB	IRS	DRS	CRS	CRS	CRS	3
Number of NBFI	n	6	4	5	2	1	

Notes: CRS–(Constant Returns to Scale); DRS–(Decreasing Returns to Scale); IRS–(Increasing Returns to Scale); The NBFIs corresponds to the shaded regions have not been efficient in any year in the sample period (2000-2004) compared to the other NBFIs in the sample; MB –Merchant Bank; FC–Finance Company.

The findings are interesting in that, although the merchant banks were small relative to its finance companies counterparts, and have relatively limited operations, they seem to have exhibited higher efficiency levels compared to its finance companies peers. The findings support the divisibility theory, which holds that there will be no such operational advantage accruing to large NBFIs, if the technology is divisible, that is, small scale NBFIs can produce financial services at costs per unit output comparable to those of large NBFIs, suggesting no or possibly negative association between size and performance. This was made possible as advances in technology reduced the size and cost of automated equipment, thus significantly enhance small banks' ability to purchase expensive technology, implying more divisibility in technology in the banking industry (Kolari and Zardkoohi, 1987).

Since the dominant source of the total technical X- (in) efficiency in the Malaysian NBFI sector seems to be scale related, it is worth investigating the composition of the efficiency frontier. Table 4 shows NBFIs that lie on the efficiency frontier under DEA Model A. The composition of the efficiency frontier for DEA Model A suggests that the number of 100 per cent efficient NBFIs (operating at constant returns to scale (CRS)), varies between one to six NBFIs. During the period of study, the merchant banks seem to have dominated the efficiency frontier for DEA Model A. It is also clear from the results that, two merchant banks namely, RHB Sakura Merchant Bankers and Utama Merchant Bank have appeared the most times on the efficiency frontier, a total of eight merchant banks have appeared at least once on the efficiency frontier, while only two merchant banks have failed to make it to the frontier. On the other hand, the results seem to suggest that only one finance company has managed to make it to the frontier, while nine finance companies have never made it to the efficiency frontier throughout the period of study.

5.2 Non-Performing Loans and the Gap between the Two DEA Models

Having established the basic DEA model, we now analyze the potential impact of risk and problem loans on Malaysian NBFIs efficiency. As indicated previously, these results are obtained by modifying the initial DEA model to incorporate an additional, non-discretionary input variable, in the form of provisions of loans losses. The results are presented in Table 5 and Figures 1–3. It is apparent that, controlling for problem loans has resulted in higher mean technical efficiency of Malaysian NBFIs during all years[7]. In line with the findings by Drake and Hall (2003) and Altunbas *et al.* (2000), the results seem to suggest that potential economies of scale may well be overestimated when risk factors are excluded. Likewise, it is clear that the inclusion of loan loss provisions has resulted in higher mean pure technical efficiency of Malaysian NBFIs[8]. The results support earlier findings by Altunbas *et al.* (2000) whom suggest that the mean scale efficiency estimate is much more sensitive that the mean pure technical efficiency estimate to the exclusion of risk factors.

Table 5
Summary Statistics of Efficiency Measures (DEA Model B)

The table presents mean, minimum, maximum, and standard deviation of Malaysian NBFIs technical efficiency (TE), and its mutually exhaustive pure technical efficiency (PTE) and scale efficiency (SE) components derived from DEA Model B (Inclusive of the risk factor). Panel A, B, C, D, and E shows the mean, minimum, maximum and standard deviation of TE, PTE, and SE of the merchant banks and finance companies for the years 2000, 2001, 2002, 2003, and 2004 respectively. Panel F and G presents the merchant banks and finance companies mean, minimum, maximum and standard deviation of TE, PTE and SE scores, respectively. The TE, PTE, and SE scores are bounded between a minimum of 0 and a maximum of 1. MB denotes merchant banks. FC denotes finance companies

Efficiency Measures	*Mean*		*Minimum*		*Maximum*		*Std. Dev.*	
	MB	*FC*	*MB*	*FC*	*MB*	*FC*	*MB*	*FC*
Panel A: 2000								
Technical Efficiency	0.908	0.823	0.443	0.560	1.000	1.000	0.193	0.174
Pure Technical Efficiency	0.926	0.902	0.532	0.561	1.000	1.000	0.165	0.162
Scale Efficiency	0.973	0.918	0.834	0.644	1.000	1.000	0.058	0.122
Panel B: 2001								
Technical Efficiency	0.818	0.799	0.437	0.511	1.000	1.000	0.219	0.173
Pure Technical Efficiency	0.897	0.878	0.551	0.517	1.000	1.000	0.179	0.196
Scale Efficiency	0.903	0.918	0.683	0.747	1.000	1.000	0.119	0.094
Panel C: 2002								
Technical Efficiency	0.837	0.643	0.275	0.324	1.000	1.000	0.251	0.212
Pure Technical Efficiency	0.914	0.860	0.492	0.533	1.000	1.000	0.159	0.181
Scale Efficiency	0.905	0.726	0.559	0.512	1.000	1.000	0.189	0.139
Panel D: 2003								
Technical Efficiency	0.885	0.801	0.504	0.554	1.000	1.000	0.204	0.157
Pure Technical Efficiency	0.912	0.859	0.513	0.562	1.000	1.000	0.181	0.153
Scale Efficiency	0.963	0.940	0.793	0.752	1.000	1.000	0.085	0.085
Panel E: 2004								
Technical Efficiency	0.896	0.963	0.700	0.764	1.000	1.000	0.127	0.097
Pure Technical Efficiency	0.950	0.982	0.857	0.769	1.000	1.000	0.048	0.098
Scale Efficiency	0.946	0.979	0.700	0.949	1.000	1.000	0.110	0.018
Panel F: Merchant Banks All Years								
Technical Efficiency	0.869		0.275		1.000		0.199	
Pure Technical Efficiency	0.929		0.492		1.000		0.151	
Scale Efficiency	0.927		0.559		1.000		0.123	
Panel G: Finance Companies All Years								
Technical Efficiency	0.795		0.324		1.000		0.189	
Pure Technical Efficiency	0.882		0.517		1.000		0.161	
Scale Efficiency	0.900		0.512		1.000		0.130	

Figure 1: Malaysian NBFIs Technical Efficiency

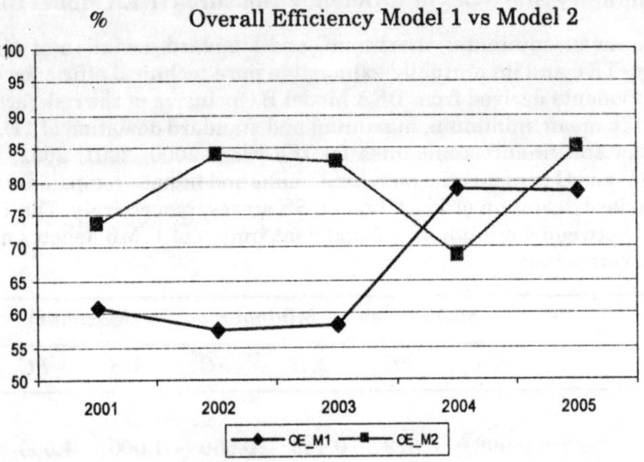

Figure 2: Malaysian NBFIs Pure Technical Efficiency

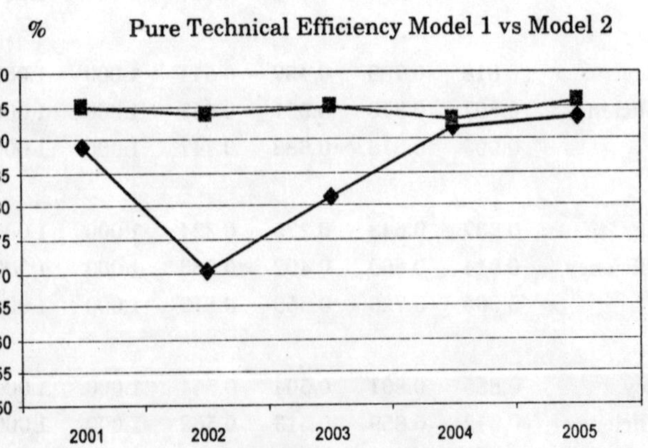

Figure 3: Malaysian NBFIs Scale Efficiency

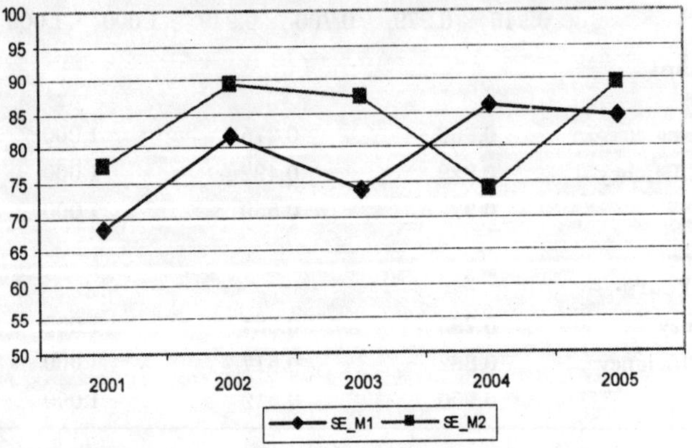

We now turn to discuss the impact of the inclusion of loan loss provisions on the evolution of the merchant banks and finance companies technical efficiency. The results from Table 5 (Panel F and G) suggest that the inclusion of risk factors has resulted in higher merchant banks and finance companies technical efficiency. It is also apparent that the inclusion of loan loss provisions has had greater positive impact on both the merchant banks and finance companies scale efficiency. A closer look at the results, it seems that while the magnitude of the increase in the finance companies pure technical and scale efficiency is higher compared to their merchant banks peers. One clear reason is that during the period of study, the finance companies have higher amount of defaulted loans relative to its merchant banks peers.

The empirical findings clearly demonstrate the importance of risk in explaining financial institutions efficiency, in particular scale efficiency. If anything could be deduced from the results, the omission of risk factors may significantly overestimate financial institutions' potential economies of scale, which could lead to bias conclusions and consequently policy recommendations. The findings are particularly important for the Malaysian policy makers in its quest to consolidate the banking system further to achieve greater economies of scale and efficiency. The Malaysian government has always believe that such a move would result in a larger institutions, which could withstand greater competition from foreign players, as well as any shocks to the financial system. As the actual potential economies of scale may significantly be lower than initially expected, policy makers should be more cautious in promoting mergers as a mean to achieve greater financial institutions' efficiency by attaining better economies of scale.

Furthermore, most of the research conducted on explaining the causes of bank or thrift industry failures have found that failing institutions carried a large proportion of non-performing loans in their books prior to failure (Dermiguc-Kunt, 1989; Whalen, 1991; Barr and Siems, 1994). Berger and Humphrey (1992), Barr and Siems (1994), and Wheelock and Wilson (1995) have found that banks approaching failure tend to have low cost efficiency and experiencing high ratios of problem loans and that failing banks tend to be located far from the best practice frontiers.

The composition of the efficiency frontier and the nature of the returns to scale for DEA Model B are discussed next. Table 6 presents the results of the nature of returns to scale in Malaysian NBFI sector derived from DEA Model B. Unlike the results from DEA Model A, the composition of the efficiency frontier for DEA Model B suggests that the number of 100 per cent efficient NBFIs has increased substantially to between six and 10 NBFIs. The results from DEA Model B are very much similar to the results from DEA Model A, where the merchant banks seem to have dominated the efficiency frontier. It is apparent from Table 6 that the global leaders under DEA Model B have increased to four merchant banks, while there was only one merchant bank that failed to appear on the efficiency frontier throughout the period of study. Unlike DEA Model A, the results from DEA Model B suggest that seven finance companies have managed to appear on the efficiency frontier, while there were only three finance

Table 6
Composition of Production Frontiers (DEA Model B)

Bank	*Type*	*2000*	*2001*	*2002*	*2003*	*2004*	*Count*
Affin Merchant Bank	MB	IRS	DRS	DRS	CRS	CRS	2
Affin-ACF Finance	FC	DRS	DRS	DRS	DRS	IRS	0
Alliance Finance	FC		DRS	DRS	DRS	CRS	1
Alliance Merchant Bank	MB		DRS	DRS	IRS	IRS	0
Arab-Malaysian Finance	FC	CRS	DRS	DRS	DRS	DRS	1
Arab-Malaysian Merchant Bank	MB	CRS	DRS	DRS	DRS	CRS	2
Aseambankers	MB	CRS	DRS	CRS	CRS	CRS	4
Bumiputra-Commerce Finance	FC	CRS	CRS	DRS	DRS	CRS	3
Commerce International Merchant Bankers	MB	CRS	CRS	CRS	CRS	DRS	4
EON Finance Berhad	FC	CRS	DRS	DRS	DRS		1
Hong Leong Finance	FC	DRS	DRS	DRS	IRS	DRS	0
Malaysian International Merchant Bankers	MB	IRS	CRS	CRS			2
Mayban Finance	FC	DRS	DRS	DRS	CRS	CRS	2
Public Finance	FC	DRS	CRS	CRS	CRS		3
Public Merchant Bank	MB		CRS	CRS	CRS	CRS	4
RHB Delta Finance	FC		IRS	DRS	CRS	CRS	2
RHB Sakura Merchant Bankers	MB	CRS	CRS	CRS	DRS	CRS	4
Southern Finance	FC	DRS	DRS	DRS	DRS	IRS	0
Southern Investment Bank	MB	CRS	IRS	IRS	CRS	IRS	2
Utama Merchant Bank	MB	IRS	DRS	CRS	CRS	CRS	3
Number of NBFI	n	8	6	7	9	10	

Notes: CRS–(Constant Returns to Scale); DRS–(Decreasing Returns to Scale); IRS–(Increasing Returns to Scale); The NBFIs corresponds to the shaded regions have not been efficient in any year in the sample period (2001-2005) compared to the other NBFIs in the sample; MB –Merchant Bank; FC–Finance Company.

companies that have never made it to the efficiency frontier throughout the period of study.

5.3 Univariate Test Results

After examining the DEA results, the issue of interest now is whether the two samples are drawn from the same population i.e., whether the merchant banks and finance companies possess the same technology. The null hypothesis tested is that the merchant banks and finance companies are drawn from the same population or environment and have identical technologies. We tested the null hypothesis that merchant banks and finance companies are drawn from the same population and have identical technologies by using a series of parametric (ANOVA and *t*-test) and non-parametric (Kolmogorov-Smirnov, Mann-Whitney [Wilcoxon Rank-Sum] and Kruskall-Wallis) univariate tests. The results are presented in Table 7.

Table 7
Summary of the Null Hypothesis Tests of Identical Technologies between Merchant Banks and Finance Companies

The table present results from the parametric (ANOVA and t-test) and nonparametric (Kolmogorov-Smirnov, Mann-Whitney and Kruskall-Wallis) tests. The tests are performed to test the null hypothesis that domestic and foreign banks are drawn from the same population (environment). Test methodology follows among others, Aly *et al.* (1990), Elyasiani and Mehdian (1992) and Isik and Hassan (2002). *** indicate significant at the 5% level.

	Test Groups				
	Parametric Test		*Non-Parametric Test*		
Individual Tests	*Analysis of Variance (ANOVA) test*	*t-test*	*Kolmogorov-Smirnov [K-S] test*	*Mann-Whitney [Wilcoxon Rank-Sum] test*	*Kruskall-Wallis Equality of Populations test*
Hypotheses	$Mean_{mb} = Mean_{fc}$		$Distribution_{mb} = Distribution_{fc}$	$Median_{mb} = Median_{fc}$	
Test Statistics	*F (Prb > F)*	*t (Prb > t)*	*K-S (Prb > K-S)*	*z (Prb > z)*	χ^2 *(Prb >* χ^2*)*
Panel A: 2000					
TE Model A	15.606***	-3.950***	1.572***	8.500***	7.316***
TE Model B	0.851	-0.922	1.000	21.500	1.387
PTE Model A	1.107	-1.052	0.857	22.000	2.128
PTE Model B	0.083	-0.289	0.500	26.000	0.524
SE Model A	14.699***	-3.834***	1.601***	7.500***	7.868***
SE Model B	1.318	-1.148	0.750	22.500	1.136
Panel B: 2001					
TE Model A	0.634***	-3.678***	1.342	11.500***	8.541***
TE Model B	0.045	-0.213	0.671	44.000	0.211
PTE Model A	0.040	-0.996	0.671	35.000	1.541
PTE Model B	0.051	-0.225	0.447	44.000	0.283
SE Model A	17.639***	-4.200***	1.565***	12.000***	8.314***
SE Model B	0.095	-0.308	0.447	47.000	0.053
Panel C: 2002					
TE Model A	19.470***	-4.412***	1.565***	11.000***	8.824***
TE Model B	3.911	-1.978	1.342	24.000	4.033***
PTE Model A	0.053	-0.230	0.671	40.000	0.685
PTE Model B	1.530	-1.237	0.894	34.000	1.753
SE Model A	42.959***	-6.554***	2.012***	2.000***	13.367***
SE Model B	3.494	-1.869	1.342	28.000	2.887
Panel D: 2003					
TE Model A	0.021	-0.147	0.991	37.000	0.427
TE Model B	0.866	-0.753	0.798	33.000	1.073
PTE Model A	0.614	-0.783	0.822	31.000	1.460
PTE Model B	0.489	-0.699	0.822	33.000	1.190
SE Model A	0.140	0.374	1.016	32.000	1.128
SE Model B	0.034	-0.185	0.547	33.000	1.074
Panel E: 2004					
TE Model A	0.198	0.445	0.657	32.500	0.114
TE Model B	0.168	0.409	0.457	35.000	0.012
PTE Model A	1.149	-1.072	0.572	28.000	0.743
PTE Model B	0.816	-0.903	0.514	33.000	0.150
SE Model A	1.564	1.250	0.915	24.000	1.333
SE Model B	2.158	1.469	0.686	36.000	0.000

Based on most of the results for DEA Model A, we failed to reject the null hypothesis at the 5 per cent levels of significance that the merchant banks and finance companies are drawn from the same population and have identical technologies, while the results for DEA Model B failed to reject the null hypothesis during all years. This implies that, there is no significant difference between the merchant banks and finance companies technologies (frontiers) and that it is appropriate to construct a combined frontier. Furthermore, the results from the Levene's test for equality of variances do not reject the null hypothesis that the variances among merchant banks and finance companies are equal, implying that we can assume the variances among merchant banks and finance companies to be equal. The findings corroborate with the findings by among others, Sathye (2001), and Isik and Hassan (2002).

6. CONCLUSIONS

The paper attempts to investigate the efficiency of Malaysian Non-Bank Financial Institutions (NBFIs) during the period of 2000-2004. The preferred non-parametric Data Envelopment Analysis (DEA) methodology has allowed us to distinguish between three different types of efficiency namely, technical, pure technical and scale efficiencies. Additionally we have performed a series of parametric and non-parametric tests to examine whether the merchant banks and finance companies are drawn from the same population.

During the period of study, the results suggest that, the Malaysian merchant banks have exhibited mean overall or technical efficiency of 69.6 per cent while the finance companies have exhibited lower mean technical efficiency of 44.7 per cent. In other words, during the period of study, the merchant banks could have produced the same amount of outputs by only using 69.6 per cent of the inputs that it currently employed. Similarly, the finance companies could have reduced 55.3 per cent of the amount of inputs it employed currently without affecting the amount of outputs that it currently produces. Overall, the results suggest that scale inefficiency dominates pure technical inefficiency effects in determining Malaysian NBFIs total technical inefficiency. The findings also seem to suggest that scale efficiency tend to be much more sensitive to the exclusion of risk factors, implying that potential economies of scale may be overestimated when risk factors are excluded.

The empirical findings clearly demonstrate the importance of risk in explaining financial institutions efficiency, particularly scale efficiency. If anything could be deduced from the results, the exclusion of risk factors may significantly overestimate financial institutions potential economies of scale, which could result in bias conclusions and consequently policy recommendations. The findings are important for policy makers in its quest to consolidate the banking system further to achieve greater economies of scale and efficiency. As the actual potential economies of scale may significantly be lower than initially expected, policy makers should be more cautious in promoting mergers as a mean to achieve greater financial institutions' efficiency by attaining better economies of scale.

The findings suggest that during the period of study, the merchant banks have dominated the efficiency frontier under both models. The merchant banks have also appeared to be the global leader by appearing the most times on the frontier. The results are interesting as although the merchant banks were smaller in terms of size, have smaller market share relative to its finance companies peers, they seem to have followed the best practice during the period of study. Further, despite being smaller, the results imply that although size is important for firms to be able to catch up to the frontier, however, it is not a dominant factor for firms to be able to catch up to the frontier, and in terms of innovations and technological advancements. The findings thus support for the divisibility theory, which suggest that there will be no or possibly negative association between size and firms ability to catch up to the frontier as technology is becoming cheaper.

It should be acknowledge that the scope of this paper is limited and several interesting questions are not answered. It is suggested for further analysis on the efficiency of the Malaysian NBFI sector to investigate changes in cost, allocative and technical efficiencies over time. In addition, the paper modelled Malaysian NBFIs according to the intermediation function. Given that NBFIs are multi-output firms, considering the production function along with the intermediation function at the same time could be another extension of the paper. Finally, the non-parametric frontier analysis used in this paper could also be combined with the stochastic frontier analysis method of estimating the frontier. This should testify to the robustness of the results against alternative estimation methods.

Notes

1. The figure is at end-2003, prior to the consolidation of finance companies into their respective commercial banking parents.
2. Good reference books on efficiency measures are Avkiran (2002), Cooper *et al.* (2000), and Thanassoulis (2001).
3. Avkiran (1999) and Hababou (2002) provide a relatively thorough discussion of the merits and limits of the DEA.
4. Humphrey (1985) presets an extended discussion of the alternative approaches over what a bank produces.
5. For a detailed discussion on the optimal number of inputs and outputs in DEA, see Avkiran (2002).
6. Investment is not significant in the case of Mann-Whitney [Wilcoxon Rank-Sum] and Kruskal-Wallis tests at any conventional levels. To conserve space, we do not report the results here but are available from the authors upon request.
7. Except for the merchant banks during the year 2000.
8. Except for the merchant banks during the year 2000.

References

Altunbas, Y., Liu, M-H., Molyneux, P. and Seth, R. (2000), 'Efficiency and Risk in Japanese Banking,' *Journal of Banking and Finance*, 24 (10): 1605-1628.

Aly, H. Y., Grabowski, R., Pasurka, C. and Rangan, N. (1990), 'Technical, Scale and Allocative Efficiencies in U.S. Banking: An Empirical Investigation,' *Review of Economics and Statistics*, 72 (2): 211-218.

Avkiran, N. K. (1999), 'An Application Reference for Data Envelopment Analysis in Branch Banking: Helping the Novice Researcher,' *International Journal of Bank Marketing*, 17 (5): 206-220.

Avkiran, N. K. (2002), *Productivity Analysis in the Service Sector with Data Envelopment Analysis*. Camira: N.K. Avkiran.

Bank Negara Malaysia (2001), *Financial Sector Masterplan: Building a Secure Future*. Kuala Lumpur: Bank Negara Malaysia Press.

Bank Negara Malaysia (2004), Annual Report. Bank Negara Press: Kuala Lumpur.

Barr, R. and Siems, T. (1994), 'Predicting Bank Failure Using DEA to Quantify Management Quality,' Working Paper, Federal Reserve Bank of Dallas.

Bauer, P. W., Berger, A. N., Ferrier, G. D. and Humphrey, D. B. (1998), 'Consistency Conditions for Regulatory Analysis of Financial Institutions: A Comparison of Frontier Efficiency Methods,' *Journal of Economics and Business*, 50 (2): 85-114.

Benston, G. J. (1965), 'Branch Banking and Economies of Scale,' *Journal of Finance*, 20 (2): 312-331.

Berger, A. N. and Humphrey, D. B. (1992), Measurement and Efficiency Issues in Commercial Banking, in Z. Griliches, (eds.), *Measurement Issues in the Service Sectors*. National Bureau of Economic Research: University of Chicago Press, 245-279.

Berger, A. N. and Humphrey, D. B. (1997), 'Efficiency of Financial Institutions: International Survey and Directions for Future Research,' *European Journal of Operational Research*, 98 (2): 175-212.

Berger, A. N. and Mester, L. J. (1997), 'Inside the Black Box: What Explains Differences in the Efficiencies of Financial Institutions," *Journal of Banking and Finance*, 21 (7): 895-947.

Bhattacharya, A., Lovell, C. A. K. and Sahay, P. (1997), 'The Impact of Liberalization on the Productive Efficiency of Indian Commercial Banks,' *European Journal of Operational Research*, 98 (2): 332-345.

Canhoto, A. and Dermine, J. (2003), 'A Note on Banking Efficiency in Portugal: New Vs. Old. Banks,' *Journal of Banking and Finance*, 27: 2087-2098.

Charnes, A., Cooper, W. W. and Rhodes, E. (1978), 'Measuring the Efficiency of Decision Making Units,' *European Journal of Operational Research*, 2 (6): 429-444.

Charnes, A., Cooper, W.W., Huang, Z.M. and Sun, D.B. (1990), 'Polyhedral Cone–Ratio DEA Models with an Illustrative Application to Large Commercial Banks,' *Journal of Econometrics*, 46 (1-2): 73-91.

Coelli, T. (1996), "A Guide to DEAP Version 2.1," *CEPA Working Paper* 8/96, University of New England, Armidale.

Coelli, T., Prasada-Rao, D. S. and Battese, G. E. (1998), *An Introduction to Efficiency and Productivity Analysis*. Boston: Kluwer Academic Publishers.

Cooper, W. W., Seiford, L. M. and Tone, K. (2000), *Data Envelopment Analysis*. Boston: Kluwer Academic Publishers.

Dermiguc-Kunt, A. (1989), 'Deposit Institutions Failure: A Review of the Empirical Literature,' *Federal Reserve Bank of Cleveland Economic Review* 25 (4): 2-18.

Drake, L. and Hall, M. J. B. (2003), 'Efficiency in Japanese Banking: An Empirical Analysis,' *Journal of Banking and Finance*, 27 (3): 891-917.

Dysön, R. G., Allen, R., Camanho, A. S., Podinovski, V. V., Sarrico, C. S. and Shale, E. A. (2001), 'Pitfalls and Protocols in DEA,' *European Journal of Operational Research*, 132 (2): 245-259.

Elyasiani, E. and Mehdian, S. (1992), 'Productive Efficiency Performance of Minority and Non-Minority Owned Banks: A Non-Parametric Approach,' *Journal of Banking and Finance*, 16 (5): 933-948.

Evanoff. D. D. and Israelvich, P. R. (1991), 'Productive Efficiency in Banking,' *Economic Perspectives*, Federal Reserve Bank of Chicago, 11-32.

Ferrier, G. and Lovell, C. A. K. (1990), 'Measuring Cost Efficiency in Banking: Econometric and Linear Programming Evidence,' *Journal of Econometrics*, 46 (1-2): 229-245.

Fried, H. O., Lovell, C. A. K. and Eeckaut, P. V. (1993), 'Evaluating the Performance of U.S. Credit Unions,' *Journal of Banking and Finance*, 17 (2-3): 251-65.

Gregoriou, G. N. and Zhu, J. (2005), *Evaluating Hedge Funds and CTA Performance: Data Envelopment Analysis Approach*. John Wiley: New York.

Grifell–Tatje, E. and Lovell, C. A. K. (1997), 'The Sources of Productivity Change in Spanish Banking,' *European Journal of Operational Research*, 98 (2): 364-80.

Hababou, M. (2006), 'Tutorial in DEA,' *http://members.tripod.com/moezh/DEAtutorial/DEAtutorial.html*, (accessed on 20 March 2006).

Humphrey, D.B. (1985), '*Cost and Scale Economies in Bank Intermediation*,' in Aspinwall, R. and Eisenbeis, R. (ed.), Handbook for Banking Strategy. New York: John Wiley and Sons.

Isik, I. and Hassan, M. K. (2002), 'Technical, Scale and Allocative Efficiencies of Turkish Banking Industry,' *Journal of Banking and Finance*, 26 (4): 719-766.

Katib, M. N. and Mathews, K. (2000), 'A Non-Parametric Approach to Efficiency Measurement in the Malaysian Banking Sector,' *The Singapore Economic Review*, 44 (2): 89-114.

Kolari, J. and Zardkoohi, A. (1987), *Bank Costs, Structure and Performance*. Lexington Books: USA.

Kumbhakar, S. C. and Lozano-Vivas, A. (2005), 'Deregulation and Productivity: The Case of Spanish Banks,' *Journal of Regulatory Economics*, 27 (3): 331-351.

Kwan, S. H. (2003), 'Operating Performance of Banks Among Asian Economies: An International and Time Series Comparison,' *Journal of Banking and Finance*, 27 (3): 471-489.

Okuda, H. and Hashimoto, H. (2004), 'Estimating Cost Functions of Malaysian Commercial Banks: The Differential Effects of Size, Location and Ownership,' *Asian Economic Journal*, 18 (3): 233-259.

Sathye, M. (2001), 'X-Efficiency in Australian Banking: An Empirical Investigation,' *Journal of Banking and Finance*, 25 (3): 613-630.

Sealey, C. and Lindley, J. T. (1977), 'Inputs, Outputs and a Theory of Production and Cost at Depository Financial Institutions,' *Journal of Finance*, 32 (4): 1251-1266.

Sherman, H. D. and Gold, F. (1985), 'Bank Branch Operating Efficiency: Evaluation with Data Envelopment Analysis,' *Journal of Banking and Finance*, 9 (2): 297-315.

Thanassoulis, E. (2001), *Introduction to the Theory and Application of Data Envelopment Analysis*. Kluwer Academic Publishers: Boston.

Whalen, G. (1991), 'A Proportional Hazards Model of Bank Failure: An Examination of its Usefulness as an Early Warning Tool,' *Federal Reserve Bank of Cleveland Economic Review* 27 (1): 21–31.

Wheelock, D. C. and Wilson, P. W. (1995), 'Explaining Bank Failures: Deposit Insurance, Regulation and Efficiency,' *Review of Economics and Statistics*, 77 (4): 689-700.

ACCESS TO CREDIT BY THE POOR IN SOUTH AFRICA: Evidence from Household Survey Data 1995 and 2000*

Francis Nathan Okurut

Department of Economics, University of Botswana, Gaborone

This study investigated factors that influenced access to credit by the poor in South Africa using income and expenditure survey data 1995 and 2000. Multinomial logit models and Heckman probit models with sample selection were estimated.

The results suggest that the poor have limited access to organized credit markets (formal and semi-formal). Access to bank credit by the poor is positively and significantly influenced by being male, provincial location (Western Cape, Gauteng and Mpumalanga) and being Coloured. Access to semi-formal credit by the poor is positively and significantly determined by household per capita expenditure, provincial location (Western Cape, Northern Cape, North West and Gauteng) and being Indian. Access to informal credit by the poor is positively and significantly influenced by provincial location (Kwazulu Natal and Gauteng).

The policy implication is that improving access to organized credit markets by the poor remains an important instrument in the fight against poverty.

Jel: *N27, D14, G2*

Keywords: credit, poverty, South Africa

1. INTRODUCTION

This study of the determinants of credit market access in South Africa was motivated by the need to measure the extent of financial sector deepening through household participation, especially among the poor and Blacks. This was in line with the strategic black economic empowerment policies of the government through increased access to education, credit markets and employment opportunities. The study formed part of a larger research programme in the Department of Economics at the University of Stellenbosch, which was funded by the European Union and the National Treasury through CAGE, the Conflict and Governance Facility. The larger research programme dealt with *Monitoring poverty, inequality and polarisation: Trends and prospects,*

* The author gratefully acknowledges the financial support from the CAGE Project of the Department of Economics, University of Stellenbosch and technical assistance from Professors Servaas van der Berg and Andrie Schoombee

Corresponding Author: *E-mail: okurutf@mopipi.ub.bw*

and the issue of access to credit was clearly one that fitted into this framework. The study specifically investigated the factors that influenced credit market access by the poor and Blacks in the formal, semi-formal and informal financial sectors in South Africa over the two survey periods of 1995 and 2000.

Credit access can be defined as the supply side phenomenon of credit markets, because it is the lenders who decide whether borrowers can access credit or not. The credit process involves two distinct stages. In the first stage, borrowers who have demand for credit decide how much funds to apply for and from which particular lender (formal or informal sector) at the prevailing market interest rates. This process constitutes the demand side. In the second stage, the lenders decide who accesses credit and what amount, which constitutes the supply side (Zeller, 1994).

Market imperfections and information asymmetry problems raise the probability of default risk, thus lenders do not sell loan contracts to every willing buyer (borrower) at the prevailing market price (interest rate). The interest rate as the price for credit therefore fails to play its market-clearing role of equating credit demand and supply, thus giving rise to an equilibrium with credit rationing (Stiglitz and Weiss, 1981).

The financial sector, comprised of the formal and informal sectors, plays a key role in financial intermediation (Levacic and Rebmann, 1982) in devloping countries. The banks are major players in formal credit markets, while informal institutions (such as relatives, friends, moneylenders, rotating savings and credit associations, microfinance institutions) are active in informal financial markets (Aryeetey and Nissanke, 1998; Yadav et al, 1992; Soyibo, 1994; Aryeetey, 1994). In this study, formal credit was defined to include debts from commercial banks (including mortgage finance and car loans), semi-formal credit included consumption credit (for household assets such as furniture and open accounts in retail stores), and informal credit specifically referred to debts from relatives and friends.

The poor are argued to have constrained access to formal sector credit due to both institutional and household level factors (Nwanna, 1995). At the institutional level, the banks incur high information costs to assess the creditworthiness of small borrowers, and low returns due to the small loan amounts involved. This motivates the formal lenders to adopt strict collateral requirements as a screening mechanism to minimize default risk, hence rationing out the poor from the formal credit market. At the household level, the low levels of income and asset accumulation and highly skewed income and asset distribution render the poor households to have a high risk profile, which makes them less attractive to formal lenders (Dallimore and Mgimeti, 2003).

The poor with no access to formal sector credit have to revert to the informal financial sector to meet their credit demand (Montiel et al, 1993), for both productive investment (Binswanger and Khandker, 1995) and consumption smoothing (Heidhues, 1995; World Bank, 1989b). Ardington et al (2003) further argued that poor households' limited access to formal financial risk management instruments (savings, credit and insurance) constrains their ability to cope with shocks and further increases vulnerability to poverty.

2. DETERMINANTS OF CREDIT ACCESS

Household access to financial services (in both the formal and informal sectors) is influenced by institutional factors, product features and household socio-economic characteristics.

From the institutional perspective, the location of the financial service providers and their conditions greatly influence the probability of access. Porteous (2003) observed that access to formal financial services in South Africa tends to be limited to salaried workers, hence excluding the poor, the unemployed, self-employed and informally employed. This scenario prevails because of the common practice of banks to demand a pay slip as a precondition for opening an account. Dallimore and Mgimeti (2003) also contended that the long distances and high transport cost constrains the rural poor's access to formal financial services mainly located in urban areas.

The financial product features that influence access include interest rates and collateral requirements. Kochar (1997) examined the effect of formal sector interest rates and choice of informal credit. Empirical evidence suggested a positive and significant relationship between the formal sector interest rate and the probability of access to informal credit (at the 5% significance level). This result can be interpreted in the context of those households that participate in both the formal and informal financial markets, where the borrower considers not only the formal sector interest rates, but also the associated transaction costs (financial and non-financial). This may explain the positive relationship between formal sector interest rates and informal credit demand.

The specific borrower characteristics that influence the household access to credit markets include the strength of previous business relationships, borrowers' reputation in the market, borrowers' acceptance of interlinked credit contracts, borrowers' debt-service capacity and borrowers' wealth status. Aleem (1990), in a study of informal market lenders and their clients in Chambar, Pakistan, argued that informal lenders mainly used their established relationship with borrowers as a screening mechanism. Lenders did not generally entertain loan requests from people who had not had previous dealings with them either in the form of the sale of harvested output through them or purchase of farm inputs. The longer the period of the previous business relationship, the higher will be the probability of the borrower having credit access. This is due to the fact that these business relationships provide the lender with important information about the potential borrower, including his marketable surplus and the way he conducts business. Evidence by Kochar (1997) also suggested that the probability of access to informal credit is positively and significantly influenced by whether personal guarantees are given for informal loans. This result may be explained in terms of personal guarantees serving as alternative collateral that is valued by informal lenders.

Bell *et al.* (1997) found that interlinked credit contracts and visible household assets positively and significantly influenced the amount of credit supplied by informal lenders. Baydas *et al.* (1994) observed that the amount of informal credit supplied was significantly positively influenced by interest rates, loan period, business profits and education level.

Vaessen (2001), in a study of accessibility of rural credit in Northern Nicaragua, showed that access to credit is influenced by both the lender and household characteristics. At the institutional level, the lender makes decisions based on the target group (either women or men or both), the selection criteria of clients, the geographic area of operation, and the features of financial products to be provided to address sustainability concerns, all of which influence credit supply. At thc household level, being part of the specific target group or living in the targeted geographical area influences credit access. The logit regression results suggested that the probability of credit access is positively and significantly influenced by education level, family size, off-farm activities, and access to a network of information/recommendation. The off-farm activities, captured by the trader dummy, were used as a proxy for repayment capacity. The network of information and recommendation acts as a screening mechanism where potential clients are required to be recommended or guaranteed by existing clients, thereby acting as social collateral.

Zeller *et al.* (1994) suggested that access to credit from the Gambian Cooperative was positively and significantly influenced by age and household income, while being female had a negative and significant effect. What these results suggest is that older persons who control household resources may be rated to be more creditworthy, while women are discriminated against in the credit market.

Collateral requirements are a major factor that influences credit access, especially in the formal sector. This view was supported by Daniels (2001), who observed that the low levels of collateral among the poor to a great extent explained their limited access to financial instruments in the formal banking sector.

3. METHODOLOGY AND DATA

This study used data from the South African Income and Expenditure Surveys of 1995 and 2000, which contained information on the amount of debt outstanding. These two household surveys were conducted by Statistics South Africa and are linked to the October Household Survey and the Labour Force Survey of the same date respectively. The surveys provide stratified samples of about 30 000 households each, representative of the total South African population. Unfortunately, though, comparability issues make direct comparison of the 1995 and 2000 data problematic, particularly regarding changes in poverty. For this reason, the term "the poor" is used in this paper not to identity the population below a fixed poverty line, but rather to refer to the bottom 40 per cent of all households in each survey.

Multinomial logit models were used to estimate the factors that influence access to different forms of credit for the whole sample, Heckman probit models with sample selection were used for estimation of the factors that influence access to credit by the poor, while probit models were used for estimation of determinants of credit access by blacks.

The Heckman probit model with sample selection involves the specification of the model of interest and the selection model. For the model of interest, the

Table 1
Definition of variables of the study

Variable	*Definition*
bankdu	Dummy for access to formal sector credit (=1 if formal)
semforma	Dummy for access to semi-formal sector credit (=1 if semi formal)
infsector	Dummy for access to informal sector credit (=1 if informal)
rbank	Amount of formal sector credit accessed in constant 2000 prices
rsemid	Amount of semi-formal sector credit accessed in constant 2000 prices
rinformad	Amount of informal sector credit accessed in constant 2000 prices
age	Age of household head, in years
agesq	Square of logarithm of age
male	Dummy for male household head (=1 if male)
household size	Household size
lnexp	Logarithm of per capita household expenditure
education	Education level of household head, measured in years
rural	Dummy for rural area (=1 if rural)
western cape	Dummy for Western Cape Province
eastern cape	Dummy for Eastern Cape Province
northern cape	Dummy for Northern Cape Province
free state	Dummy for Free State Province
kwazulu natal	Dummy for Kwazulu Natal Province
north west	Dummy for North West Province
gauteng	Dummy for Gauteng Province
mpumalanga	Dummy for Mpumalanga Province
limpopo	Dummy for Limpopo Province (Reference category)
blacks	Dummy for black household head (Reference category)
coloured	Dummy for coloured household head
indian	Dummy for indian household head
white	Dummy for white household head
poor	Being in the bottom 40% of the distribution of per capita expenditure for the whole population

dependent variable was the probability of credit access either in the formal, semi-formal or informal markets *(=1 if accessed credit, otherwise zero)*. For the selection models, the dependent variable was the probability of being poor *(=1 if household was poor, otherwise zero)*.

The specification of the Heckman probit model with sample selection for credit access was as follows:

Prob(access) = $\beta_0 + \Sigma\beta_i X_i + \varepsilon_i$, select (poor = $\Omega_0 + \Sigma\,\Omega_i K_i + \varepsilon_i$)..........(1)

Where:

Prob (access) = $\beta_0 + \Sigma\beta_i X_i + \varepsilon_i$ is the model of interest

$Prob(poor) = \Omega_0 + \Sigma\, \Omega_i\, K_i + \mu_i$ is the selection model

β_0 , Ω_0 = constant terms

β_i, Ω_i = vector of coefficients

X_i = vector of household socio-economic characteristics

K_i = socio-economic characteristics vector that is not identical to X_i.

$\varepsilon_{i,}\, \mu_i$ = error terms

The dependent variable for the ith observation is only observable if $(\Omega_i\, K_i + \mu_i) > 0$, where

$\varepsilon_i \sim N(0,1)$, $\mu_i \sim N(0,1)$, $corr(\varepsilon_{i,}\, \mu_i) = \rho$ and $\rho \neq 0$.

Access to various credit markets were captured by the following dummy variables: *infsector (=1 if accessed informal credit), semforma (=1 if accessed semi formal credit), bankdu (=1 if accessed formal credit)*. The specific variables used in the study are as defined in Table 1.

4. ECONOMETRIC RESULTS FOR DETERMINANTS OF CREDIT ACCESS BY THE POOR

4.1 Multinomial Logit Model for Credit Access for Whole Sample

A multinomial logit model for determinants of access to each of the different credit sources was estimated for the whole sample, using the following variables as the reference categories: those with no access to credit, Blacks and Limpopo province. The results (see Table 2) suggest that access to bank credit in both periods was positively and significantly influenced by age, being male, household size, per capita expenditure, education level, and race (being White, Indian or Coloured). Access to bank credit was negatively and significantly influenced in both periods by being poor, indicating that there is an additional effect from being from the bottom two quintiles of households, apart from the effect of per capita expenditure already controlled for. This result suggests that the poor, who usually cannot satisfy the collateral requirements, are regarded as risky borrowers and rationed out of the formal credit markets.

Access to semi-formal credit was positively and significantly influenced in both periods by household size, per capita expenditure, provincial location (Eastern Cape, Northern Cape, Free State and North West) and being Coloured. The factors that negatively and significantly influenced access to semi-formal credit in both periods included being male, rural location, being poor and being White. This might suggest that Whites and Indians possibly prefer bank credit to finance consumption needs as compared to semi-formal credit, which is more expensive.

Informal credit access was positively and significantly influenced in both periods only by being located in Eastern Cape. The negative and significant determinants of informal credit access in both periods include education level and being Coloured or White. This might suggest that those with higher levels of education may have preference for banks or semi-formal credit, which is relatively cheaper (in terms of interest rates charged).

Table 2
Multinomial Logit Model for Access to Credit Whole Sample

Explanatory Variable	*1995* *Coefficient*		*2000* *Coefficient*	
Bank Credit				
Age	0.7827	***	0.1720	***
Age squared	-0.0011	***	-0.0019	***
Male	0.4674	***	0.3910	***
Household size	0.2215	***	0.2760	***
Per capita expenditure	0.6832	***	0.9472	***
Education Level	0.0639	***	0.0286	***
Rural	-0.0660		-0.7387	***
Poor	-1.5462	***	-0.6269	***
Western Cape	0.2410		0.4316	**
Eastern Cape	0.0891		0.2998	
Northern Cape	-0.2932		0.5981	***
Free State	-0.3574	*	0.0427	
Kwazulu Natal	-0.4215	***	0.0117	
North West	-0.2075		-0.2251	
Gauteng	-0.4308	***	-0.0038	
Mpumalanga	-0.9089	***	-0.0067	
Coloureds	0.8159	***	0.5693	***
Indians	1.0103	***	0.8796	***
White	1.2313	***	0.9570	***
Constant	-12.9106	***	-17.1174	***
Semi Formal Credit				
Age	-0.0113		0.0267	**
Age squared	0.00002		-0.0003	**
Male	-0.3089	***	-0.0986	**
Household size	0.1455	***	0.1607	***
Per capita expenditure	0.2879	***	0.3416	***
Education Level	0.0073		0.0050	
Rural	-0.1767	***	-0.1989	***
Poor	-0.3808	***	-0.5910	***
Western Cape	0.3437	**	0.1621	
Eastern Cape	1.0151	***	0.2391	***
Northern Cape	0.9247	***	0.7854	***
Free State	0.2871	**	0.6353	***
Kwazulu Natal	0.0241		-0.1572	*
North West	0.9503	***	0.5370	***
Gauteng	0.0508		0.1310	
Mpumalanga	-0.2232		0.7926	***

contd. table 2

Coloureds	0.1662	**	0.1481	*
Indians	-0.2513	*	-0.1495	
White	-1.2379	***	-1.0586	***
Constant	-5.2790	***	-5.6720	***
Informal Credit				
Age	-0.0588	***	0.0777	***
Age squared	0.0005	**	-0.0009	***
Male	-0.6391	***	-0.0197	
Household size	0.0515	*	-0.0270	*
Per capita expenditure	0.1298		-0.0343	
Education Level	-0.0512	**	-0.0197	***
Rural	0.1543		-0.1698	**
Poor	0.0111		0.1307	
Western Cape	0.3168		0.3313	
Eastern Cape	1.1011	***	0.7865	***
Northern Cape	-0.3636		0.5569	**
Free State	-0.3658		0.9626	***
Kwazulu Natal	0.2327		0.5511	***
North West	0.1496		0.3212	*
Gauteng	0.2216		0.5416	***
Mpumalanga	0.1220		1.0638	***
Coloureds	-0.8288	***	-0.5863	***
Indians	0.0182		-0.4059	
White	-0.6580	**	-1.3044	***
Constant	-4.0564	***	-4.3368	***
Number of observations	28,585		22,111	
LR	chi2 (57)=3188.3		chi2(57)=3982.19	
Prob>chi2	0.0000		0.0000	
Pseudo R2	0.1300		0.1145	
Reference categories	Black race and Limpopo Province			
Base Category	No access to credit			

*** significant at 1%, ** significant at 5%, * significant at 10%

4.2 Heckman Probit Model with Sample Selection for Credit Access by the Poor

4.2.1 Determinants of Informal Credit Access by the Poor

The Heckman probit model with sample selection was used to estimate the factors that influence access to informal credit by the poor. The dependent variable for the equation of interest was *infsector (=1 if accessed informal credit)*, while the dependent variable for the selection equation was *poor (=1 if poor)*.

The results in Table 3 suggest that the age of the household head had an inconclusive effect on informal credit access. The coefficient was negative and significant in 1995 but positive and significant in 2000. However, age squared had a positive and significant effect on informal credit access in 1995, but a negative and significant effect in 2000. Being male had a negative but insignificant effect in both survey periods on the probability of informal credit access. This result may suggest that women are not discriminated against in the informal credit markets in South Africa. These results are however in sharp contrast to Zeller et al (1994), whose results indicated discrimination against women in the informal credit markets in Gambia.

Education level had a positive but insignificant effect on informal credit access. This suggests that education levels do not influence participation in informal credit markets in South Africa. These results are not consistent with Vaessen (2001), who concluded that the education level had a positive and significant effect on informal credit access in Nicaraqua.

Being located in a rural area had an insignificant effect on informal credit access by the poor in both periods. Relative to Limpopo Province (reference category), being located in Kwazulu Natal and Gauteng had a positive and significant effect on access to informal credit by the poor in both periods. However, being located in the Western Cape, Eastern Cape, Northern Cape, Free State or Mpumalanga had positive and significant effects (at least at 10% level) on informal credit access only in the 2000 model.

The race of the household head had a significant effect on informal credit access. Relative to Blacks (reference category), being in the other race groups (Coloured, Indian and White) had a negative and significant effect in 2000.

4.2.2 Determinants of Semi-formal Credit Access for the Poor

Access to semi-formal sector credit by the poor was significantly influenced by the following factors in at least one period: age, being male, per capita expenditure, education level, being rural based, provincial location and race (see Table 4). The age of the household head had a positive effect and age squared had a negative effect on semi-formal credit access in 2000. This result may suggest that older household heads have more control of household resources, hence making them more credit worthy. But the effect only applies to a certain threshold, after which age reduces creditworthiness. Being male had a positive and significant effect on semi-formal credit access only in 2000, which is indicative of discrimination against women in semi-formal credit markets.

Household per capita expenditure, which is a measure of household wealth, had a positive and significant effect on access to semi-formal credit in both survey periods. Wealth is an indicator of the repayment capacities of a household. These results are consistent with Ardington et al (2003), according to which household income in South Africa is central in determining access to formal or semi-formal financial credit markets, where a lack of income drives a wedge between potential borrowers and suppliers in these markets.

Being located in a rural area negatively and significantly affected semi-formal credit access in 2000. This may be explained by the fact that the providers of semi-formal financial services are urban based and may prefer to lend to urban households that have diversified income sources to service the loans. Relative to Limpopo province (reference category), being located in all other

Table 3
Heckprobit Model with Sample Selection for Access to Informal Credit by the Poor

Explanatory Variable	*1995* Coefficient		*2000* Coefficient	
Equation of Interest: Dependent variable - infsector (=1 if accessed informal credit)				
Age	-0.0214	**	0.0462	***
Age squared	0.0002	*	-0.0005	***
Male	-0.1373		-0.0606	
Household size	-0.0833		0.0123	
Per capita expenditure	0.0698		-0.0091	
Education Level	0.0040		0.0026	
Rural	0.1414		-0.0170	
Western Cape	-0.0927		0.3496	**
Eastern Cape	0.3023		0.4103	***
Northern Cape	-0.0345		0.3678	***
Free State	-0.3639		0.3931	***
Kwazulu Natal	0.2192	*	0.3121	***
North West	0.1465		0.2411	**
Gauteng	0.7581	***	0.3963	***
Mpumalanga	0.1387		0.4417	***
Coloureds	-0.0734		-0.3594	***
Indians	1.2068	**	-5.0314	***
White	-1.3519		-5.0079	*
Constant	-1.2478		-2.9067	***
Selection Equation : Dependent variable - poor (=1 if poor)				
Age	0.0050	***	-0.0004	
Male	-0.2965	***	-0.4082	***
Household size	0.1937	***	0.2433	***
Western Cape	-0.0646		-0.6956	***
Eastern Cape	0.4348	***	0.1035	***
Northern Cape	0.5564	***	0.1437	***
Free State	0.5088	***	0.0846	**
Kwazulu Natal	-0.1182	***	-0.1489	***
North West	0.2051	***	-0.3224	***
Gauteng	-0.7739	***	-0.7929	***
Mpumalanga	0.0211		-0.3906	***
Coloureds	-0.3989	***	-0.3255	***
Indians	-1.5085	***	-1.6181	***
White	-2.1156	***	-2.1351	***
Constant	-0.9884	***	-0.6323	***
anthro	-0.7352		0.1041	
Number of observations	29,309		22,111	
Censored observations	17,757		13,829	
Uncensored observations	11,552		8,282	
Wald	chi2(18)=219.03		chi2(18)=7287.38	
Prob>chi2	0.0000		0.0000	

**** significant at 1%, ** significant at 5%, * significant at 10%*

Table 4
Heckprobit Model with Sample Selection for Access to Semi-formal Credit by the poor

Explanatory Variable	*1995* *Coefficient*		*2000* *Coefficient*	
Equation of Interest: Dependent variable - semforma (=1 if accessed semi formal credit)				
Age	0.0024		0.0240	**
Age squared	-0.0001		-0.0003	**
Male	0.0043		0.1577	***
Household size	0.0058		0.0046	
Per capita expenditure	0.2326	***	0.4805	***
Education Level	0.0105	*	0.0007	
Rural	0.0628		-0.1903	***
Western Cape	0.5354	***	0.2806	**
Eastern Cape	0.6464	***	0.0813	
Northern Cape	0.5960	**	0.1928	*
Free State	0.2597		0.2110	***
Kwazulu Natal	0.3180	***	-0.2522	***
North West	0.4383	***	0.3143	***
Gauteng	0.6714	***	0.2278	*
Mpumalanga	0.1379		0.3656	***
Coloureds	0.2923	***	0.1125	
Indians	0.8744	*	1.1144	***
White	1.2082	**	0.8729	
Constant	-3.3760	***	-5.01307	***
Selection Equation : Dependent variable - poor (=1 if poor)				
Age	0.0050	***	-0.0005	
Male	-0.2971	***	-0.4055	***
Household size	0.1937	***	0.2440	***
Western Cape	-0.0638		-0.6929	***
Eastern Cape	0.4347	***	0.1079	***
Northern Cape	0.5539	***	0.1431	***
Free State	0.5080	***	0.0845	**
Kwazulu Natal	-0.1172	***	-0.1474	***
North West	0.2053	***	-0.3191	***
Gauteng	-0.7735	***	-0.7902	***
Mpumalanga	0.0224		-0.3904	***
Coloureds	-0.3990	***	-0.3260	***
Indians	-1.5088	***	-1.6171	***
White	-2.1148	***	-2.1353	***
Constant	-0.9869	***	-0.6345	***
anthro	-0.6571		-0.6254	***
Number of observations	29,309		22,111	
Censored observations	17,757		13,829	
Uncensored observations	11,552		8,282	
Wald chi (18)	280.7		chi2(18)=375.45	
Prob>chi2	0.0000		0.0000	

**** significant at 1%, ** significant at 5%, * significant at 10%*

provinces in South Africa had a positive and significant effect on access to semi-formal credit at least in one period, with the exception of Kwazulu Natal, which was negative in 2000. In addition, the poor of all other races other than Blacks (reference category) had higher access to semi-formal credit, as indicated by the positive and significant coefficients in 1995. Interestingly, in 2000 Whites and Coloureds no longer had *significantly* better access to semi-formal credit than Blacks, the reference group, once other factors had been controlled for.

4.2.3 Determinants of Formal Credit Access by the Poor

Access to formal sector credit by the poor was significantly influenced by age, being male, household size, education level, being rural, provincial location and race, in at least one period (see Table 5).

The age of the household head had a negative and significant effect on bank credit access by the poor only in 1995. Being male had a positive and significant effect on formal credit access in both periods, which is indicative of discrimination against women in formal credit markets. Household size had a negative and significant effect on access to formal credit in 1995. This result may suggest that households with larger sizes may be construed to have lower repayment capacity and are therefore more likely to be constrained in their access to credit in formal markets.

Education level had a positive and significant effect on formal sector credit access in 2000. This may be explained by the bank account opening requirements in South Africa of at least one pay cheque. The poor with low education levels are more likely to have casual jobs without pay cheques, thereby constraining their access to formal bank services. Being located in a rural area negatively and significantly affected formal credit access by the poor in 2000.

Provincial location, relative to Limpopo province (reference category), had significant effects on formal credit access. Being located in the Western Cape, Gauteng and Mpumalanga had positive and significant effects on formal credit access by the poor in both survey periods. However, being located in the Eastern Cape, Northern Cape and Free State had negative and significant effects only in 1995. The poor from other races were more likely to access formal sector credit as compared to Blacks.

4.3 Probit Models for Credit Access by Blacks

Separate probit models were estimated for factors that influence access to the different credit markets by specifically the black population in South Africa.

4.3.1 Determinants of Informal Credit Access by Blacks

The age of the household head had an inconclusive effect on informal credit access by Blacks in South Africa, as the sign of the coefficient changed between 1995 and 2000. Being male had a negative and significant effect only in 1995 but positive and insignificant in 2000, implying positive bias in favour of women in informal markets. Education level had a negative and significant effect on informal credit access in both periods. This suggests that Blacks with higher levels of education have a preference for formal or semi-formal credit, which is

Table 5
Heckprobit Model with Sample Selection for Access to Bank Credit by the Poor

Explanatory Variable	*1995* Coefficient		*2000* Coefficient	
Equation of Interest: Dependent variable - bankdu (=1 if accessed bank credit)				
Age	-0.0054	**	0.0595	
Age squared	0.0005		-0.0007	
Male	0.3018	***	0.2755	*
Household size	-0.1775	***	-0.0353	
Per capita expenditure	0.0477		0.1674	
Education Level	0.0004		0.0148	***
Rural	0.0108		-0.3195	**
Western Cape	0.3346	***	0.8518	***
Eastern Cape	-0.2067	***	-0.0049	
Northern Cape	-0.3098	***	0.4814	
Free State	-0.2625	***	0.4059	
Kwazulu Natal	0.3077	***	0.3722	
North West			0.4473	
Gauteng	0.9961	***	0.9293	***
Mpumalanga	0.1810	***	0.8431	***
Coloureds	0.3897	***	0.3682	*
White	1.3065	***		
Constant	0.2556		-4.8826	**
Selection Equation : Dependent variable - poor (=1 if poor)				
Age	0.0050	***	-0.0005	
Male	-0.2964	***	-0.4081	***
Household size	0.1937	***	0.2433	***
Western Cape	-0.0633		-0.6970	***
Eastern Cape	0.4355	***	0.1029	***
Northern Cape	0.5560	***	0.1385	**
Free State	0.5079	***	0.0848	**
Kwazulu Natal	-0.1191	***	-0.1485	***
North West	0.2055	***	-0.3223	***
Gauteng	-0.7746	***	-0.7929	***
Mpumalanga	0.0215		-0.3900	***
Coloureds	-0.3994	***	-0.3232	***
Indians	-1.5082	***	-1.6189	***
White	-2.1157	***	-2.1345	***
Constant	-0.9873	***	-0.6320	***
anthro	-3.9258	***	-0.5738	
Number of observations	29,309		22,111	
Censored observations	17,757		13,829	
Uncensored observations	11,552		8,282	
Wald	chi2 (16) 3383.52		chi2(16)=115.18	
Prob>chi2	0.0000		0.0000	

**** significant at 1%, ** significant at 5%, * significant at 10%*

relatively cheaper. Being poor increases the probability of access to informal credit markets, which is the main option available to them. Some provincial locations, relative to Limpopo, had positive and significant effects on informal credit access in 2000 by Blacks (see Table 6).

Table 6
Probit Model for Access to Informal Credit by Blacks

	1995		*2000*	
Explanatory Variable	*Coefficient*		*Coefficient*	
Dependent variable : infsector (=1 if accessed informal credit)				
Age	-0.0280	***	0.0307	***
Age squared	0.0003	***	-0.0003	***
Male	-0.2818	***	0.0015	
Household size	0.0119		-0.0284	***
Per capita expenditure	0.0521		-0.0264	*
Education Level	-0.0228	**	-0.0088	**
Poor	0.0260		0.1439	***
Rural	0.0834		-0.0403	
Western Cape	0.3476	**	0.2340	**
Eastern Cape	0.4082	***	0.3462	***
Northern Cape			0.1165	
Free State	-0.1535		0.4244	***
Kwazulu Natal	0.0250		0.2675	***
North West	-0.0267		0.0967	
Gauteng	0.0322		0.2504	***
Mpumalanga	0.0464		0.4360	***
Constant	-1.9921	***	-2.1891	***
Number of observations	18,309		17,565	
LR	chi2(15)=110.42		chi2(16)=138.85	
Prob>chi2	0.0000		0.0000	
Pseudo R2	0.0470		0.0192	

**** significant at 1%, ** significant at 5%, * significant at 10%*

4.3.2 Determinants of Semi-formal Credit Access by Blacks

Access to semi-formal credit markets by blacks was positively and significantly influenced by household size, per capita expenditure, education level and provincial location (Eastern cape, Northern Cape, Free State and North West) in both survey periods. Being poor and located in a rural area had negative and significant effects on semi-formal credit access by Blacks (see Table 7).

4.3.3 Determinants of Formal Credit Access by Blacks

The probability of access to formal credit markets by Blacks was positively and significantly influenced by age, being male, per capita expenditure, household size, and education level in both periods. With the exception of household size, all these variables may be used by commercial banks as measures of households' repayment capacity to determine their creditworthiness. Poverty had no significant additional impact (see Table 8).

Table 7
Probit Model for Access to Semi-formal Credit by Blacks

	1995		*2000*	
Explanatory Variable	*Coefficient*		*Coefficient*	
Dependent variable : semforma (=1 if accessed semi formal credit)				
Age	-0.0004		0.0224	***
Age squared	-0.00002		-0.00028	***
Male	-0.1551	***	-0.0685	***
Household size	0.0733	***	0.0932	***
Per capita expenditure	0.1873	***	0.2304	***
Education Level	0.1385	***	0.0047	**
Poor	-0.1312	***	-0.2356	***
Rural	-0.0627	*	-0.0931	***
Western Cape	0.2135	**	0.0334	
Eastern Cape	0.6152	***	0.1080	**
Northern Cape	0.4194	***	0.5651	***
Free State	0.3002	***	0.3524	***
Kwazulu Natal	0.0413		-0.1597	***
North West	0.5624	***	0.3013	***
Gauteng	0.1211	*	0.0763	
Mpumalanga	0.0093		0.4267	***
Constant	-3.5216	***	-3.8145	***
Number of observations	18,719		17,565	
LR	chi2(16)=552.96		chi2(16)=1059.71	
Prob>chi2	0.0000		0.0000	
Pseudo R2	0.0627		0.0715	

****** significant at 1%, ** significant at 5%, * significant at 10%*

Table 8
Probit Model for Access to Bank Credit by Blacks

	1995		*2000*	
Explanatory Variable	*Coefficient*		*Coefficient*	
Dependent variable : bankdu (=1 if accessed bank credit)				
Age	0.0362	**	0.1008	***
Age squared	-0.0004	**	-0.0011	***
Male	0.2350	***	0.1086	*
Household size	0.1189	***	0.1110	***
Per capita expenditure	0.4361	***	0.4538	***
Education Level	0.0386	***	0.0136	***
Poor	-0.2096		-0.0170	
Rural	-0.1198		-0.3770	***
Western Cape	0.3067	*	-0.0441	
Eastern Cape	0.1467		-0.0687	
Northern Cape			0.1684	
Free State	-0.0997		-0.0957	
Kwazulu Natal	-0.1982		-0.0035	
North West	0.0465		-0.1499	
Gauteng	0.1661		-0.0403	
Mpumalanga	-0.4032	**	-0.0643	
Constant	-7.8790	***	-8.7980	***
Number of observations	18,309		17,565	
LR	chi2(15)=422.22		chi2(16)=602.00	
Prob>chi2	0.0000		0.0000	
Pseudo R2	0.2210		0.1807	

****** significant at 1%, ** significant at 5%, * significant at 10%*

5. CONCLUSIONS

The financial market in South Africa is segmented into the formal, semi-formal and informal sectors. The poor and Blacks have limited access to the formal and semi-formal financial sectors. In selecting the variables that explain access to different credit markets, the criteria were that they should be significant and that the sign of the coefficient should be consistent in both the 1995 and 2000 models.

At the national level, access to bank credit was positively and significantly influenced by age, being male, household size, education level, household per capita expenditure and race (being Coloured, Indian or White). Being poor had a negative and significant effect on formal credit access. Semi-formal credit access was positively and significantly influenced by household size, per capita expenditure, provincial location (Eastern Cape, Northern Cape and Free State and North West) and being Coloured. The negative and significant factors in determining access to semi-formal credit included being male, rural location, being poor and being White. Informal credit access was negatively and significantly influenced by education level and race (being Coloured or White).

Among the poor, access to bank credit was positively and significantly influenced by being male, provincial location (Western Cape, Gauteng and Mpumalanga) and being Coloured. Access to semi-formal credit was positively and significantly determined by household per capita expenditure, provincial location (Western Cape, Northern Cape, North West and Gauteng) and being Indian. Access to informal credit by the poor was positively and significantly influenced by provincial location (Kwazulu Natal and Gauteng).

Within the black population, access to bank credit was positively and significantly influenced by age, being male, household per capita expenditure and education level. Semi-formal credit access by Blacks was positively and significantly influenced by household size, household per capita expenditure, education level and provincial location (Eastern Cape, Northern Cape, Free State and North West). However, being male, poor and located in a rural area negatively affected access to semi-formal credit by Blacks. Informal credit access by Blacks was negatively influenced by education level, but positively influenced by being in the Western and Eastern Cape.

In conclusion it can be argued that improved access to organized credit markets (i.e formal and semi-formal credit markets) by the poor and Blacks is an important policy instrument in the fight against poverty.

References

Aleem, I. (1990), "Imperfect Information, Screening, and the Costs of Informal Lending: A Study of a Rural Credit Market in Pakistan", *The World Bank Economic Review*, 4(3), 329-349.

Ardington, C., Lam, D. and Levinsohn, J. (2003), "Savings, Insurance and Debt over the Post-Apatheid Period" Report for Office of the Presidency.

Aryeetey, E. (1994), *"Financial Intergration and Development in Sub-saharan Africa: A Study of Informal Finance in Ghana"*, Overseas Development Institute, Working Paper 78.

Aryeetey, E. and Nissanke, M. (1998), "Microfinance within a Financial Systems Approach to Development in Africa", Poverty Research Unit at Sussex, PRUS Working Paper 3, 61-77.

Bell, C. (1990), "Interaction Between Institutional and Informal credit Agencies in Rural India", *The World Bank Economic Review*, 4 (3), 297 - 327.

Bell, C., Srinivasan, T. N. and Udry, C. (1997), "Rationing, Spillover and Interlinking in Credit Markets: The Case of Rural Punjab", *Oxford Economic Papers*, 49, 557-585.

Daniels, R. C. (2001), "Consumer Indebtedness Among Urban South African households: A Descriptive Overview", *Working Paper No 01/55*, Development Policy Research Unit, University of Cape Town.

Dallimore, A. and Mgimeti, M. (2003), "Democratic Banking in the New South Africa: Challenging Contemporary Banking Practices at Grass Roots" Unpublished Report, Durban: Development Research Africa, February.

Greene, W. H. (2000), *Econometric Analysis*, New Jersey: Prentice-Hall, Inc. Fouth Edition.

Heckman, J. (1976), "The Common Structure of Statistical Models of Truncation, Sample Selection, and Limited Dependent Variables and a Simple Estimator for such Models", *Annals of Economic and Social Measurement*, 5, 475–492.

Heckman, J. (1990), "Varieties of Selection Bias" *American Economic Review*, 80, 313–318.

Heidhues, F. (1995), "Rural Finance Markets- An Important Tool to Fight Poverty", *Quarterly Journal of International Agriculture*, 34 (2), 105–108.

Kochar, A. (1997), "An Empirical Investigation of Rationing Constraints in Rural Credit Markets in India", *Journal of Development Economics*, 53, 339–371.

Levacic, R. and Rebmann, A. (1982), *Macro-economics: An Introduction to Keynesian Neoclassical Controversies*, London: McMillan Education Ltd.

Mohieldin, M. S. and Wright, P. W. (2000), "Formal and Informal Credit Markets in Egypt", *Economic and Cultural Change*, 657-670.

Montiel, P. J., Agenor, P. R. and Ul Haque, N. (1993), *Informal Financial Markets in Developing Countries: A Macroeconomic Analysis*, London: Blackwell Publishers.

Nwanna, G. I. (1995), "Financial Accessibility and Rural Sector Development", *Savings and Development,* X1X(4),453-491.

Porteous, D. (2003), "The Landscape of Access to Financial Services in South Africa", *Labor Markets and Social Frontiers No. 3*, South African Reserve Bank, Pretoria.

Schoombee, A. (2000), "Getting South African Banks to serve Micro-entrepreneurs: An Analysis of Policy Options", *Development Southern Africa*, 17(5), 751-767.

Soyibo, A. (1994), *"Financial Linkage and Development in Sub-saharan Africa: A Study of the Informal Finance Sector in Nigeria"*, Overseas Development Institute.

Stiglitz, J. E. and Weiss, A. (1981), "Credit Rationing in Market with Imperfect Information", *American Economic Review,* 71(3), 393-410.

Vaessen, J. (2001), "Accessibility of Rural Credit in Northern Nicaragua: The Importance of Networks of Information and Recommendation", *Savings and Development*, XXV(1), 5–31.

World Bank (1989), *World Development Report*, Washington DC: World Bank.

Yadav, S., Otsuka, K. and David, C. C. (1992), "Segmentation in Rural Financial Markets: The Case of Nepal", *World Development*, 20(3), 423–436.

Zeller, M. (1994), "Determinants of Credits Rationing: A Study of Informal Lenders and Formal Credit Groups in Madagascar", *World Development*, 22 (12), 1895-1907.

Zeller, M., Braun, J. V., Johm, K. and Puetz, D. (1994), "Sources and Terms of Credit for the Rural Poor in the Gambia", *African Review of Money Finance and Banking,* 1, 167-186.

SOCIAL INFRASTRUCTURE IN INDIA:
The Present Scenario and Future Perspective

Rudra Prakash Pradhan
Indian Institute of Technology, Kharagpur

The paper discusses the status of output aspects of social infrastructure in India particularly with respect to education and health. While literacy has been taken as an indicator to education, life expectancy and infant survival rate have been taken as the indicators to health. The findings ascertained that India's achievement on social infrastructure has been very satisfactory. However, it is bounded by the existence of regional disparity across its states. While the status of social infrastructure is significantly high in Kerala, Punjab, Haryana, Maharashtra, Tamil Nadu and Gujarat, it is noticeably low in Orissa, Bihar, Madhya Pradesh, Uttar Pradesh and Assam. But no state is extremely good or bad in all the dimensions of social infrastructure except Kerala, who is supreme position in all the spheres of same. The paper in the final section provides some suggestions to improve the future status of social infrastructure in India and across its states.

I. INTRODUCTION

Close to sixty years after independence, India is indeed become one of the fastest and vibrant growing economies in the world (Jalan, 2006; Kondap, 2005). Its comparative advantage in the globe has changed for the better because of various factors. Some of the most notable among them are: our skills (the growing mass of educated people), integration of financial markets (free flow of capitals), changing of technology, strong foreign exchange reserve, increasing FDI inflows and the booming stock markets. In the same time, India is also low performer in other aspects such as growing fiscal deficit, low tax-GDP ratio, regional disparity, infrastructural deficiencies, poor governance, weak public delivery systems, lack of accountability, bureaucratic hurdles and so forth (Ahluwalia, 2002; Kanda *et al.*, 2001). Hence, India can not achieve a sustainable economic growth in the long run unless the country addresses these problems in a more effective way. The present paper consequently makes an attempt to analyze the issue of infrastructure in India particularly with respect to social infrastructure only. The broad objective of this study is to examine the status of output aspects of social infrastructure in India and their future perspective. That is mostly on education and health.

The remaining of the paper is organized as follows: Section II describes the concept and importance of Infrastructure. Section III outlines the futures of infrastructure. Section IV highlights the importance of education and health.

Section V describes the methodology and database. Section VI follows results and its discussion. Section VI concludes with future perspective.

II. INFRASTRUCTURE: THE CONCEPT AND IMPORTANCE

The role and imperativeness of infrastructure in spearheading economic development of a country and also setting its pace can hardly be overemphasized. Like the foundation in an edifice, place of infrastructure and its soundness are very crucial to the reliability of nation's total development. In fact, provision of infrastructure and its maintenance is very needful for the achievement of sustainable economic growth. In the recent years, it is debated more frequently in the development literature. This is since infrastructure is considered as an engine of economic growth and the basic determinants of quality of future social development (WDR, 2003). But unfortunately, infrastructure has not been explicitly defined in precise and generally acceptable manner. A number of interchangeable words such as 'social overhead', 'economic overhead', 'overhead capital', 'basic economic facilities', etc. have been usually used to denote infrastructure services in the economy.

Infrastructure, in general, defines as a basic system and services without which no economic (under primary, secondary and tertiary) activities can be undertaken in the society. It refers to social, economic and institutional framework facilities that are very essential for a country or a region or an organization. These are all very indispensable not only to facilitate socio-economic development of the country but also to accelerate its space (Kapila and Kapila, 2002; Raghuram *et al.*, 1999). Infrastructure services are usually classified into two broad groups such as Economic Infrastructure (EIS) and Social Infrastructure (SIS). EIS, sometimes called as Economic Overhead Capital (EOC), primarily supports and promotes Direct Productive Activities (DPA) in the economy. It represents the physical framework of facilities through which goods and services are provided to the public. The items cover under this head are power, transport, communication, telecommunication, provision of water, sanitation, safe disposal of waste and other pollutants (See Figure 1).

The WDR (1994) stressed several important linkages of EIS to economic growth in both developed and developing countries. For instance, public investment in transport and communications, which include roads, railways and telephones, has been found significant positive impact on economic growth, particularly in the developing countries. An analysis of the value of EIS stocks in recent years shows that their composition changes significantly as per capita income increases. In the first stage, more basic infrastructure such as water supply, roads, etc. become the dominant component for low income countries. In the second stage, when the economy matures into the middle income stage, the share of agriculture declines and more transport infrastructure is to be developed. Finally, economy moves to high income stage and during that phase, the share of power and telecommunications becomes most important.

SIS, on the contrary, is often termed as Social Overhead Capital (SOC) and mostly useful for the growth of human capital in the economy. This includes education, health and the process of urbanization (Sengupta, 1998). Social

Figure 1: The Structure of Infrastructure

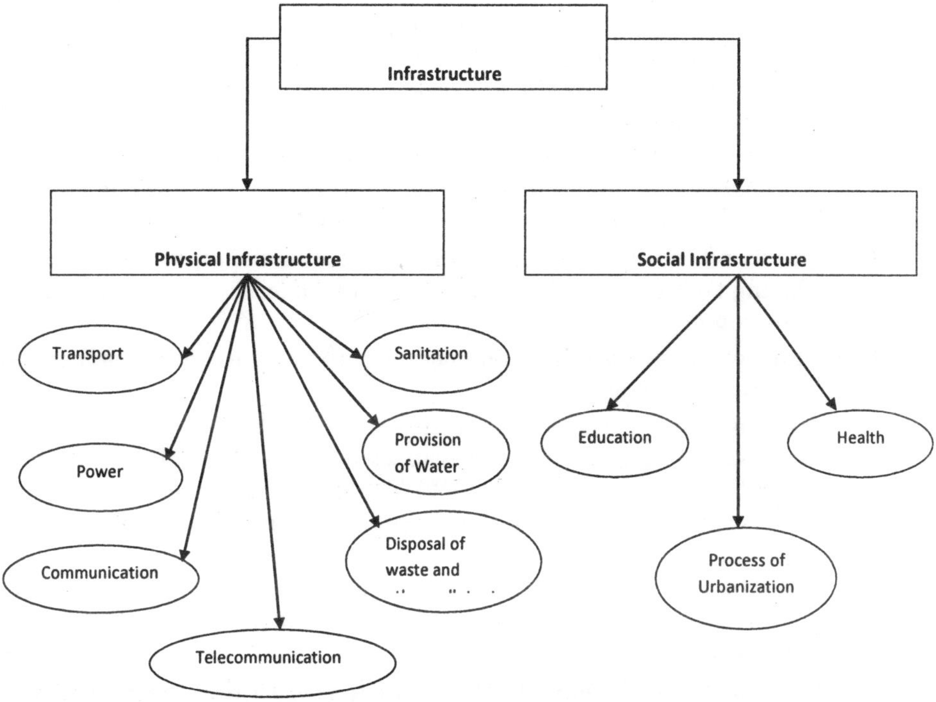

Source: Sengupta, 1998

indicators are sometimes used as a proxy measure for these services. In the economic theory, they are the public goods that characterized as positive externalities. SIS is not only useful for the production activities but also helps in increasing income, raising standard of living, alleviating poverty and declining income inequalities. To be brief, the availability of social infrastructure has multiple effects on labour productivity as well as quality of life.

III. THE FEATURES OF INFRASTRUCTURE

The above section analyzed the concept of infrastructure under two broad heads such as economic and social. However, they are very complementary and interdependent to each other in propelling basic activities of the economy. Here we highlight the basic features of overall infrastructure that are very useful for attaining sustainable economic growth in the economy.

- Infrastructure services are usually provided by public agencies or private agencies subject to some public control. They are provided either free of charge or at a rate that is regulated by public agencies.
- It is normally obtainable/ available to each and every section of the people in the society.

- Infrastructural services can not be transferable and imported easily. Once it is made available means it will continue for ever, though it requires some maintenance at a reasonable cost. It is more or less considered as one time investment for the longer period of time. Briefly, infrastructure systems are both geographically extensive and long-lived (Mishalani and McCord, 2006).
- It is a source of external economies. For example, once a road/ railway are constructed, all people on that locality can get benefit from it. However, all people may not get equal benefit form the same.
- Infrastructure has strong technological dimension, which helps in reducing technical inefficiencies and financial losses in an organization or an economy.
- It falls in the category of public goods, which has the significant features of positive externality.
- Its expansion is costly affairs in the country. This is because it needs huge investment and beyond the capacity of an individual/ organization to establish the same (Nurkse, 1952). That is why it has been undertaken by either government alone or any collaboration by government.
- It is a kind of investment that promotes innovation in the subsequent stages of the economy. Infrastructure usually creates a condition whereby it is very possible for producers to adopt modern techniques (Youngson, 1967).
- Development of the export sector, which so critical in the new growth theory, depends very significantly on the high quality of economic as well as social infrastructure. For instance, the recent advances in transport and communications have accelerated the pace of world trade in the globalization era.
- The expansion of infrastructure certainly expands market base in the economy. Therefore, it encourages international competitiveness in the global economy.
- Infrastructure investment ordinarily works through employment multiplier, income multiplier and investment multiplier (Kaur and Kaur, 2000). Thus, it enhances employment, income and investment opportunities in the country (Ghosh and Dee, 1998).
- It stimulates Direct Productive Activities (DPA) in the economy. According to Hrischman (1958), DPA could not be possible without the development of infrastructure. In fact, access to an area by sea, road, rail or air is indispensable before other economic activities unfold there (Owen, 1964).

The above mentioned features clarified that there is significant need of infrastructure in the economy. The lack/ absence of the same are certainly an obstacle to economic development. In the below, we highlight some of the developmental issues, which can not be fully accomplished without proper infrastructural support in the economy.

- Increasing production and lowering cost;
- Efficient allocation of resources;
- Diversifying production and expanding trade;
- Controlling population, poverty and inequalities;
- Increasing employment and income; and
- Improving environmental condition and the quality of life.

Over and above, economic infrastructure supports and promotes direct productive activities, while social infrastructure ensures the freedom from ignorance, disease and fear to provide human welfare or quality of life to the public. Though both are equally important in the process of socio-economic development, it is the social infrastructure (that is typically by education and health) that affects the most on country's economic growth and progress (Bhandari, 2006; Goyal, 1998). But it is important to note that social infrastructure usually interprets in the form of both inputs as well as outputs. While the inputs of social infrastructure represents hospitals, dispensaries, educational institutions, medical institutions, Primary Health Centres (PHCs), Community Health Centres (CHCs) and the like, output of social infrastructure represents, literacy, life expectancy, infant mortality rate and so forth. But as far as the impact of social infrastructure on economic growth is concerned, it is the output of social infrastructure that determines the same but not the inputs. This is because the inputs of social infrastructure are usually meant to improve the outputs of social infrastructure in the economy. Consequently, our present paper is basically based on the output aspects of social infrastructure and that's mostly on education and health. In the subsequent section, we first highlight the importance of education and health and then we apply an empirical investigation to examine their status in India.

IV. THE IMPORTANCE OF EDUCATION AND HEATH

The importance of education and health should not be overemphasized. This is since both are the most important wealth for a person or an organization or a society. They are very interdependent to each other and equally important for the achievement of sustainable economic growth in the country. They are the most intellectual property in the economy and have been more valuable than that of immovable property (Karnik, 2006). But in India, by both large-survey-based studies as well as case studies, it has noticed the following features: (1) inadequate and inferior infrastructure; (2) poor public service delivery; (3) lack of quality choices for consumers; (4) lack of access specially for the poor, which is due to a high dependence on relatively expensive privately provided services; and so like (See Bhandari, 2006; Misra et al., 2003; Pant and Pandey, 2001).

The lack of education (i.e., illiteracy) is considered as a trap and education simply frees somebody from that trap. Education increases people's awareness of opportunities for the advancement and imparts of ability to seize them. Self-help is very easier for an educated person. Knowledge of one's rights empowers a person and a literate person is able to acquire that knowledge. Literacy is an ability of a person to choose among different states of existence for himself. This can be made clear from the following schematic diagram (See Figure 2). The various states of existence in the diagram may be thought of as diverse combinations of income, leisure, social esteem, political freedom, etc. These states may alternatively be thought of as 'opportunities'. To make use of these opportunities, a person needs basic capabilities like literacy, health, rights, liberty and so forth (see Sekhar, 2005; Dreze and Sen, 1995; Nussbaum and Sen, 1993; Nussbaum, 1992).

Figure 2: The Concept of Development

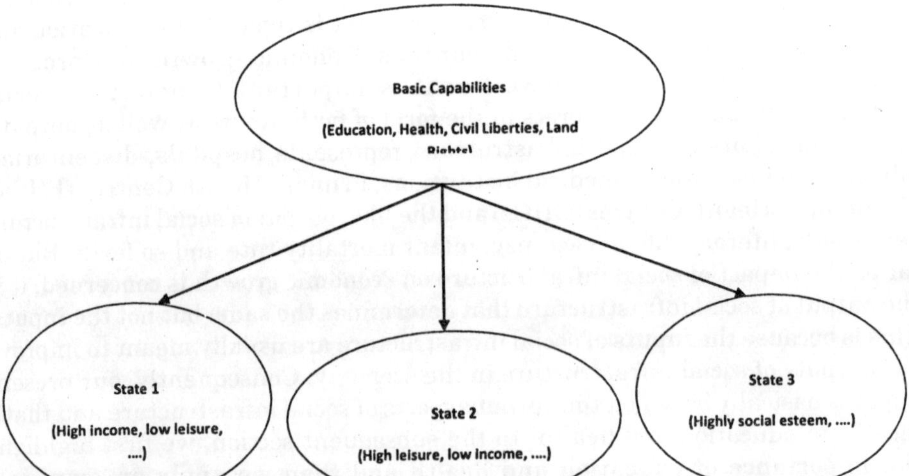

Source: Sekhar, 2005.

Literacy is the first and foremost condition of socio-economic empowerment. The economic return on education is usually very high and also noticeably high in contrast to physical capital. Private returns to education are higher than that of social returns and the return of primary education is logistically more counter to higher education (Tilak, 1995). Provision of universal primary education is also an effective anti-poverty measures that promotes equity in the economy. The poor are poor, as they have very low access of land, capital and skills. Various research studies point out that giving capital to the poor would require large resources and may not be very effective (Parikh, 2004). This is because they have no substantial skills to use this capital efficiently. Providing skills (either formal or informal way) to them is also not practically feasible, if he/she does not have basic education to acquire the same. Basic literacy is the most crucial in this context. Provision of basic literacy to the poor and disadvantaged sections will not only provide them economic opportunities but also enable them to organize better for participating in the political processes (by improving their level of awareness about policies). In brief, literacy plays a major role in broadening the base of economic growth by making the growth sustainable and help in improving the participation of poor in the political process.

The importance of education has, however, been growing much faster during the globalization era. This is because an illiterate person can not participate in the new-knowledge-based society driven by information technology. In fact, globalization also forces the people to acquire knowledge, as they know that it is very difficult for them to survive or get justice in the society without improving their skills. Technological progress, which may be in the form of new ideas, products and process, has been the main driving force behind the economic development in the globalization era. But its outcome may not be efficient, if there is significant presence of illiterate in the economy. Thus, the role of the government is to increase the basic capabilities for a more participatory economic growth and that is crucial for the success of economic reforms.

The modern economy is normally characterized as knowledge economy and that requires highly educated people. That's why the first and foremost need for a country is to make the primary education compulsory and also substantial emphasis on higher education. So far as status of India is concerned, it has been received significant progress on education. The level of literacy has been increased from a low of 16.1% in 1941 to a high of 65.38% in 2001 (See Table 1). This progress has been visible both in male front as well as female front. While the male literacy has been increased from a low of 24.9% to a high of 75.85%, female literacy has been increased from a low of 7.3% to a high of 54.16% during the same period (See Figure 3). In the state-wise comparison, Kerala (both in male front as well as female front) along with Maharashtra and Tamil Nadu are at the highest level, whereas Bihar along with Uttar Pradesh, Rajasthan and Assam are at the bottom level (See GOI, 2001; 2000).

Like education, health is also equally important, as it provides basic welfare to the human being. For making a productive life, one has to be healthy. Usually a healthy man's productivity is significantly higher in contrast to a weak man and hence, his contribution is also considerably high in the economic development. According to Viner (1953), the first requirements of higher labour productivity under modern conditions are that the majority of the population should be literate, healthy and sufficiently well-fed to be strong energetic. Health is more desirable in itself, since a sickness (or ill-health) imposes a burden on other members of the family and also on the society. Absenteeism can result in a loss of production and productivity. In fact, to emerge as a wealthy nation, a healthy society is absolutely desirable. Health, however, can not be ensured simply by individual efforts. Social action is highly needed especially in the areas of sanitation, water supply, clean air, waste disposal and an environment which does not breed diseases or result in epidemics. Public policy is very critical in ensuring adequate infrastructure for a health society. Public action is also important for the health of the poor as they are not unable to take care of themselves to the same extent as the rich.

So far as the status is concerned, India has been achieved a substantial progress in health, which is basically visible in the fonts of life expectancy,

Infant Mortality Rate (IMR), birth rate and death rate (See Table 1). The level of life expectancy has been increased from 32.1 years in 1941 to 64.9 years in 2001. While the male life expectancy has been increased from 32.4 year to 64 years, female life expectancy has been increased from 31.7 years to 65.6 years during the same period (See Figure 3). The level of IMR has been substantially declined from 97 (per 1000) to 63 (per 1000) in 2002 and projected to fall to 55 by 2006 (See Table 1) and 25.9 by 2020 (See Figure 4). While the male IMR has been declined from 96 to 69, female IMF has been declined from 98 to 40 during same period (See Figure 3). In the state-wise, Kerala is at the top level in both the spheres of social infrastructure, i.e. on education and health. The other states that have favorable achievement on social infrastructure are Punjab, Haryana, Maharashtra, Tamil Nadu and Gujarat. On the contrary, the states that have low status of social infrastructure are Bihar, Orissa, Madhya Pradesh, Assam and Uttar Pradesh (See GOI, 2001; 2000). This has also been empirically verified in the subsequent section.

Table 1
The Status of Social Infrastructure in India

Years	X_1	X_2	X_3	X_4	X_5
1941	32.1	16.10	39.9	27.4	192
1951	41.3	18.33	41.7	22.8	140
1961	45.6	28.30	41.1	19.0	114
1971	49.7	34.45	36.9	14.9	129
1981	55.4	43.57	33.9	12.5	110
1991	60.3	52.21	29.5	9.8	80
2001	64.9	65.38	24.8	8.9	63
2006	NA	NA	22.0	8.2	55

Note: X_1: Life Expectancy; X_2: Literacy Rate; X_3: Birth Rate; X_4: Death Rate; X_5: Infant Mortality Rate.

Source: Census of India (Various Issues); CIA World Fact Books.

IV. METHODOLOGY AND DATA DESCRIPTIONS

The broad objective of this paper is to study the status of social infrastructure in India, particularly with respect to output aspects of education and health. The methodology used for the same is the construction of composite indices such as Social Quality of Life Index (SQLI) and Gender Development Index (GDI). While SQLI measures an average development of the country with respect to health and education, GDI adjusts an average achievement to reflect the inequalities between man and women (See Shaljan, 2004; Mitra, 2003). We have taken literacy as an indicator to educational infrastructure and Infant Survival Rate (ISR) and Life Expectancy (LE) as the indicators to health infrastructure. Our structure is very similar to Morri's approach of Physical Quality of Life Index (See Komlos and Snowdon, 2005; Ram, 1982; Mukherjee, 1980; Hicks and Streeten, 1979; Morris, 1979). The only difference is the consideration of ISR in place of Infant Mortality Rate (IMR). We have taken the same in the sense that ISR is a positive measure of well being, while IMR is a negative measure of standard of living (See Shanmugam and Bhaduri, 2000). The other difference is the consideration of dimension index rather than original indicators.

Figure 3: Literacy Rate and Life Expectancy in India (Male and Female comparison)

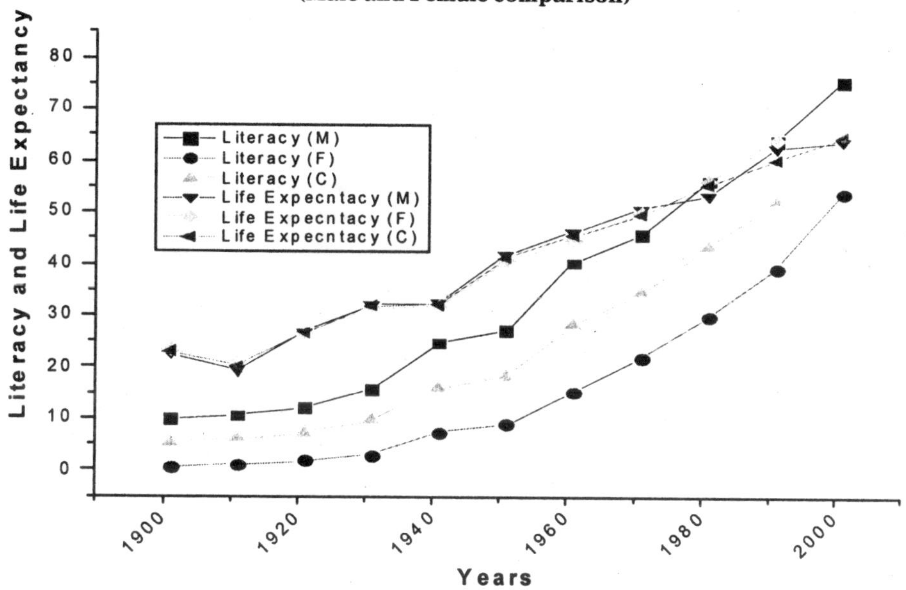

Source: GOI, 2000; 2001

Figure 4: Infant Mortality Rate in India

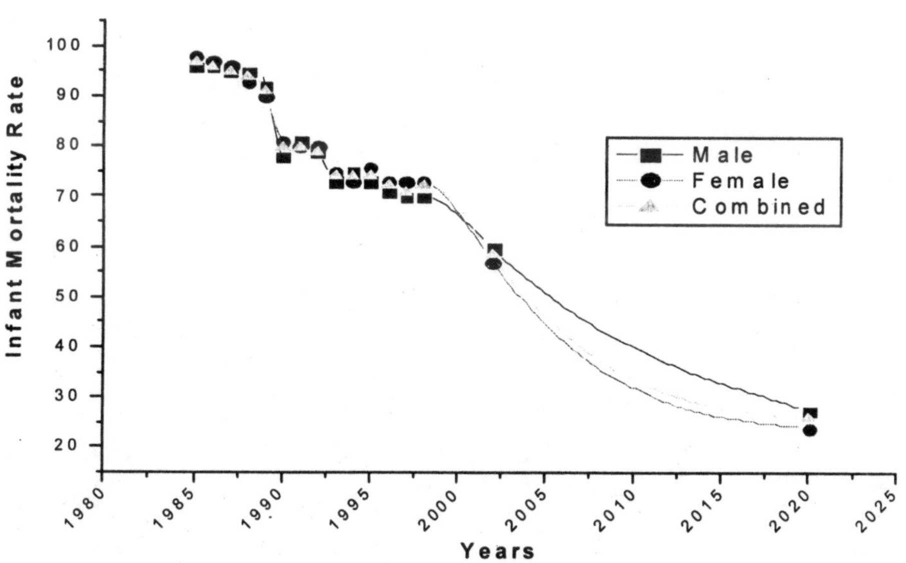

Source: GOI, 2002; US Bureau of the Census, Institutional Programs Centre, International Data Base.

In other words, we use unit free indicators for the construction of SQLI. But equal weights are assigned to all the three dimensions. This is, in fact, very similar feature of Morri's PQLI.

The structure of GDI is very similar to UNDP approach. But the only difference is about the inclusion and exclusion of some parameters. While the original idea of UNDP's GDI is the average achievement and adjustment of education (adult literacy rate and gross enrollment ratio), health (life expectancy), and command over the resources (income), our structure follows the average achievement and adjustment of literacy rate, life expectancy and ISR. A brief outline of these two composite indices is represented in Figures 5 and 6. The detail technical procedures

Figure 5: The Structure of Social Quality of Life Index Social Infrastructure

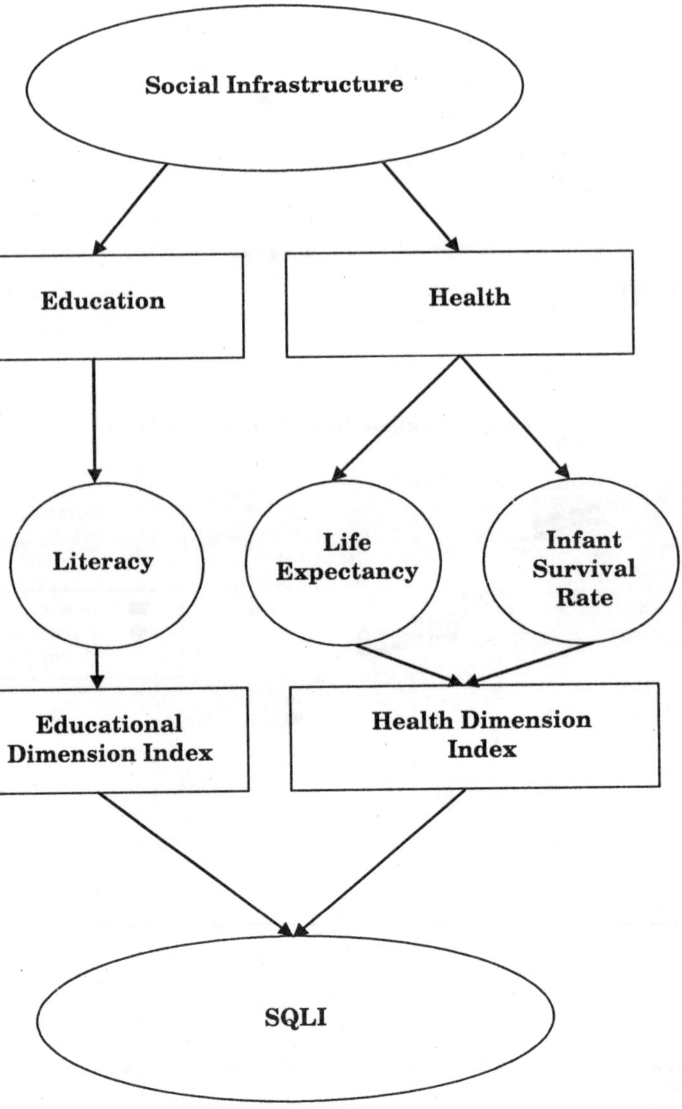

of obtaining social quality of life index and the gender development index are as follows:

A. Social Quality of Life Index

The construction of Social Quality of Life Index (SQLI) follows two step procedures, which are as follows:

Figure 6: The Structure of Gender Development Index Social Infrastructure

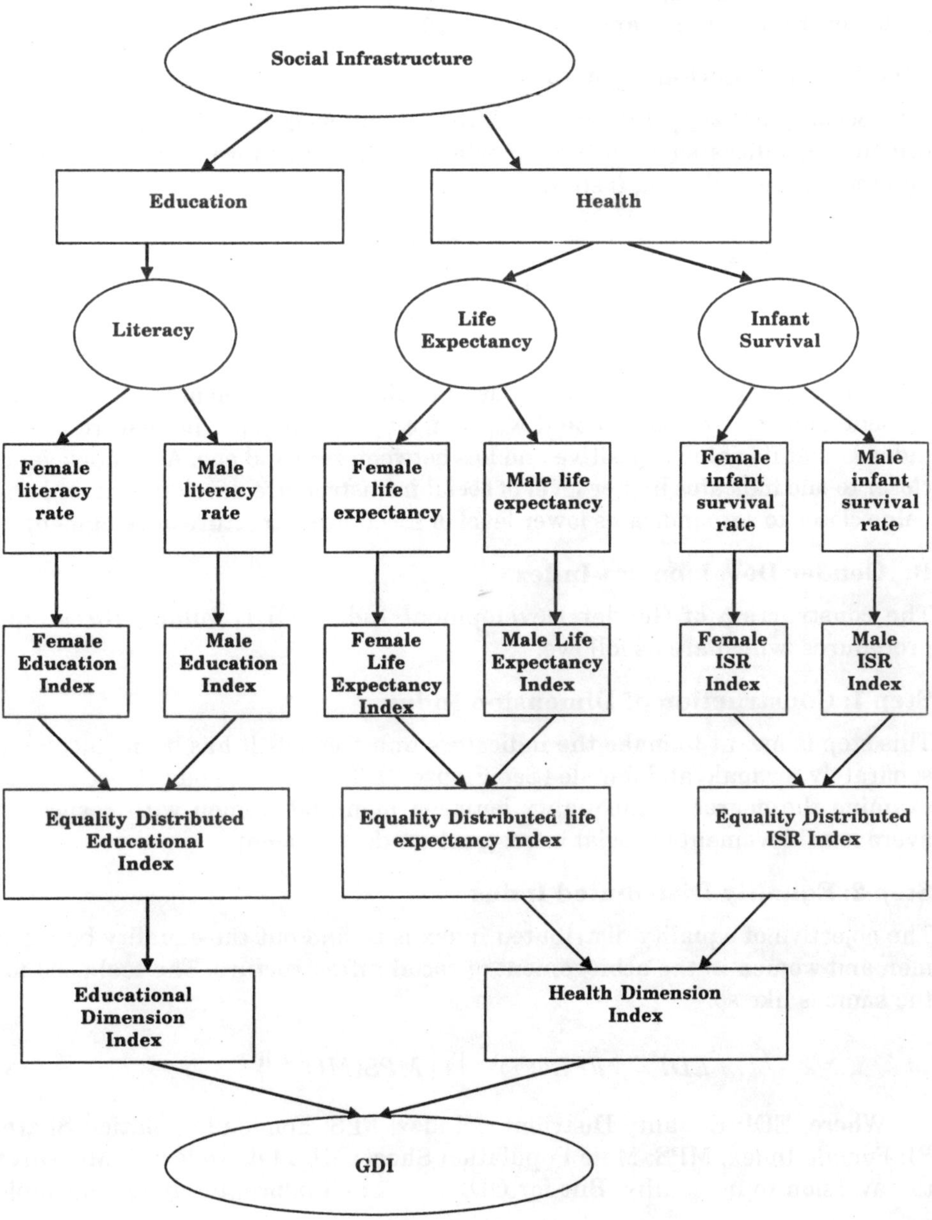

Step 1: Construction of Dimension Index

The basic objective of this step is to make the chosen indicators unit free. The index is prepared in the following fashion:

$$DI = \frac{(X_{ij} - X_{min})}{(X_{max} - X_{min})} \quad (1)$$

Where, DI: Dimension Index; X_{ij}: Denotes i^{th} indicators in j^{th} state; X_{max}: Relates maximum value of ith indicator; X_{min}: Pertains minimum value of ith indicator; i = 1, 2 and 3; and j = 1, 2, ... 15.

Step 2: Construction of SQLI

The Social Quality of Life Index (SQLI) is the weighted average of chosen dimension indices such as life expectancy, ISR and literacy. This has been obtained in the following fashion:

$$SQLI = \frac{\sum_{i=1}^{3} \alpha_i DI_j}{\sum_{ii=1}^{3} i} \quad (2)$$

Where, α_i represents weightage factor to all the dimension indices. But in the present context, we assign equal weightage to all. The specific feature of this index is that its value is positive and lies between zero and one. Any index value closer to one indicates higher level of social infrastructure development and any value closer to zero indicates lower level of social infrastructure development.

B. Gender Development Index

The construction of Gender Development Index (GDI) follows three step procedures, which are as follows:

Step 1: Construction of Dimension Index

This step is meant to make the indicators unit free but it has been calculated separately for male and female (See Figure 6). This is since our objective is to examine the degree of inequality between men and women with respect to average achievement of social infrastructure development.

Step 2: Equality Distributed Index

The objective of equality distributed index is to find out the equality between men and women in the achievement of social infrastructure. The tool used for the same is like so:

$$EDI = \left\{\left[FPS(FI)^{1-\varepsilon}\right] + \left[MPS(MI)^{1-\varepsilon}\right]\right\}^{1/1-\varepsilon} \quad (3)$$

Where, EDI: Equality Distributed Index; FPS: Female Population Share; FI: Female Index; MPS: Male Population Share; MI: Male Index; ϵ: Measures the aversion to inequality. But for GDI, ϵ = 2 and hence, the index is simple represents the harmonic mean of the female and male indices (See Kohli *et al.*, 2005; HDR, 2002; Hemlata, 2002).

Step 3: Gender Development Index

The Gender Development Index (GDI) is the average achievement and adjustment of equality between men and women in the sphere of social infrastructure development. The device used for the same is as follows:

$$GDI = \frac{\sum_{i=1}^{3} EDI_i}{\sum_{ii-1}^{3} i} \quad (4)$$

Where, GDI: Gender Development Index; EDI: Equality Distributed Index. It is to be noted that the value of GDI is also nonnegative like SQLI and lies between zero and one. Any value closer to one indicates complete equality in the achievement of social infrastructure development and indicates lesser gender discrimination. Again any value closer to zero indicates complete inequality in the achievement of social infrastructure development and implies greater gender discrimination in the output of social infrastructure. The data used for the empirical investigation of the status of social infrastructure in India are secondary in nature and that have been obtained from various sources. These include: Census of India (GOI, 2001); Selected Socio-Economic Statistics (GOI, 2000); Women and Men in India (GOI, 2002); and Economic Survey (GOI, 2004). The study is based on state-wise analysis of India for three cross sectional years such as 1981, 1991 and 2001.

VI. RESULTS AND DISCUSSION

In this section, we scan the empirical results and its discussion thereof. The estimated results of Social Quality of Life Index (SQLI) and Gender Development Index (GDI) as well as their dimension indices are presented in Tables 2-3 and Figures 7-8. While the performance of individual indicators is presented in Tables 2 and 3, their average performances are presented in Figures 7 and 8. The findings guaranteed that India's achievement on social infrastructure is very satisfactory. The composite indices of SQLI and GDI have been increasing over the years. The value of SQLI is about 0.507 in 1981 and has been increased to 0.553 in 1991 and 0.647 in 2001. On the contrary, the status of GDI has been increased from 0.456 in 1981 to 0.538 in 1991 and 0.641 in 2001. Since its trend has been increasing over the years and closer towards one, it reflects a maximum achievement of social infrastructure with perfect gender equality. In the state-wise comparison, the status of social infrastructure is significantly high in Kerala and that is followed by Punjab, Haryana, Maharashtra, Tamil Nadu and Gujarat. On the contrary, it is noticeably low in Orissa, Bihar, Madhya Pradesh, Uttar Pradesh, Assam and Rajasthan. But their progress has been increasing over the years (See Figure 7). The pattern and structure is also very similar in the gender disparity of social infrastructure (See Figure 8). That means where SQLI is high, GDI is also high there and vice versa.

Table 2
The State-wise Dimension Indices of Social Quality of Life Index

Year / States	*1981*				*1991*				*2001*			
	X_1	X_2	X_3	X_4	X_1	X_2	X_3	X_4	X_1	X_2	X_3	X_4
Andhra Pradesh	0.73	0.50	0.25	0.49	0.64	0.58	0.42	0.55	0.67	0.60	0.61	0.63
Assam	0.54	NA	NA	—	0.60	0.54	0.53	0.56	0.63	0.53	0.64	0.60
Bihar	0.63	0.44	0.32	0.46	0.66	0.51	0.39	0.52	0.69	0.62	0.60	0.60
Gujarat	0.61	0.48	0.52	0.54	0.66	0.56	0.61	0.61	0.70	0.59	0.70	0.66
Haryana	0.74	0.54	0.44	0.57	0.66	0.61	0.56	0.61	0.67	0.65	0.69	0.67
Karnataka	0.63	0.54	0.46	0.54	0.62	0.61	0.56	0.60	0.71	0.61	0.67	0.66
Kerala	0.79	0.66	0.82	0.76	0.92	0.70	0.90	0.84	0.95	0.76	0.91	0.87
Madhya Pradesh	0.34	0.41	0.34	0.36	0.42	0.51	0.44	0.46	0.57	0.51	0.64	0.57
Maharashtra	0.68	0.54	0.56	0.59	0.70	0.61	0.65	0.65	0.78	0.67	0.77	0.74
Orissa	0.38	0.42	0.41	0.40	0.38	0.52	0.49	0.46	0.55	0.53	0.64	0.57
Punjab	0.63	0.61	0.48	0.57	0.74	0.64	0.59	0.66	0.74	0.72	0.70	0.72
Rajasthan	0.57	0.45	0.30	0.44	0.61	0.55	0.39	0.52	0.60	0.58	0.61	0.60
Tamil Nadu	0.73	0.50	0.54	0.59	0.72	0.58	0.63	0.64	0.76	0.67	0.73	0.72
Uttar Pradesh	0.51	0.35	0.33	0.40	0.52	0.45	0.42	0.46	0.59	0.60	0.57	0.59
West Bengal	0.69	0.48	0.49	0.55	0.65	0.57	0.58	0.60	0.75	0.66	0.69	0.70
India	0.62	0.46	0.44	0.50	0.60	0.54	0.52	0.55	0.67	0.62	0.65	0.65

Note: X_1: ISR Dimension Index; X_2: Life Expectancy Dimension Index; X_3: Educational Dimension Index; X_4: Social Quality of Life Index

Source: Author's Calculation

Table 3
The State-wise Dimension Indices of Gender Development Index

Year / States	*1981*				*1991*				*2001*			
	X_1	X_2	X_3	X_4	X_1	X_2	X_3	X_4	X_1	X_2	X_3	X_4
Andhra Pradesh	0.175	0.641	0.577	0.464	0.350	0.550	0.603	0.501	0.573	0.594	0.642	0.603
Assam	NA	0.427	0.500	—	0.535	0.529	0.522	0.529	0.649	0.560	0.587	0.599
Bihar	0.246	0.482	0.523	0.417	0.382	0.542	0.587	0.504	0.480	0.620	0.685	0.595
Gujarat	0.493	0.497	0.564	0.518	0.603	0.551	0.605	0.586	0.718	0.634	0.654	0.669
Haryana	0.585	0.675	0.667	0.642	0.691	0.645	0.675	0.670	0.793	0.693	0.702	0.729
Karnataka	0.404	0.580	0.607	0.514	0.518	0.561	0.618	0.566	0.647	0.653	0.655	0.652
Kerala	0.757	0.727	0.757	0.747	0.861	0.921	0.802	0.861	0.879	0.957	0.792	0.876
Madhya Pradesh	0.284	0.077	0.472	0.278	0.415	0.270	0.499	0.395	0.658	0.475	0.574	0.569
Maharashtra	0.415	0.531	0.636	0.567	0.640	0.635	0.664	0.646	0.790	0.726	0.726	0.747
Orissa	0.300	0.228	0.475	0.334	0.418	0.171	0.509	0.366	0.590	0.450	0.570	0.537
Punjab	0.543	0.535	0.707	0.595	0.640	0.682	0.722	0.681	0.746	0.765	0.785	0.765
Rajasthan	0.263	0.452	0.532	0.416	0.379	0.487	0.578	0.481	0.617	0.520	0.635	0.591
Tamil Nadu	0.465	0.665	0.591	0.573	0.575	0.612	0.631	0.606	0.697	0.722	0.717	0.712
Uttar Pradesh	0.405	0.406	0.536	0.449	0.503	0.427	0.569	0.500	0.621	0.523	0.667	0.604
West Bengal	0.509	0.588	0.618	0.571	0.594	0.614	0.629	0.612	0.697	0.698	0.715	0.704
India	0.412	0.516	0.560	0.496	0.518	0.501	0.594	0.538	0.656	0.606	0.676	0.646

Note: X_1: Equality Distributed Educational Index; X_2: Equally Distributed ISR Index; X_3: Equally Distributed Life Expectancy Index; X_4: Gender Development Index.

Source: Author's Calculation.

Figure 7: The State-Wise Social Quality of Life Index in India

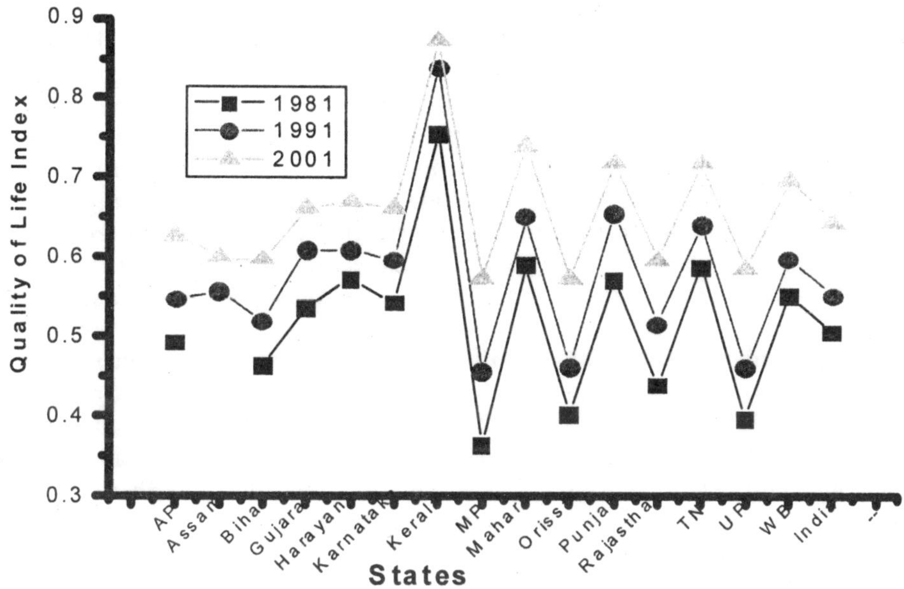

Source: Author's Calculation

Figure 8: The States-Wise Gender Development Index in India

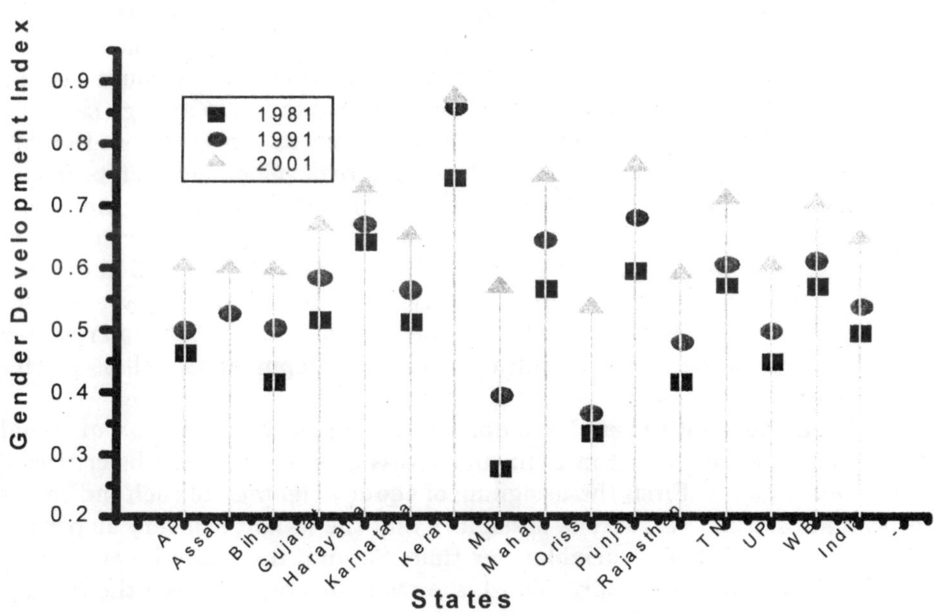

In the dimension-wise, Kerala dominates other states in the aspects of social infrastructure, that is particularly with respect to education and health. However starting with education, the better performing states are Kerala, Haryana, Punjab, Tamil Nadu, Gujarat and Andhra Pradesh. On the contrary, the low performing states are Bihar, Assam, Orissa and Rajasthan. In the health front, the states achieved well are Kerala, Haryana, Andhra Pradesh, Tamil Nadu, West Bengal and Punjab and the states that achieved at a low rate are Madhya Pradesh, Orissa, Uttar Pradesh and Rajasthan. Again if you compare the performance among the states, one can observe that poor states have remained poor and the rich states become rich over the years. This implies that as the social infrastructure increased in the state, its progress is much faster than others.

Over and above, Kerala along with Punjab, Haryana, Maharashtra, Tamil Nadu and Gujarat have achieved well in social infrastructure. On the contrary, Orissa, Bihar, Assam, Madhya Pradesh and Uttar Pradesh have low achievement of the same. But no single state is extremely bad or good in all these three dimension indices. For instance, Maharashtra 3rd position in ISR dimension index but attains 7th and 3rd positions in life expectancy and educational dimension indices. Similarly, Orissa is 15th position in ISR dimension index but stands 10th and 14th position in educational and life expectancy dimension indices. Again Madhya Pradesh secures 15th position in life expectancy dimension index but holds 9th and 14th position in educational and ISR dimension indices. In the similar way, we can represent the status of other states in India.

The results also indicated that all the states move up and down their ranks in different dimension indices except Kerala. The state Kerala is very peculiar and exceptional, who achieved highest position in all the fronts of social infrastructure. The state is also very favorable position in the outcome of gender development. That means there is no discrimination in the achievement of social infrastructure development in Kerala. This is probably due to its high sex ratio than any other states of India (see GOI, 2001). The results also clear that Kerala's achievement in higher level of social infrastructure development and its gender development is not due to a single indicator but due to all the indicators simultaneously. This clarifies that to achieve higher status of social infrastructure and the gender equity; it is required to stress all the social infrastructure indicators simultaneously. This is because they are very interdependent to each other. The lack of one leads to lack of others and resulted an overall degradation of social infrastructure development as well as gender development.

Though the study provides empirical evidence to the status of social infrastructure development in India and across its states, it could be criticized under four grounds. First, the assigning of equal weightage to each indicators of social infrastructure; there is possibility that the weight can very as per the relative importance of a variable over time. Second, the study ignores other aspects of social infrastructure. Third, the study has not explored the linkage between inputs and outputs aspect of social infrastructure. Fourth, the empirical analysis has been followed three cross sectional years only. The ranking and status could be otherwise, if one can go by time series analysis. This is, in fact, not easily possible to investigate, since the time series data are not available in India and across its states.

VII. CONCLUSION AND FUTURE PERSPECTIVE

The paper examined the status of social infrastructure in India. It mostly focused on the output aspects of social infrastructure, particularly with respect to education and health. While literacy has been chosen as an indicator to education, Infant Survival Rate (ISR) and life expectancy have been taken as the indicators to health. The analysis followed with the construction of composite indices such as Social Quality of Life Index (SQLI) and Gender Development Index (GDI). While SQLI represents an average development of the country with respect to literacy rate, life expectancy and ISR, GDI adjusts an average achievement to reflect the inequalities between men and women. The special features of these indices are that their values lie between zero and one. Any value closer to one indicates higher level of social infrastructure development as well as gender development and vice versa. Our investigation followed the state-wise analysis of India for three cross sectional years such as 1981, 1991 and 2001.

The estimated results confirmed that India's progress on social infrastructure development has been very satisfactory. While the value of SQLI has been increased from 0.507 in 1981 to 0.647 in 2001, the value of GDI has been increased from 0.456 to 0.641 during the same period. The implication of these results is that India has achieved a maximum of social infrastructure development with perfect gender equity. However, this achievement is not at all balanced; t is bounded by the existence of regional disparity across its states. While the status of social infrastructure development is substantially high in Kerala, Punjab, Haryana, Tamil Nadu, Maharashtra and Gujarat, it is noticeably low in Orissa, Bihar, Madhya Pradesh, Uttar Pradesh and Assam. But the dimension indices clarified that no state is extremely good or bad in all the areas of social infrastructure except Kerala. For instance, some states have achieved better in educational front but not better in health front. The reverse is also significantly true for other states. That means some states have achieved better in health front but not better in educational front. Kerala is the only state in India, whose achievement in social infrastructure is very best in all the dimensions. As a result, its both SQLI and GDI are at the highest level. Kerala's achievement on social infrastructure development reflects that a mere improvement in single dimension of infrastructure will not ensure higher SQLI and GDI in the economy. This is because the components of social infrastructure are very interdependent to each other. The lack of one leads to lack of others and resulted overall degradation of both SQLI and GDI. With these specific findings, the paper in the bellow provides some suggestions to improve the future status of social infrastructure in India and across its states.

- There is need of balanced infrastructural development in the Indian economy. For this, a massive dose of public investment is urgently required, particularly in the disadvantages states like Orissa, Bihar, Assam, Madhya Pradesh and Uttar Pradesh.

- Though government intervention is sole essential in this journey, greater private sector participation along with public-private partnership is also essential in the social infrastructure development. This is not only due the constraint of government but also to improve the quality of social infrastructure.
- A complete exclusion of either market forces or the state from the infrastructure spheres is totally inappropriate and may prove counter-productive. The state can provide the enabling environment and produce desired results through a judicious mix of market-excluding and market-complementing interventions depending on whether the type of error by the market is a commission or an omission.
- A structural reform in the infrastructure sector is urgently required for promoting greater efficiency and viability by freeing them from bureaucratic and political hurdles.
- People's participation is very helpful and urgent need for social infrastructure development in the economy. An effort must be taken to strengthen the grass-roots level democratic institutes, which includes Panchayats, Non-Governmental Organizations, Community Based Organizations, Self-Help Groups and so forth.
- The role of civil society lies in creating pressure on the government for positive action through the organs of the free press, judiciary and mass media, which the democratic polity of India provides.
- There is need to decentralization of planning, which implies the involvement of government at the local level. This is very essential in the sense that local government can ensure better development, as per the need of social infrastructure in the locality.
- As you know India has endowment of a young population and its pool of well-educated knowledge-edge-professionals is uniquely positioned. No other country has such level skills with scalability and a comparatively low-cost base than that of India. If we can add some innovation to this, we certainly dominate the global knowledge economy at least in some areas of economic development.
- The last but not the least is to integrate physical infrastructure with social infrastructure. This will bring the best outcome of social infrastructure development in the economy.

To conclude, the output of social infrastructure, particularly on the aspects of education and health, is part and parcel of economic development in the country. A piece-meal approach to such a vital need could be of serious consequences. So what is required is to design and implement the infrastructural related policies and programmes in a right earnest way. It will not be a daunting task, if there is adequate political will in the country.

References

Ahluwalia, M. S. (2002), State Level Performance under Economic Reforms in India, in Krueger, A. O. (ed.), *Economic Policy Reforms and the Indian Economy*, pp. 91-125, Oxford University Press, New Delhi.

Bhandari, L. (2006), Social Infrastructure: Urban Health and Education, in *India Infrastructure Report,* pp. 232-257, Oxford University Press, New Delhi.

Dreze, J. and Sen, A. (1995), India: Economic Development and Social Opportunity, Oxford University Press, New Delhi.

Ghosh, B. and De, P. (1998), Role of Infrastructure in Regional Development: A Study over the Plan Period, *Economic and Political Weekly*, 33 (40), pp. 3039-3048.

Goyal, I. C. (1998), An Introspection on Some Aspects of Infrastructure, *Yojana*, 42 (2), pp. 21-25.

GOI (2004), Indian Economic Survey, Ministry of Finance, Government of India (GOI), New Delhi.

GOI (2002), Women and Men in India, Central Statistical Organization (CSO), Government of India (GOI), New Delhi.

GOI (2001), Population Census of India, Office of Registrar General, Government of India (GOI), New Delhi.

GOI (2000), Selected Socio-Economic Statistics, Central Statistical Organization (CSO) Government of India (GOI), New Delhi.

HDR (2002), *Human Development Report*, United Nations Development Programme (UNDP), Oxford University Press, New York.

Hemlata, J. (2002), Educational Development Index- Rajasthan, Spatio-Temporal Appraisal at Panchayat Samiti/Block Level, Institute of Development Studies, Jaipur.

Hicks, N. and Streeten, P. (1979), Indicators of Development: The Search for a Basic Needs Yardstick, *World Development*, 7 (6), pp. 567-580.

Hrischman, A. O. (1958), The Strategy of Economic Development, Yale University, Press, New Haven.

Jalan, B. (2006), Cloud on Silver, *Outlook*, 56 (13), pp. 34-38.

Kanda, D., Reynolds, P. and Towe, C. (2001), Structural Reforms n India", in Callen, T., Reynolds, P. and Towe, C. (eds.), *India at the Cross Roads: Sustaining Growth and Reducing Poverty*, pp. 170-189, International Monetary Fund (IMF), Washington.

Kapila, R. and Kapila, U. (2002), India's Economy in the 21st Century, Academic Publications, New Delhi.

Karnik, K. (2006), Education for Innovation, *The Economic Times*, 7 September.

Kaur, K. and Kaur, M. (2000), Physical Infrastructure and Performance of Corporate Sector-An Interrelationship, in Corporate Sector Research (Conference Volume, held at Navi Mumbai, during May 12, 2000), pp. E-5-E9.

Kohli, A., Samra, A. and Samra, A. (2005), Gender Educational Development Index and Its Impact on Women Status, *Asian Economic Review*, 47 (3), pp. 391-401.

Komlos, J. and Snowdon, B. (2005), Measures of Progress and Other Tall Stories: From Income to Anthropometrics, *World Economics*, 6 (2), pp. 87-135.

Kondap, N. M. (2005), Mergers and Acquisitions in the Indian Industry and Its Effects on People Management, *Management Review*, 17 (2), pp. 9-15.

Mishalani, R. G. and McCord, M. R. (2006), Infrastructure Condition Assessment, Deterioration Modeling, and Maintenance Decision Making: Methodological Advances and Practical Considerations, *Journal of Infrastructure Systems*, 12 (3), pp. 145-146.

Misra, R., Chatterjee, R. and Rao, S. (2003), The Current Health Scenario, *India Health Report*, pp. 18-43, Oxford University Press, New Delhi.

Mitra, K. (2003), Gender, Development and Women's Health in India, *Indian Journal of Social Development*, 3 (1), pp. 74-83.

Morris, M. D. (1979), Measuring the Condition of the World's Poor: The Physical Quality of Life Index, Pergamon Press, New York.

Mukherjee, M. (1980), Physical Quality of Life Index, Centre for Monitoring Indian Economy (CMIE), Mumbai.

Nurkse, R. (1952), Problems of Capital Formation in Underdeveloped Countries, Oxford University Press, London.

Nussbaum, M. (1992), Human Functioning and Social Justices, *Political Theory*, 20 (2), pp. 202-247.

Nussbaum, M. and Sen, A. (1993), The Quality of Life, Clarendon Press, Oxford.

Owen, W. (1964), Strategy for Mobility, Brooking Institute, Washington D. C.

Pant, S. K. and Pandey, A. (2001), Social Sector in Liberalized Era, in R. Datt (ed.), *Second Generation Economic Reforms in India*, Deep and Deep, New Delhi.

Parikh, K. S. (2004), Social Infrastructure as Important as Physical Infrastructure, Indian Development Report, 2004-05, pp. 103-115, Oxford University Press, New Delhi.

Raghuram, G., Jain, R., Sinha, S., Pangotra, P. and Morris, S. (1999), Infrastructure Development and Finance, MacMillan Publications, New Delhi.

Ram, R. (1982), International Inequality in the Basic Needs Indicators, Journal of Development Economics, 10 (1), pp. 113-117.

Sengupta, J. K. (1998), Infrastructure and Economic Growth, in *New Growth Theory-An Applied Perspective*, pp. 209-218, Elgar Publications, United Kingdom.

Sekhar, C. S. (2005), Economic Growth, Social Development and Interest Groups, *Economic and Political Weekly*, 41 (50), pp. 5338-5347.

Shaljan, A. M. (2004), Population, Gender and Development in Maldives, *Economic and Political Weekly*, 39 (18), pp. 1835-1840.

Shanmugam, K. R. and Bhaduri, S. N. (2000), Composite Indices of Basic Human Needs and Income in India, *Artha Vijnana*, 52 (2), pp. 115-126.

Tilak, J. B. G. (1995), Costs and Financing of Education in India: A Review of Issues, Problems and Prospects, Studies on Human Development in India, Discussion Paper No. 5, Centre for Development Studies, Thiruvananthapuram.

Viner, J. (1953), International Trade and Economic Development, Oxford University Press, Oxford.

WDR (2003; 1994), World Development Report, United Nations Development Programme (UNDP), Oxford University Press: Washington.

Youngson, A. J. (1967), Overhead Capital, Edinburgh University Press, Edinburgh.

THE ROLE OF CREDIT ACCESS IN IMPROVING COCOA PRODUCTION IN WEST AFRICAN COUNTRIES

Joachim Nyemeck Binam
International Institute of Tropical Agriculture, Cameroon

Jim Gockowski
International Institute of Tropical Agriculture, Messa

Guy Blaise Nkamleu
International Institute of Tropical Agriculture, Nigeria

This study uses survey data to examine the role of access to credit on cocoa production, in West African countries. The study specifies and estimates econometric models to simulate the counterfactual of what cocoa production would be in the absence of credit facilities. The results show that the cocoa farmer's capacity variables as well as the level of infrastructural development in the village, the lending reputation of the region are more important determinants to extent cocoa farmer access to credit. We also find that access to credit by cocoa farmers has a positive spillover effect on cocoa production. The research concludes that there is a need to promote credit institutions specialized in saving mobilization and credit supply to farmers in general and specifically cocoa farmers.

JEL Classification: *Q12, Q14, Q18*

Key words: *access to credit, cocoa production, farmers' ability, farmers' capacity, West African countries.*

INTRODUCTION

Cocoa is one of the most widely produced agricultural crops in the West African countries. It is a vital source of foreign exchange, investment, and economic growth. Cocoa also occupies a pivotal role in the livelihoods of rural people. Million of people in rural area are thought to be directly or indirectly involved in its production and marketing (NRI, 2004).

The four largest cocoa producers in this region are Cote d'Ivoire, Ghana, Nigeria and Cameroon with roughly 95% of their production coming from smallholder farmers (Vos *et al.* 2002).

Since the early 1980s dramatic changes in export commodity markets, and other shocks resulted in a drop in the price of cocoa and other raw material in the world market, the cocoa sub sector had to be reformed with the support of the World Bank and the International Monetary fund. The recommended policy

---

Corresponding Author: *E-mail: b.nyemeck@cgiar.org; nyemeckbijoa@yahoo.fr*

was the retreat of the states from economic life and the opening up of economic activities to the free play of market forces.

Following the implementation of liberalization policies in West African countries, there has been a decline in the availability of adequate and appropriate rural banking and credit facilities that could help to support future tree crop development such as cocoa (NRI, 2004).

The availability and timely delivery of inputs is probably one of the most effective ways of rising productivity. Access to inputs (e.g. seeds, chemicals and fertilizers) has often become more difficult as input distribution has passed from the public to the private sector and subsidies have been reduced or removed. Shortfalls in input availability have contributed to other on-farm problems, for example, one of the most severe problems faced by cocoa farmers is pest and disease control. Yield losses due to disease are estimated to range between 10% and 80% (Natural Resources Institute, 2004). Chemicals, cultural practices and biological control can all be used to control pest and diseases, but depressed produce prices do not encourage farmers to use inputs or undertake appropriate cultural practices involving costly labour. Prior to liberalization, many cocoa farmers received free or subsidized pesticides, and many who relied on state-sponsored pest and disease control services have not continued to treat their trees after state systems were withdrawn. This together with other factors, for example limited replanting and lack of access to quality planting material, poor level of technical knowledge and technology transfer, have caused declining yields.

Because of the need for purchased inputs to achieve on-farm yields, and high quality requirements throughout the supply chain to be competitive in world markets, processed product such as cocoa require a great deal of coordination to be produced, processed, and marketed competitively. Unfortunately, the consequent denial of access to affordable credit is probably the major constraint facing the farmers in developing countries in general (Killick, 1999) and specifically, cocoa farmers in West Africa.

It has been a long-held belief among researchers and policymakers that cocoa farmers in West African countries lack adequate access to credit. This lack of adequate access to credit is in turn believed to have significant negative consequences on various aggregate and household level-incomes, including technology adoption, agricultural productivity, and the overall household welfare.

Several studies in the past two decades have substantially increase scientists' understanding of the workings of financial credit institutions in developing countries (Alderman and Paxson, 1992; Besley, 1995; Delgado, 1995; Zeller et al. 1997; Zeller et Sharma, 1998; Diagne and Zeller, 2001). These studies have revealed the complex strategies used by farmers to increase their productive capacity, share risks, and smooth consumption. These strategies generally work through self-enforcing informal contracts among friends, neighbours, and members of extended family, and arranged within networks of informal institutions of diverse natures (Diagne, 1999; Diagne and Zeller, 2001).

These nonmarket informal institutions, the economic rationales of which have long eluded the attention of researchers and policymakers, have often been found to outperform the financial institutions governments have set up to serve rural population. One hypothesis that is often advanced by researchers and policymakers to explain this phenomenon is that government and non government organizations (NGO) supported credit programs often crowd out the financial services offered by these informal institutions. Hence, understanding how informal credit institutions serve the financial need of cocoa farmers and interact with the cocoa production is important.

Access to credit affects cocoa farmers' outcomes through different pathways. The more prominent is through the alleviation of capital constraints on cocoa production: expenditures on cocoa inputs are incurred during the cocoa husbandry process, whereas returns are received only after the cocoa are harvested and commercialized. Most cocoa farmers show a negative cash flow during the proceeding season. Therefore, to finance the purchase of production inputs, the farmer must either dip into its savings or obtain credit. Access to credit can therefore significantly increase the ability of cocoa farmers with little or no savings to acquire agricultural inputs. Furthermore, easing potential capital constraints through the credit reduces the opportunity costs of capital-intensive assets relative to family labour, thus encouraging the adoption of high-yielding technologies such as Integrated crop and pest management (ICPM) and therefore increasing land and labour productivity, a crucial factor in encouraging development, in particular in many West African cocoa countries. The analysis is based on a data set collected in 2002 and 2003 among cocoa farmer households in Cote d'Ivoire, Ghana, Nigeria and Cameroon.

The paper is organized as follows: section 2 present the methodology of the paper and discusses the conceptual framework between the two regimes of cocoa farmers (those who have access to credit and those who do not have access to credit). Section 3 briefly describes the structure of data collected and used in this paper. Section 4 presents the results of the econometric analysis. Section 5 concludes the paper with some final remarks on the policy implications of the findings of the paper.

2. METHODOLOGY

To allow the most flexible form of interaction between credit and cocoa production activities, we use the methodology performed by de Janvry *et al.* (2005) by separately considering two cocoa production regimes: households producing cocoa without credit access, regime 0; and households producing cocoa with credit access, regime 1. We start by introducing the notation, used in this section.

Let y_{0i} be the total production for each individual i in regime 0. We assume a linear model for its logarithm:

$$\log y_{0i} = E\log y_{0i} + \mu_{0i} = \beta_0 X_i + \gamma_0 \hat{\lambda}_i + \mu_{0i},$$

where $E\log y_{0i}$ is expected log-production conditional on observed characteristics and regime participation, X_i are observed characteristics of the farmers/farms, $\hat{\lambda}_i$ (defined later) is function of observed characteristics and observed regime participation, and μ_{0i} accounts for unobserved characteristics. Estimation of this model will give an estimated expected log-production: $\hat{E}\log y_{0i} = \hat{\beta}_0 X_i + \hat{\gamma}_0 \hat{\lambda}_i$ from which one can derive an estimated expected production $\hat{E}y_{0i} = \exp\left(\hat{E}\log y_{0i} + 0.5\,\hat{\text{var}}\,\mu_{0i}\right)$.

Using the estimation results, we also generate a predicted unobserved term $\hat{\mu}_{0i}$, and derive the predicted log-production and corresponding production:

$$\hat{\log} y_{0i} = \hat{\beta}_0 X_i + \hat{\gamma}_0 \hat{\lambda}_i + \hat{\mu}_{0i} \text{ and } \hat{y}_{0i} = \exp\left(\hat{\log} y_{0i}\right).$$

Similar expressions are defined for cocoa production in regime 1, y_{1i}.

2.1 Effect of the Credit Access on Cocoa Production and Revenue

To identify the impact of the credit access on cocoa production and revenue, we compare the observed farmer production distribution with a counterfactual production distribution without credit access. We first estimate farmer production equations from observed values; then use the production equations to simulate what farmer production would be if the household produce cocoa without credit; finally we compare the simulated and observed production distributions, and derive the contribution of the credit access to cocoa production.

We are interest in predicting the total production for each individual i in regime 0, y_{0i}. For farmer non-having access to credit, this is the observed production; for those who have access to credit, this is the predicted production they would earn if they had not credit facilities. The prediction requires (i) the estimation of the a model of cocoa production under regime 0, and (ii) using the estimated conditional mean and variance of production to generate a counterfactual predicted production $\hat{y}_{0i}$ for farmer i.

Estimation for the cocoa production in regime 0 is done with a standard selection model:

$$\begin{cases} P_i^* = \alpha Z_i + \varepsilon_i \quad P_i = 1\,(P_i^* \succ 0) \\ \log y_{0i} = \beta_0 X_i + \mu_{0i}^*, \; \textit{observed for } P_i = 0 \end{cases} \tag{1}$$

where P_i^* is non-observed continuous latent variable and P_i is an observed binary variable, equal to 1 if the farmer has credit facilities; Z_i and X_i are vectors of independent variables of the belonging regime and production equations; $(\varepsilon_i, \mu_{0i}^*)$ are unobserved terms following a bivariate Normal distribution. This distributional assumption on the unobserved terms implies that, conditional on the belonging regime:

$$E(\log y_{0i}|P_i) = \beta_0 X_i + \gamma_0 \lambda_i, \text{ with } \lambda_i = E(\varepsilon_i|P_i) = \begin{cases} -\phi(\alpha Z_i)/(1-\Phi(\alpha Z_i)) & \text{for } P_i = 0. \\ \phi(\alpha Z_i)/\Phi(\alpha Z_i) & \text{for } P_i = 1. \end{cases} \quad (2)$$

The model is estimated with the two-step Heckman procedure (Heckman, 1979). From the estimated probit equation (1), we compute an estimated value $\hat{\lambda}_i$ for λ_i, by replacing α by its estimated value $\hat{\alpha}$ in equation (2). The log-production in regime 0 is then estimated on the group $P_i = 0$:

$$\log y_{0i} = \beta_0 X_i + \gamma_0 \hat{\lambda}_i + \mu_{0i}, \quad (3)$$

with $E(\mu_{0i}|P_i) = 0$, $\text{var}(\mu_{0i}|P_i) = \sigma_0^2$. For this sub-sample of observations, y_{0i} is total farmer production (equal to y_i).

Using estimated parameters, we can now predict individual log-production, $\hat{\log} y_{0i}$, for all farmers *i*.

Equation (3) includes two terms: a conditional expected value, $E \log y_{0i} = \beta_0 X_i + \gamma_0 \hat{\lambda}_i$, based on the observable variables and characteristics of the farmer, and unobserved term μ_{0i}. a prediction of the conditional expected value of farmer log-production in regime 0 is given by:

$$\hat{E} \log y_{0i} = \hat{\beta}_0 X_i + \hat{\gamma}_0 \hat{\lambda}_i.$$

To generate unobserved terms for group in regime 1, we construct a random value:

$$\hat{\mu}_{0i} = \hat{\sigma}_0 \Phi^{-1}(r)$$

where $\hat{\sigma}_0$ is the estimated standard error of μ_{0i} for the group in regime 0, *r* stands for a random number between 0 and 1, and Φ^{-1} is the inverse of the cumulative probability function of the standard normal distribution. For the non access to credit farmers, we use the observed residual.

Combining these two terms gives a predicted log-production in regime 0 for all farmers:

$$\hat{\log} y_{0i} = \begin{cases} \log y_i = \hat{\beta}_0 X_i + \hat{\gamma}_0 \hat{\lambda}_i & \text{for } P_i = 0 \\ \hat{\beta}_0 X_i + \hat{\gamma}_0 \hat{\lambda}_i + \hat{\mu}_{0i} & \text{for } P_i = 1 \end{cases} \quad (4)$$

and the corresponding predicted production $\hat{y}_{0i} = \exp(\hat{\log} y_{0i})$ in regime 0.

In particular, we are interested in assessing whether the farmers that had credit facilities would be better or worse farmers without credit; whether having credit facilities enhance or reduce farmer production; and finally whether the farmers that have credit facilities are those that benefit the most from credit. To answer these questions, we use the expected farmer production in each regime estimated for each farmer.

This method requires an estimation of the expected log-production from farming in each regime ($\hat{E}\log y_1^a, \hat{E}\log y_0^a$) for the two population groups. The predicted of the expected log-production from farming $\hat{E}\log y_0^a$ in regime 0 was done, since in that regime the total production is:

$$\hat{E}\log y_{0i}^a = \hat{E}\log y_{0i} = \hat{\beta}_0 X_i + \hat{\gamma}_0 \hat{\lambda}_i. \tag{5}$$

Similarly, we estimate an equation for the log-production from farming for the group of farmers in regime 1:

$$\hat{E}\log y_{1i}^a = \beta_1 X_i + \gamma_1 \hat{\lambda}_i + \mu_{1i} \tag{6}$$

from which we can derive the expected log-production from farming in regime 1:

$$\hat{E}\log y_{1i}^a = \hat{\beta}_1 X_i + \hat{\gamma}_1 \hat{\lambda}_i. \tag{7}$$

Using equations (5) and (7) and the estimated variance of μ_{0i} and μ_{1i}, and the method described previously, we can predict the counterfactual expected cocoa production of the farmers that have credit facilities based on regime 0, $\hat{E}y_0^a|_{P=1}$, and the expected cocoa production of the farmer that haven't credit facilities based on regime 1, $\hat{E}y_1^a|_{P=0}$. This allows some interesting comparisons:

(a) The difference in expected cocoa production within regime 0 is measured by the difference between the average observed cocoa production $Ey_0^a|_{P=0}$ of the farmers without credit facilities with the average predicted expected cocoa production $\hat{E}y_0^a|_{P=1}$ for credit facilities' farmers.

(b) The impact of credit facilities on cocoa production is obtained by comparing the average observed production $Ey_0^a|_{P=0}$ with the average predicted expected production from farming $\hat{E}y_1^a|_{P=0}$, also a measure of the average predicted production $\hat{y}_1^a|_{P=0}$, for non-credit facilities' farmers, and similarly by comparing average of $y_1^a|_{P=1}$ and $\hat{E}y_0^a|_{P=1}$ credit facilities' farmers.

3. DATA

The present study will be based on data collected by the International Institute of Tropical Agriculture (IITA) in 2002 in Côte d'Ivoire, Ghana, Nigeria and Cameroon.

A baseline survey of major cocoa growing regions of West and Central Africa was conducted to provide base parameters of cocoa based systems in the sub-region. In all of the countries indicated, villages and clusters of households were randomly selected and household heads interviewed using structured questionnaires. In Nigeria, 1083 households were visited in 35 villages and towns of Ondo State, which accounts for 40 to 50 per cent of annual production in Nigeria. In Cameroon, 1003 households in 83 villages in the Southwest, Center and South Provinces were visited with production from these sites accounting for over 80 percent of national production. In Ghana, the survey was conducted with 1000 households from 85 villages in the Brong Ahafo, Ashanti, Eastern and Western regions which together account for approximately 90% of national production. In Cote d'Ivoire, a list of farmers obtained from a national census of cocoa and coffee producers conducted in 1998 made it possible in selecting households using a random number procedure. 1372 households from 20 sub-divisions and 134 villages, hamlets and cocoa "camps" across the cocoa belt of Cote d'Ivoire were interviewed.

Table 1
Number of Villages and Farmers Surveyed

	Villages	*Farmers*
Cote d'Ivoire	134	1372
Ghana	85	1000
Nigeria	35	1083
Cameroon	83	1003
Total	337	4458

The main objective of this survey was to understand the general constraints and opportunities of cocoa based systems in the humid forest zone of West and Central Africa, in view to increase the productivity of agricultural land and labor employed by asset-poor households, and thus contribute to alleviation of rural poverty. The objective should feature in the introductory part of the article

Conducted in close consultation with research collaborators in Cameroon, Côte d'Ivoire, Ghana, and Nigeria, data were collected with a questionnaire that was made of six parts:

1. Agricultural systems and rural livelihoods (demographics, other enterprise, farm size, capital inventory).
2. Rural service provision (input markets, credit markets, market and production information, rural organization).
3. Tree stocks by age, replanting, uprooting and new planting.
4. Agronomic practices and output by plot.
5. Labour practices.
6. Post harvest practices and cocoa marketing.

4. SPECIFICATION OF THE CREDIT ACCESS AND PRODUCTION EQUATION

Two major categories of factors determine a farmer's liability to have credit facility: first, the factors that affect the relative return of cocoa production; second, and the factors that determine the capacity of the cocoa farmer to negotiate a credit. We can assume that these two set of factors are determine by cocoa farmer's endowment in physical and human capital and by environment where it is located. In the credit access equation, we introduce the following independent variables:

(i) The cocoa land area operated by the farmer. For the cocoa farmer, land is the main form of physical capital.

(ii) The average number of years of schooling of cocoa farmers. Many researchers have shown that farmers with higher education level are more likely to negotiate extra income for agricultural activities (de Janvry *et al.*, 2005).

(iii) The gender of the farmer

(iv) The average yield per hectare.

(v) The distance of the plot from the main access road.

(vi) The social capital variable measuring if the cocoa farmer is a member of a cocoa farmer organization.

For the production equation, the following variables have been introduced: (i) the number of worker in the cocoa farm, (ii) the productive cocoa area, (iii) the amount of expenditure on pesticide, (iv) the average age of the cocoa farm.

Table 2 presents descriptive statistics from the sample of cocoa farmers. Average cocoa production in the sample was 247.67kg/ha in Cameroon, and 375 kg/ha in Nigeria.

Cocoa farmers that have access to credit in Cameroon have a significant higher level of production (2307.5 kg or 325.50 kg/ha) than those that do not have access to credit (950kg or 184.5 kg/ha). In Nigeria, the same observation can be made where farmers with credit facilities exhibit a higher level of production (2088.2 kg or 429.67 kg/ha) than their counterparts that do not have access to credit (1406.7 kg or 307.14 kg/ha).

The lower part of table 2 summarizes farmer characteristics. The difference between the two groups is significant in term of human resources, the average number of workers that have access to credit is 5.76 in Cameroon and, 3.29 in Nigeria, higher than that of farmers that do not have access to credit (3.59 and 2.70 in Cameroon and Nigeria respectively). Also, the average expenditure on pesticides (US$ 343.9 in Cameroon and, US$ 175.08 in Nigeria) is higher than that of the latter (US$ 100.9 and US$ 132.77). In terms of community organization, majority of cocoa farmers that have access to credit are members of farmer organization (39% in Cameroon and, 29 % in Nigeria), as opposed to cocoa farmers that do not have access to credit (37% and 19%) suggesting that farmer organizations give credits opportunities to their members. However, about the location from the town, the situation is opposite. Cocoa farmers that

Table 2
Descriptive statistics

	Cameroon				*Nigeria*			
	All farmers	*Non access to credit*	*Access to credit*	*Difference*	*All farmers*	*Non access to credit*	*Access to credit*	*difference*
Total cocoa production (kg)	1453.8	950.2	2307.5	1358*** (9.698)	1770	1406.7	2088.2	681.5*** (4.39)
Total cocoa farm size (ha)	5.87	5.15	7.089	1.94*** (3.69)	4.72	4.58	4.86	0.28 (0.28)
Number of workers (man/day)	4.40	3.59	5.76	2.17*** (6.55)	3.01	2.7	3.28	0.58*** (4.29)
Total expenditure on pesticides used (US$)	191.19	100.9	343.9	243*** (7.25)	155.3	132.77	175.08	42.31*** (3.91)
Age of the farms (years)	30.24	34.78	22.56	-12.22*** (-10.36)	24.55	24.89	24.26	-0.63 (-0.91)
Age of the farmer (years)	50	51	50	-1 (-0.91)	56	55	56	1(0.67)
Gender of the farmer (% of men)	97	97	98	1(0.67)	89	0.9	0.88	-0.02 (-0.86)
Rural organization (%)	37.8	37	39	2 (0.61)	24.11	19	29	8*** (3.67)
Number of years of education	7.58	7.8	7.2	-0.68** (2.475)	1.59	1.65	1.52	-0.13 (-0.96)
Distance between the household and the major urban market centre (km)	18.73	15.05	24.97	9.92*** (7.18)	2.85	2.08	3.52	1.44** (5.68)

t-statistics are in brackets. *** significant at 1%; ** significant at 5%

do not have access to credit are relatively closer to the town (15.05 km in Cameroon and, 2.08 km in Nigeria) than those that have access to credit (24.97 km and 3.52 km). In summary, cocoa farmers acceding to credit are richer in work force, have higher cocoa farms, and invest in pesticides expenditures.

5. RESULTS AND DISCUSSION

The results of our analysis are presented in two parts. First, we estimate the credit access and production equations. These two equations allow us to (1) identify the determinants of credit access and estimate the cocoa production equation, and (2) simulate the production given the credit status of the cocoa farmer. Second, we compare the level of production between the two groups of farmers.

5.1 Estimation of Credit and Production Equations

The model used three sets of regressors. The first set includes farmer characteristics: (1) farmer ability as proxied by age of the farmer; education of the farmer measured as number of years of schooling, the gender of the farmer, and (2) farmer's capacity as proxied by the size of the Cocoa area operated by the farmer; the age of the cocoa farms; the social capital as proxied by the farmer organization. The second set, information variables such as the lending reputation of the region as proxied by the regional dummy variables. Finally, there are other exogenous variables depicting, for example the level of infrastructural development in the village. The former variable is a distance indicating the distance of the village from major urban marketing centres.

The estimates for the credit access equation, using the Probit model are reported in table 2, in all countries several regression cases were run, but only the most statistically sound ones are presented and discussed here, and some regressors were dropped for statistical problems as the case of regional variable in Nigeria.

The Chi-square statistic was significant in all regressions, indicating that the models are good.

Table 3
Estimation of the Credit Access Equation (Probit)

Endogenous variable=1 if the farmer has credit facilities	*Cameroon*	*Nigeria*
Constant term	-0.740 (-0.851)	-0.818 (-1.242)
Number of years of education	-0.002 (-0.268)	-0.011 (-0.184)
Cocoa area operated by the farmer	0.184*** (2.673)	0.011 (0.224)
Age of the cocoa farm	0.074 (0.896)	-0.044 (-0.538)
Age of the farmer	-0.137 (-0.709)	0.199 (1.168)
Gender of the farmer	-0.511 (-1.559)	-0.044 (-0.332)
Farmer organization		0.339*** (3.440)
Distance	0.022 (0.539)	0.242*** (5.863)
Regional variable South west	1.935*** (12.636)	
Mbam	0.299 (1.590)	
Lekie	-0.238 (-1.179)	
Chi-square	*$\chi^2(9) = 382.144$*	*$\chi^2(8)=55.109$*
Percentage of correct prediction	83%	60%
Sample	824	1041

t-statistics are in brackets. *** significant at 1%; ** significant at 5%; * significant at 10%.

Results show that in Cameroon, the cocoa area operated by the farmer and the lending reputation of the region contribute significantly to the accessibility of credit. This suggests that if households have the capacity to farm cocoa, then the existence of the credit opportunities will raise their loan demand. This positive effect can be attributed to the fact that seasonal agricultural loans come as input packages. In Nigeria, accessibility to credit is positively and significantly responsive to the social capital variable (farmer organization) and the level of infrastructural development in the region, suggesting that both farmer-specific variables and the general level of infrastructural development in the locality are more important determinants of access to credit in Nigeria. Finally, as the regression results show the gender of the farmer, educational level, and age have no significant effect on access to credit.

Table 4 shows the estimates of the production equations in each of the two regimes. Except the variable labour in Cameroon, the coefficients of the main exogenous variables have the expected signs. It appears that cocoa farm size,

Table 4
Estimation of the Farm Production Equation (Probit with the two-step Heckman procedure)

	Cameroon N=824		*Nigeria N=1041*	
	Regime		*Regime*	
	0	*1*	*0*	*1*
Constant term	4.42***	4.84***	4.77***	4.81***
	(20.25)	(3.59)	(16.1)	(18.8)
Cocoa area operated by the farmer	0.38***	0.32**	0.33***	0.35***
	(6.26)	(3.68)	(7.08)	(7.56)
Age of the cocoa farm	0.03	-0.03	0.10	0.08
	(0.48)	(-0.49)	(1.57)	(1.29)
Pesticides	0.29***	0.29***	0.29***	0.35***
	(11.31)	(8.80)	(7.88)	(10.1)
Labour	-0.00	0.41***	0.26***	0.26***
	(-0.24)	(6.15)	(4.89)	(5.01)
Inverse Mills Ratio	0.14	-0.10	-0.03	-0.34*
	(0.21)	(-0.15)	(-0.16)	(-1.8)
Regional variable				
South west	0.89	0.22		
	(1.29)	(0.25)		
Mbam	0.56***	0.11		
	(4.67)	(0.44)		
Lekie	0.36***	0.11		
	(3.88)	(0.38)		
Idanre/Owena			-	-
Akure/Owo			-0.29***	0.03
			(-3.44)	(0.32)
Ile-Oluji/Ondo/Ijesha			-0.25***	-0.26**
			(-3.09)	(-3.21)
R^2				
Number of observations	0.49	0.42	0.42	0.46
	518	306	486	555

t-statistics are in brackets. *** significant at 1%; ** significant at 5%; * significant at 10%.

the expenses in pesticide use and some regional variables significantly increase cocoa farmer production in Cameroon and Nigeria whereas the number of workers significantly increases the cocoa production in Nigeria in the two regimes. This effect is only positive and significant in regime 1 in Cameroon.

The Inverse Mills Ratio (IMR) reflects the correlation between the unobserved terms in the credit and production equations. In table 4, the coefficients of the IMR are negative in general. Since the selection criterion is 'access to credit', the IMR is negative in regime 0 for the cocoa farmer without credit facilities and positive for the cocoa farmer with credit facilities. The selection effect thus implies that, conditional on observed characteristics, cocoa farmers that have no access to credit have a higher farm production than an average farmer would have in their regime. In other words, there is a positive selection in the decision to produce cocoa without credit facilities. By contrast, for cocoa framers that have access to credit, the negative effect of the IMR suggests that these farmers have a lower farm production than their counterparts would if they were in this regime.

The results of this regression are used to predict what the cocoa production of farmers that have access to credit would if they produce cocoa without credit facilities.

5.2 Cocoa farm Production Difference between the two Groups of Farmers

Following the methodology presented in section 3.2, we can predict for each farmer with access to credit the cocoa production obtained in regime 0; we can also predict for each farmer without access to credit the cocoa production it would obtained in regime 1, Results are reported in table 5. Comparisons of observed farm cocoa production with their counterfactuals in the other regime allow us to derive two conclusions. The first is that the cocoa production of farmers that have access to credit, had they stayed in the opposite side (2029.47 kg in Cameroon and; 1256.59 kg in Nigeria), would be much more than that of cocoa farmers without credit facilities (950.16 kg) in Cameroon and; less (1406.72kg) in Nigeria.

Hence, the farmers that produce cocoa with credit facilities are the best farmers in Cameroon, and their cocoa production premium is 114% in Cameroon and; -11% in Nigeria. This is also true if they produce cocoa without credit. Implying 123% and, -3% premium in Cameroon and Nigeria respectively.

The second conclusion is that access to credit in cocoa production creates spillover effects on cocoa production. For those who have access to credit, spillovers raise cocoa production from 2029.47 kg to 2307.92 kg in Cameroon and; from 1256.59 kg to 2088.15 kg in Nigeria, a 14 and 40% production gains respectively. If farmers that produce cocoa without access to credit were to benefit in credit facilities, their cocoa production would increase by 9% and 53% in Cameroon and Nigeria respectively, from 950.16kg to 1036.17kg in Cameroon and, 1406.72 kg to 2153.41kg in Nigeria. Hence, access to credit help raise total factor productivity in cocoa production, expectedly by helping relax the constraints on cocoa farming imposed by the pervasive credit and market failures that characterize less developed countries such as Cameroon and Nigeria.

Table 5
Average farm Production of the Two Groups of Cocoa Farmers in Each Regime

		Region	*Cocoa farmers without credit facilities*	*Cocoa farmers with credit facilities*
			$(\overline{Y_0^\alpha\|_{P=0}}$, *observed production in kg)*	$(\overline{Y_0^\alpha\|_{P=1}}$, *simulated production in kg)*
	Regime 0	Lekie	723.26	860.62
		Mbam	1008.33	1305.50
		South	563.46	718.94
		South West	2216.83	2269.50
		Total	950.16	2029.47
		Region	$(\overline{Y_1^\alpha\|_{P=0}}$, simulated production in kg)	$(\overline{Y_1^\alpha\|_{P=1}}$, observed production in kg)
		Lekie	730.78	718.11
		Mbam	868.00	1068.33
		South	710.42	1010.81
		South West	2501.72	2598.52
Cameroon		Total	1036.17	2307.92
		Region	*Cocoa farmers without credit facilities*	*Cocoa farmers with credit facilities*
			$(\overline{Y_0^\alpha\|_{P=0}}$, *observed production in kg)*	$(\overline{Y_0^\alpha\|_{P=1}}$, *simulated production in kg)*
		Idanre/Owena	2016.75	1513.18
		Akure/Owo	1007.18	898.83
		Ile-Oluji/Ondo/Ijesha	1121.88	1021.05
	Regime 0	Total	1406.72	1256.59
		Region	$(\overline{Y_1^\alpha\|_{P=0}}$, simulated production in kg)	$(\overline{Y_1^\alpha\|_{P=1}}$, observed production in kg)
		Idanre/Owena	2702.60	2443.51
	Regime 1	Akure/Owo	1931.12	1947.30
		Ile-Oluji/Ondo/Ijesha	1793.33	1434.45
Nigeria		Total	2153.41	2088.15

CONCLUSION

Understanding the socioeconomic factors influencing cocoa farmer access to credit, and how the latter interacts with and affects cocoa production can help in the design of credit programs targeted to the rural household in general and cocoa farmers in particular. This paper used survey data from West African cocoa production countries to examine the role of access to credit in improving cocoa production and then revenue in the study area. There are several conclusions drawn from the analysis.

Our study shows that about 54% of cocoa farmers have access to credit in Nigeria, and 37% in Cameroon, while in Ghana and Côte d'Ivoire, only 18% and 13% cocoa farmers have access to credit respectively.

Second, we find that the cocoa farmer's capacity such as, the cocoa farm size, and the mutuality status of the farmer are more important as determinants of cocoa farmers access to credit. We also find that another set of variables such as the level of infrastructural development in the village, the lending reputation of the region as more determinant of extent cocoa farmer access to credit.

Third, we find that access to credit by cocoa farmers has a positive spillover effect on cocoa production. In West African cocoa countries, the rural credit and insurance markets are seriously deficient. As a consequence, the conflict between cash shortage and cocoa agricultural investment, and between risk-taking and aversion to risk, must be generally solved internally to the household through the strategic use of their own resources. Without doubt, access to credit in cocoa production is a smart alternative in overcoming the major cocoa production constraints. Credit obtained by cocoa farmers helps enhance the investment capacity in cocoa production activities.

An important policy implication of this study concerns the promotion of credit institutions specializing in saving mobilization and credit supply to farmers in general and cocoa farmers specifically. Given the evidence that agriculture as a whole could be net lender, there appears to be a necessity as well as a scope for the promotion of appropriate financial intermediaries. These could include voluntary saving and credit cooperatives, which could pool funds from surplus units for lending to deficit farmers so as to smooth seasonal discrepancies between cocoa farmer income and expenditure. However, considering that the necessary complementary resources and economic environment are not yet in place for access to credit for cocoa countries farmers, and considering the fact that formation of sustainable rural financial institutions is such a difficult task in West African countries rural economies, our study recommend a cautious and gradual strategy for expansion of the rural financial institutions. This strategy will require direct support by government, donors, and NGOs, through an adequate legal and regulatory framework, of institutional innovations and pilot programs such as the Sustainable Tree Crops Program (STCP) in cocoa production areas that may have the potential to reduce costs in providing savings, credit, and insurance services to the rural clientele. This will probably contribute to support government and private efforts to improve the access of cocoa farmers to best production practices and their capacity of professional enterprises for the marketing, and production

References

Alderman, H., and Paxson, C. H. (1992), *Do the Poor Insure? A Synthesis of the Literature on Risk and Consumption in Developing Countries*. IFPRI Discussion Paper 164.

Besley, T. (1995), Saving, Credit and Insurance. In *Handbook of Development Economics*, Vol. III, ed. J.Behrman and T.N. Srinivasan. Amsterdam and New York: Elsevier.

De Janvry, A., Sadoulet, E., and Nong, Zhu. (2005), The Role of Non-farm Income in Reducing rural Poverty and Inequality in China. CUDARE Working paper No. 1001. University of California, Berkeley.

Delgado, C. (1995), *Africa's Changing Agricultural Development Strategies. Past and Present Paradigms as a Guide to the Future*. 2020 Vision Food, Agriculture and the Environment Discussion paper 3. International Food Policy Research Institute. Washington, D.C.

Diagne, A. (1999), Determinants of Household Access and Participation in Formal and Informal Credit Market in Malawi. FCND Discussion Paper No. 67. International Food Research Institute. Washington, D.C.

Diagne, A., and Zeller, M. (2001), *Access to Credit and its Impact on Welfare in Malawi*. Research Report No. 116. International Food Research Institute. Washington, D.C.

Heckman, J.J. (1979), Sample Selection Bias as Specification Error. *Econometrica* 47(1): 153-161.

Killick, T. (1999), *Economic Change and the Welfare of the Rural Poor*. A Report Prepared for IFAD Rural Poverty Report.

National Resources Institute-NRI (2004). *Prospects for Sustainable tree Crop Development in Sub-Saharan Africa*. Policy Series 17.

Vos, J.G.M., Krauss, U., Petithuguenin, P., Perreira, L., and Nanga, C. (2002), Global Co-ordination Group on Sustainable Cocoa Economy: Achieving more efficient knowledge transfer.

Zeller, M., and Sharma, M. (1998), *Rural Finance and Poverty Alleviation*. Food Policy Report. International Food Research Institut. Washington, D.C.

Zeller, M., Schrieder, G., von Braun, J., and Heidhus, F. (1997), *Rural Finance for Food Security Fort he Poor: Implication for Research and Policy*. Food Policy review No. 4. Washington, D.C.: International Food policy research Institute.

A NOTE ON INTRA-INDUSTRY TRADE:
The Australia Experience

Kishor Sharma
Associate Professor of Economics and Sub Dean International Research
School of Commerce, Charles Sturt University, Australia

This paper investigates the industry-specific hypotheses of the determinants of intra-industry trade (IIT) in the context of policy liberalization in Australia. Results suggest that IIT is positively related to economies of scale but negatively to foreign participation in the pre-liberalization period. However, in the post-liberalization period, IIT is positively related to economies of scale but negatively to product differentiation and foreign participation.

JEL classification codes: *F12, F13, F14*

Key words: *Intra-industry trade, economies of scale, protection, foreign investment, liberalization*

I. INTRODUCTION

Since the early 1970s the phenomenon of intra-industry trade (IIT) ie, simultaneous exports and imports of similar products, has produced a large number of cross-country and cross-industry studies. Most of these empirical studies of the determinants of IIT find strong support for country effects, but little evidence is available in support of industry-specific effects [see, Aturupane et. al. 1999)]. This is puzzling as a great deal of theoretical literature suggests that industry-specific effects are the immediate cause for the occurrence of IIT [see, Krugman (1979) and (1980) and Lancaster (1980)]. Greenaway, Hine and Milner (1995) argue that failure to segregate IIT into horizontally and vertically differentiated products may be the reason for inconsistency between theory and empirical findings as the determinants of horizontal and vertical IIT differ. While this is an issue, very limited studies have investigated the role of industry-specific effects in explaining IIT as Greenaway and Milner (1986) and Greenaway and Torstensson (1997) correctly point out. Since increased IIT can be the additional source of gains from trade arising from increasing returns to scale, product differentiation and imperfect competition, it is important to test industry-specific hypotheses of the determinants of IIT. We do this using the Australian experience. The examination of Australian case is particularly important as among the high-income OECD countries it has relatively lower level of IIT,

Corresponding Author: *E-mail: ksharma@csu.edu.au*

although its share in Australia's total trade has increased from 25 per cent in 1985 to 37 per cent by 1992/93 [see, Grimwade (1989) and Sharma (2000)].

Although a few studies have examined the pattern of IIT in Australia [see, Grubel and Lloyd (1975), Menon (1994), Menon and Dixon (1996) Ratnayake and Athukorala (1992) Ratnayake and Jayasuriya (1991) Sharma, (2000)], industry-specific hypotheses of the determinants of IIT have not been tested before in the context of policy liberalization. Australia has substantially open up its economy since the mid 1980s by dismantling barriers to trade and investment, and liberalizing the foreign exchange market. The level of effective rate of assistance (ERA) to manufacturing has fallen from 22 per cent in the mid 1980s to 9 per cent by 1995 (Industry Commission 1995). Furthermore, economic relations between Australia and New Zealand have been strengthened since the mid 1980s by further dismantling barriers to trade and investment. Resulting structural changes brought about by these reforms may have changed the industrial structure and the determinants of IIT.

The purpose of this paper is to test industry-specific hypotheses of the determinants of IIT in the context of trade liberalization in Australia. We do this using data from both the pre- and post- liberalization periods. We have access to a rich data set to investigate this issue which classifies trade and industry data under the same category (Australian Standard Industry Classification) and thereby reduces the bias emerging from the regrouping of industry data into trade classification or vice versa. Normally, in the model of IIT, the left hand side variable (ie, IIT) is computed from the Standard International Trade Classification (SITC) data while most right hand side variables reflecting industry characteristics are constructed from the Standard International Industrial Classification (SIIC) data. Although these two are not comparable classifications, this problem is overcome by regrouping the data from established classifications, usually from the three-digit SITC to the three-digit SIIC. Since there is no established rules of how this should be done, individual researchers to a large extent follow subjective judgement. Consequently, different investigators obtain different results for the same country and the same time period (Hitiris and Bedrossian, 1987). In this study we avoid this problem, as trade data is also available in the SIIC classification. Results obtained from this study, therefore, can be accepted with a greater degree of certainty. The remainder of the paper is organised as follows. In section II, methodological issues and recent trends in IIT in Australian manufacturing industries are discussed. Section III presents an econometric model and discusses the results. Paper concludes in section IV with policy recommendations.

II. METHODOLOGICAL ISSUES AND RECENT TRENDS IN IIT

The Grubel and Lloyd (GL) index is the most popular index of IIT, which is calculated as follows:

$$B_j = \left[1 - \frac{|X_j - M_j|}{(X_j + M_j)} \right] X100 \qquad (1)$$

Where,
Xj = exports of industry j
Mj = imports of industry j
j = 1...n.

The computed value of B_j lies between 0 to 100. If $X_j = M_j$, then Bj would be 100 indicating that all trade is intra-industry and when either $X_j = 0$ or $M_j = 0$ then the value of B_j would be 0 indicating that all trade is inter-industry. The closer the value of the index to 100 the greater is the degree of intra-industry trade. However, the GL index is influenced by the size of the trade imbalance. Aquino (1978) has, therefore, suggested to adjust X_j and M_j values in equation (1) by a factor representing the aggregate imbalance, before deriving the aggregate index. However, there are no theoretical reasons to adjust trade data and as far as measuring trade overlap is concerned the GL index is to be preferred [for further discussion see, Kol and Mennes (1985)]. In recent years two other measurement issues have also dominated the discussion on IIT. These include the refining the GL index to more accurately measure marginal intra-industry trade (MIIT), and adjusting IIT measures to disentangle horizontal and vertical IIT [Greenaway and Torstensson (1997)]. However, these issues are beyond the scope of this paper.

Table 1 reports the frequency distribution of the GL IIT index for the pre-liberalization (1979/80) and post-liberalization (1992/93) periods. Selections of years are mainly guided by data availability. Following the standard practice, food, beverages and tobacco, non-metallic mineral products, and petroleum and coal products are excluded from the analysis as trade in these commodities are predominantly determined by the availability of natural resources in the country in question [see, Menon (1994), Ratnayake and Athukorala (1992) and Sharma (2000)]. However, one could argue that these industries should also be included in the analysis as they are also subject to scale economies and product differentiation that determine IIT.

Table 1
Frequency distribution of IIT index at the four-digit ASIC industries

	1979/80		*1992/93*	
Range of IIT	*Frequency*	*Per cent*	*Frequency*	*Per cent*
0 and below 10	15	19.0	4	5.1
10 and below 20	15	19.0	14	17.7
20 and below 30	14	17.7	18	22.8
30 and below 40	15	19.0	15	19.0
40 and below 50	6	7.6	10	12.6
50 and below 75	10	12.6	14	17.7
75 and below 100	4	5.1	4	5.1
Total sample	79	100	79	100
Weighted				Average
(weighted by trade share)	-	28.3	-	37.3

Source: Calculated from data from Industry Commission, 1995.

As shown in table 1 above there has been an increase in IIT from 28 per cent in 1979/80 to 37 per cent in 1992/93. Growth in IIT appears to be due to several factors, including increased domestic processing, the closer economic relations between Australia-New Zealand under the bilateral trade agreements and trade liberalization. Much of this growth in IIT came mainly from textile, garments, rubber products, and machinery and equipment sub-sectors, which have experienced a substantial fall in industry protection in recent years. For example, the ERA in textiles, clothing, footwear and leather fell from 90 per cent in the late 1970s to 57 per cent by 1992/93, and in transport equipment sector it fell from 59 per cent to 28 per cent in the same period. Intra-industry trade in rubber products rose from about 7 per cent in 1979/80 to 22 per cent in 1992/93, and in motor vehicles and parts it increased from about 17 per cent to about 31 per cent in the same period. The biggest growth was observed in textile and garments which recorded an increase in IIT from 17 per cent in 1979/80 to 37 per cent in 1992/93. A rising trend in IIT suggests that the short-term adjustment costs associated with trade liberalization are likely to be lower in terms of income and employment losses.

In 1979/80, about 19 per cent of industries (or 15 out of 79 sample industries) had a lower level of IIT (ranged between 0-10 per cent) which fell to about 5 per cent by 1992/93, indicating that manufacturing industries are increasingly specialised (see table 1). Higher IIT (over 50 per cent) is found in industries producing chemical products, machinery and equipment, fashion-ware (jewellery etc), and electric and telephone cable. Although an increasing number of industries-especially textile, garments, rubber products, and motor vehicle and parts- have recorded growth in IIT in recent years, the range of IIT in these industries is still less than 50 per cent.

III ECONOMETRIC MODEL AND RESULTS

(a) The Model

Following Greenaway *et al.* (1995), we develop an eclectic model to test the industry-specific hypotheses of the determinants of IIT in the context of policy liberalization in Australia. Krugman (1979 and 1980) and Lancaster (1980) have shown that product differentiation and increasing returns to scale are the major industry-specific factors that determine IIT. Krugman and Obstfeld (1994) argue that industry-specific technological know-how and production processes are also an important source of comparative advantage in international trade. Hence, trade by research intensive industries involves the intra-industry exchange of technologically differentiated goods. This led us to believe that IIT is higher in R&D intensive industries. In the presence of demand for different varieties of the same products, the production of which is subject to economies of scale, there may be a tendency for foreign direct investment (FDI) and IIT to go hand in hand [Greenaway and Milner (1986) and Sharma (2000)]. On this ground one would expect a positive link between FDI and IIT. Markusen (1995), however, argues whether or not FDI contributes to a higher level of IIT depends on the motive behind such investment. If the motive behind foreign participation is to fragment the production process geographically by stage of production (vertical investment) then there would be inter-industry not intra-industry trade. Thus, the nature of the link between FDI and IIT is not clear.

The above considerations lead to the following specification of the model, with expected signs is given in parentheses.

$$IIT_i = \delta_0 + \delta_1 PD_i + \delta_2 ES_i + \delta_3 RD_i + \delta 4 FDI_i \quad (2)$$

Where,

IIT = Intra-industry trade

PD = Product differentiation

ES = Economies of scale

RD = Research and development intensity

FDI = Foreign Direct Investment

$i = 1, \ldots$ N (sub-sectors)

δj = (j = 0,.....4) are parameters to be estimated.

U is a standard error term. Appendix 1 presents the definition of variables.

(b) Econometric Results

Results are reported in table 2. The model specified above is estimated using data for 1979/80 (regarded as pre-liberalization) and 1992/93 (regarded as post-liberalization) to investigate the impact of liberalization on the determinants of IIT. Note that selection of years is guided by data availability. For both periods we have 79 industry groups at the four-digit level. At the experimental stage we tested our model with the pooled data, however, it failed the RESET test and only a few variables were statistically significant. Thus, we decided to estimate the cross-sectional equations. The model is estimated separately for the pre- and post-liberalization periods to see the effects of policy liberalization on the industry-specific determinants of IIT.

We use ordinary least squares (OLS) and the logit transformation method to estimate the model. As discussed in the literature, when the value of the dependent variable lies within the range of 0 and 100, like in our case, the estimated regression equation may predict values, which lie outside that range. Therefore, to overcome this problem we apply the logit transformation method [for further discussion on this see, Gujarati (1995), pp. 556-57]. Note that there is no consensus among the researchers as to the use of OLS and the logit method in the study of IIT. For example, Tharakan (1986) and Cave (1981) support the idea of transforming the dependent variable using the logit method while Greenaway and Milner (1986) argue that there is no need for such transformation when the aim of the research is to investigate the determinants of IIT not the forecasting. On the basis of high explanatory power of the model, however, we prefer the OLS method. Note for comparison purposes we also report the logit results.

To ensure the robustness of our estimates we performed heteroskedasticity and RESET tests before estimating the final models. At the diagnostic testing stage we had to delete R&D variable from the model, because in its presence the model failed the RESET test and had poor explanatory power. Also, we introduce an interaction term between product differentiation and FDI (ie, PDFDI). Both models are statistically significant in terms of the F test, however, the explanatory power of the models is not very high which is expected in a cross-sectional analysis.

Table 2
Determinants of Inter-industry Variations IIT in Australian Manufacturing

Independent Variable	*OLS Model*		*Logit Model*	
	Pre-liberalization	*Post-liberalization*	*Pre-liberalization*	*Post-liberalization*
Intercept	24.275	49.941	-24.032	-49.442
	(1.442)	(3.148)***	(-1.442)	(-3.148))***
PD	-1.410	-4.064	1.396	4.023
	(-0.671)	(-2.067)**	(0.671)	(2.067)**
ES	1.047	0.179	-1.037	-0.177
	(2.693)***	(2.213)**	(-2.693)***	(-2.213)**
FDI	-0.698	-0.857	0.691	0.849
	(-1.909)*	(-2.148)**	(1.909)*	(2.148)**
PDFDI	0.072	0.110	-0.715	-0.109
	(1.452)	(2.335)**	(-1.452)	(-2.335)**
No. of Observation	79	79	79	79
F (4, 74)	2.216*	2.743**	2.216*	2.892**
R^2	0.11	0.19	0.11	0.13
RESET F (3, 71)	1.774	1.060	1.774	0.282
Heteroskedasticity	Corrected	Corrected	Corrected	Corrected

Note: t-ratios are Heteroskedasticity corrected using White's procedure. Significant levels are: *** = 1%, ** = 5%, and *10%.

The coefficient of product differentiation (PD) is statistically insignificant in the pre-liberalization period. However, it is significant in the post-liberalization period and has an unexpected negative sign, indicating that industries with the greater product differentiation are the industries with the lower levels of IIT. This is probably due to the fact that liberalization has made these industries (ie, industries with the greater product differentiation) less competitive and hence less scope for intra-industry exchange.

As expected the coefficients of economies of scale (ES) are statistically significant and have expected positive signs in both the pre- and post-liberalization periods. This provides support for the theoretical proposition that industries that are able to enjoy economies of scale are the industries with the higher levels of IIT regardless of the nature of the policy regime.

The coefficients of foreign direct investment (FDI) are statistically significant in both the pre-and post-liberalization periods and have negative signs, indicating that industries with foreign investment are the industries with the lower levels of IIT. In the pre-liberalization period this may be due tariff-jumping type investment, which may have attracted multinational companies to invest in import substitution industries to bypass protective trade barriers. The fact that the coefficient of FDI has a negative sign even after the liberalization indicates that FDI continue to be in import substitution industries, and hence contributes negatively to IIT in the post-liberalization period.

The coefficient of the interaction term between product differentiation and FDI (PDFDI) is statistically insignificant in the earlier period. However, it is statistically significant in the latter period and has a positive sign, indicating that product differentiation by foreign firms contributes to higher IIT. This is probably because foreign firms have well-established contacts in major markets, and hence opportunities for intra-industry exchange.

IV. CONCLUSION

This paper has investigated industry-specific hypotheses of the determinants of IIT in the context of policy liberalization in Australia. The results indicate a sharp rise in IIT, from 28 per cent in the late 1970s to 38 per cent in the early 1990s, which appears to be due to several factors, including trade liberalization that began in the mid 1980s. The rising share of IIT suggests that the short-term adjustment costs associated with trade liberalization are likely to be lower in terms of employment and income losses, and that liberalization can proceed without a huge short-term adjustment costs even in textile, clothing, footwear and motor car industries- industries which have attracted much policy debate in recent years in Australia.

Econometric evidence suggests that not all industry-specific factors are important in explaining the inter-industry variations in IIT, especially when the policy environment is restrictive and inward-oriented. Industries that enjoy economies of scale and have lower level of foreign participation are the industries with the greater IIT in the pre-liberalization period. In the post-liberalization period, economies of scale have a positive effect on IIT, but product differentiation and foreign participation result in the lower level of IIT. The interaction term between product differentiation and foreign investment (PDFDI) is statistically significant and has a positive sign in the post-liberalization, suggesting that product differentiation by foreign firms contribute to higher level of IIT.

However, these results should be interpreted with some degree of caution due to the following reasons: Firstly, we have to exclude an important industry-specific factor (ie, minimum efficient scale) due to the lack of appropriate data. Secondly, our dependent variable groups together both horizontal and vertical intra-industry trade, when in fact the determinants of horizontal and vertical IIT differ.

References

Australian Bureau of Statistics, *Research and Experimental Development All Sectors Summary Australia*, various issues, Catalogue No. 81112.0

Australian Bureau of Statistics, *International Merchandise Trade Australia*, various issues, Catalogue No. 5422.0.

Australian Bureau of Statistics, *Foreign Ownership and Control in Manufacturing*, various issues, Catalogue Nos. 5315.0 and 5314.0.

Aturupane, C., Djankov, S. and Hoekman, B. (1999), 'Horizontal and Vertical Intra-Industry Trade between Eastern Europe and the European Union,' *Weltwirtschaftliches Archiv*, 135, 62-81.

Aquino, A. (1978), 'Intra-Industry Trade and Intra-Industry Specialisation as Concurrent Sources of International Trade in Manufacturers,' *Weltwirtschaftliches Archiv*, 114, 275-96.

Caver, R. E. (1981), 'Intra-Industry Trade and Market Structure in the Industrialised Countries,' *Oxford Economic Papers*, 33, 203-223.

Greenaway, D. and Milner, C. (1984), 'A Cross-Section Analysis of Intra-industry Trade in the U. K.,' *European Economic Review*, 25, 319-44.

Greenaway, D. and Milner, C. (1986), *The Economics of Intra-industry*, Oxford: Blackwell.

Greenaway, D., Hine, R. and Milner, C (1995), 'Vertical and Horizontal IIT: A Cross-Industry Analysis for the United Kingdom,' *The Economic Journal*, 105, 1505-1518.

Greenaway, D. and Torstensson, J. (1997), 'Back to the Future: Taking Stock on Intra-Industry Trade,' *Weltwirtschaftliches Archiv*, 133: 249-269.

Grimwade, N. (1989), *International Trade, New Patterns of Trade, Production and Investment*, London: Routledge.

Grubel, H. G. and Lloyd, P. J. (1975), *Intra-Industry Trade*, London: Macmillan.

Gujarati, D. N. (1995), *Basic Econometrics*, Third Edition, New York: McGraw-Hill.

Hitiris, T. and Bedrossian, A. (1987), 'Import Penetration, Export Competitiveness, and the Pattern of UK Intra-Industry Trade: A Note', *Applied Economics*, 19, 215-20.

Industry Commission (1995), *Australian Manufacturing Industry and International Trade Data: 1968-69 to 1992-93*, Canberra: Australian Government Press.

Kol, J. and Mennes, L. B. M. (1985), 'Intra-industry Specialization: Some Observations on Concept and Measurement,' *Journal of Industrial Economics*, 33, 173-81.

Krugman, P. (1979), 'Increasing Returns, Monopolistic Competition and International Trade,' *Journal of International Economics*, 9, 469-479.

Krugman, P. (1980), 'Scale Economies, Product Differentiation and the Pattern of Trade,' *American Economic Review*, 70, 950-59.

Krugman, P. and Obsfeld, M. (1994), *International Economics*, Third Edition, New York: HarperCollins College Publishers.

Lancaster, K. J. (1980), 'Intra-Industry Trade under Perfect Monopolistic Competition,' *Journal of International Economics*, 10, 151-75.

Markusen, J. R. (1995), 'The Boundaries of Multinational Enterprises and the Theory of International Trade' *Journal of Economic Perspectives*, 9, 169-189.

Menon, J. (1994), 'Trade liberalisation, Closer Economic Relations and Intra-Industry Specialisation,' *Australian Economic Review*, 106, 31-42.

Menon, J. and Dixon, P. B. (1996), 'Regional Trading Agreements and Intra-Industry Trade,' *Journal of Economic Integration*, 11, 1-23.

Ratnayake, R. and Athukorala, P. (1992), 'Intra-Industry Trade: The Australian Experience,' *International Economic Journal*, 6, 47-62.

Ratnayake, R. and Jayasuriya, S. (1991), 'Intra-Industry Trade and Protection: Which Way Does the Causation go?,' *Economics Letters*, 36, pp. 71-76.

Sharma, K. (2000), 'Pattern and Determinants of IIT in Australian Manufacturing,' *Australian Economic Review*, 33, 245-255.

Tharakan, P. K. M (1986), 'The Intra-Industry Trade of Benelux with the Developing Countries,' *Weltwirtschaftliches Archiv*, 122, 131-149.

Appendix 1: Definition of variables and Their Sources

IIT computed from IC, 1995.

PD is defined as the number of four-digit sub-groups in each three-digit sub-groups. Data source: IC, 1995.

ES is proxied as the average value added per establishment. Data source: IC , 1995.

RD is measured as the percentage of the workforce that carry R&D in each category. Data source: Australian Bureau of Statistics (ABS), (1981/82 and 1992/93), Research and Experimental Development All Sectors Summary Australia, Catalogue No. 8112.0.

FDI is defined as the value-added share of foreign owned company in each category. Data source: ABS (1982/83 and 1992/93), Foreign Ownership and Control in Manufacturing, Catalogue Nos. 5315.0 and 5314.0.

AN EVALUATION OF FISHERIES POLICIES AVAILABLE TO AUSTRALIA FOR THE MANAGEMENT OF SOUTHERN BLUE FIN TUNA FISHERY

R. Sathiendrakumar

Senior Lecturer in Economics, Murdoch University, Australia

In the absence of proper management, fishery resource tends to be exploited as a common property resource with a tendency towards over-exploitation. In the absence of appropriate property rights, the exploitation of a common property such as the fisheries may lead to over exploitation (and possible extinction of a species but not with migratory species such as the southern blue fin tuna) and externalities both contemporaneous and inter-generational. The paper aims to identify the various economic policy instruments that may be available and then uses a 'cubic' model to select the best model suitable for the blue fin tuna fishery. Price control is selected as the appropriate policy instrument, even though individual transferable catch quota is also a possibility. Price control is based on levying a tax on catches and is oriented towards economic efficiency.

1. INTRODUCTION

It is claimed that the purpose of fisheries management should be to control the fishery in a manner, which will continue to yield net benefits for the community, and is in accord with national goals. If society exercises no control over capital and labour, fishery resources will attract excess investments and economic rents will be dissipated (Anderson and Wilson, 1977).

Furthermore, every period of good harvest or high prices tends to result in an increased inflow of new boats and gear (Department of Primary Industry, 1986). These fishermen are not easily driven out again when the market is weak, because fishermen are notably immobile (Christy, 1976, Crutchfield, 1986).

In the absence of property rights the operation of the free market does not lead to a socially rational allocation of resources, even though it may appear to the individual crew to be rational. This is because individual fishermen may impose costs on one another, such as congestion cost (a contemporaneous externality), that are not transmitted through normal market forces. Thus from a fisheries management point of view, it is important to internalise these externalities.

Maintaining a constant stock of renewable fishery resource is a necessary condition for sustainable exploitation of a fishery. Maintaining a constant stock of fishery resource is necessary to meet both the present and future needs of the population. In other words, it is aimed at maintaining inter-generational equity.

It is a well-known fact that in a common property situation, reducing the use of the resource by one individual will contribute to the available supply of the other users. Therefore, the user has no incentive to conserve the resource in a sustainable manner. This action could ultimately lead to the depletion of the renewable resource beyond recovery (not in the case of migratory tuna). Therefore, to overcome this problem some form of quasi property rights have to be given to these resources as giving pure private property rights is not possible with migratory species such as the southern blue fin tuna. This is only possible by some sort of administrative mechanism.

The other necessary conditions for sustainable fisheries management is:

- To prevent crowding externality and
- To prevent the dissipation of rent.

CROWDING EXTERNALITY

This arises because of over commitment of resources to the common property. That is too many boats and too many fishermen resulting in too much effort. The operation of the free market system in the fishing industry does not lead to a rational allocation of resources as far as the society is concerned, even though it may appear to the individual to be rational. This is because individual fishermen may impose costs on one another, such as congestion cost, that are not transmitted through normal market forces. To explain this let us take the case of a boatman travelling between two points A and B and using one channel. The demand for travel between these two points is shown in Figure 1 by a downward sloping demand curve DD.

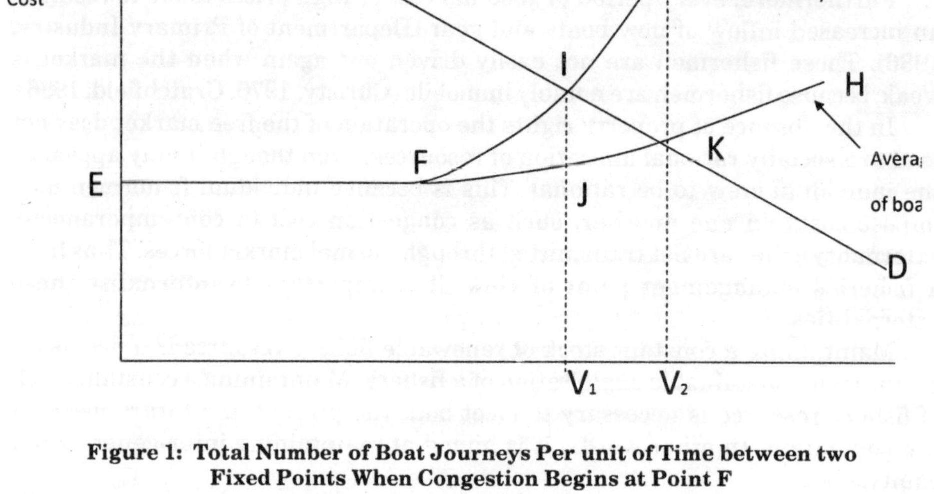

Figure 1: Total Number of Boat Journeys Per unit of Time between two Fixed Points When Congestion Begins at Point F

The average cost per boat journey is given by the curve EFJKH and the marginal cost curve by EFILG. Up to point F, the average cost is equal to the marginal cost because there is no congestion externality. However, as the congestion increases, the average cost begins to rise because of lost time, additional cost of fuel and even possibility of greater susceptibility to accidents. When average cost rises the marginal cost will be above the average cost. This happens at point F. But when average cost is constant the marginal cost will be equal to the average cost, this is between points E and F.

In a common property situation individuals base their decision on average cost and not on the collective marginal cost due to additional traffic. Given the demand curve and cost curves shown, boatman will make V_2 boat journeys per unit of time. But in terms of economic efficiency V_1 boat journeys are optimal. This is because at V_1 the demand, which measures the marginal private benefit, is equal to the marginal private cost.

V_2 journey instead of V_1 journey results in a dead weight social loss given by area IKL which is the difference between the collective marginal cost between V_1 and V_2 journeys (given by area V_1ILV_2) and the value of the additional journey to the boatman (given by area V_1IKV_2). Therefore at V_2 number of boat journey per unit of time between the two fixed points, there is a loss in economic efficiency, because the additional marginal cost exceeds the additional marginal benefit. Only at point I, the marginal cost equals the marginal benefit. Thus V_1 is the Pareto efficient point with regard to the number of boat journeys per unit of time. The efficiency aspect implies that this should be the level of effort that any management tool should try to achieve in the open access fisheries.

DISSIPATION OF RENT

In a common property situation the fishermen do not care for marginal productivity but cares only for the average productivity. This is because the average productivity is the one that indicates where the greater total catch may be obtained by any tuna boat. That is for individuals who are unable to appropriate property rights to any part of the fishery; the average revenue product of effort is the relevant measure to compare his income in alternative employment (Tisdell, 1983). Therefore the fishermen will continue to exploit the fishery up to the point where their average cost of exploitation of a tuna boat is equal to their average revenue productivity of that boat. When average product is equated to average cost, rent is dissipated. As natural resources belong to the society it is important to prevent any rent dissipation.

Therefore in a common property situation, all profits will be competed away at the point where the average revenue product of effort is equal to the average cost. In Figure 2 it is at effort level equal to E_0.

If on the other hand, private property rights prevailed in this fishery, then the marginal revenue product of individual boat's effort is the relevant measure with which to compare someone's income from alternative employment. In such a situation the marginal cost will be equated to the marginal revenue product and the rent from the resource will be maximised (Sathiendrakumar, 1996). Thus, with private property rights the optimum allocation effort will be E_1, where

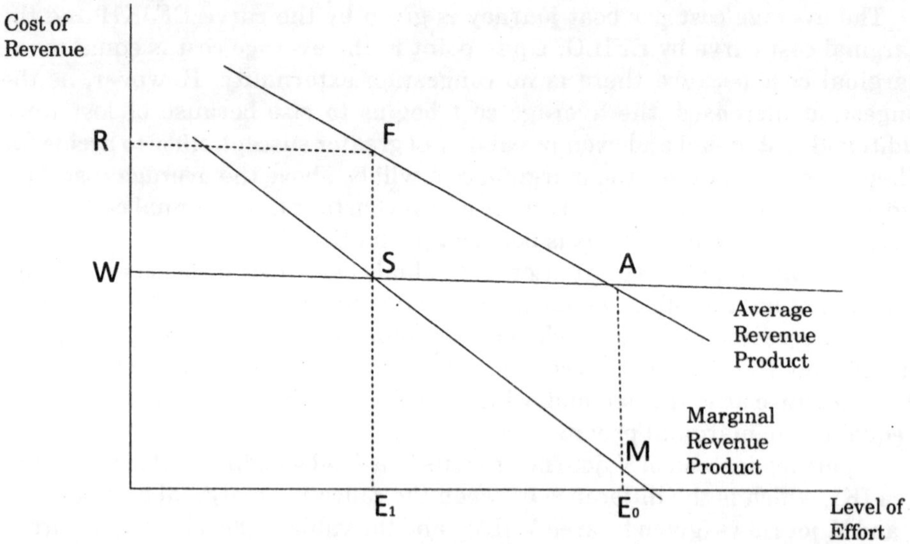

Figure 2: The Effort Levels with Common Property and Private Property Rights

the marginal cost of effort is equal to the marginal revenue product of effort (see Figure 2) and the maximum rent will be denoted by the area WRFS.

Thus, common property implies a dissipation of rent equal to area SAM, which is precisely equal to area WRFS. Also note that the average revenue product with private property rights (point F) is greater than the average revenue product with common property rights (point A), ceteris paribus. That is, with private property, production will result in higher effort productivity.

Therefore the aim of any management strategy should be to give some form of private property rights to the fishery. The allocation of property rights should not be aimed at giving those rights to the powerful and rich lobby groups only. Economically rational exploitation of fisheries would effectively raise fishermen's incomes.

2. SELECTION CRITERIA FOR TUNA FISHERY MANAGEMENT STRATEGIES

Any economic instrument used in managing the southern blue fin tuna fishery should satisfy the following three important criteria, namely:

- The economic efficiency principle or the cost minimisation principle. That is, it should provide a least cost solution, including the administrative and compliance cost.
- The equity principle. That is, its effect on the distribution of wealth and on other supplementary goals such as employment must be considered.
- The acceptability principle. That is it should be acceptable to both the politicians and the fishermen as a tool that will effectively control fishing effort. Acceptability also includes flexibility so that it will allow for proper reaction to changes in both economic and biological conditions. That is, it is dynamic in nature.

3. THE CUBIC MODEL

We could represent the above three principles, namely: efficiency, equity and acceptability principles as a 'cubic' model. The framework in Figure 3 is in the form of a cube whose surfaces represent cost effectiveness, equity and acceptability principles.

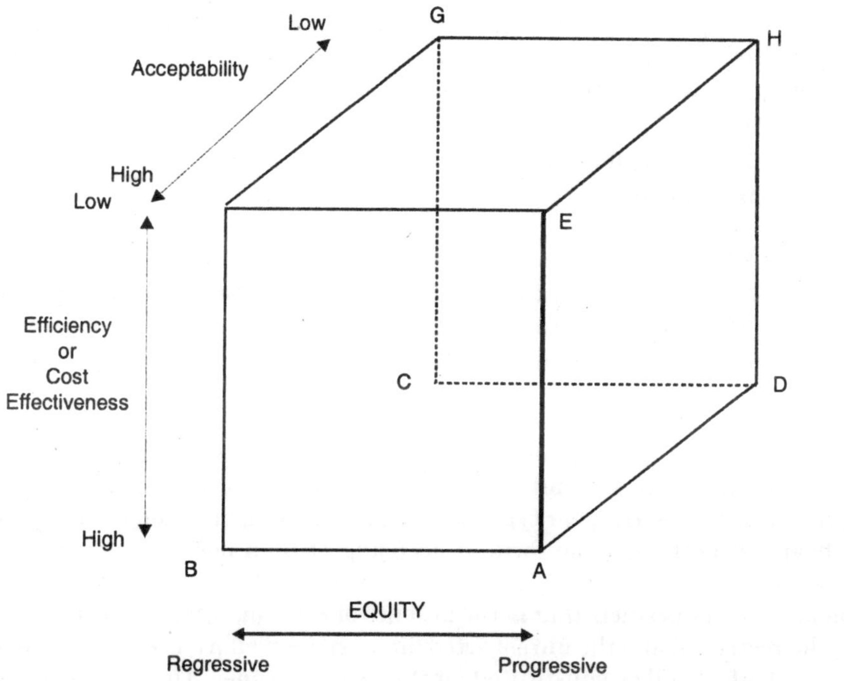

Figure 3: Framework Representing the Cost Effectiveness Equity and the Acceptability Principle

The eight corners of the cube are labelled as 'A', 'B', 'C', 'D', 'E', 'F', 'G', and 'H'. The positions 'A', 'B', 'C', and 'D' are the ones that satisfy the efficiency principle (or cost effectiveness principle). Likewise, the corners 'E', 'F', 'A' and 'B' are the ones that satisfy the acceptability principle. The corners 'A', 'D', 'E' and 'H' are the ones that satisfy the equity principle. Therefore, the policy instrument that satisfies all three principles is in position 'A'. The position that satisfies at least two of these three principles is corners 'E', 'D', and 'B'. In reality it is not possible to achieve these corner solutions. Therefore we draw concentric circles using the effectiveness of all our three objectives mentioned before for each of the policy instrument around these corners and select the policy instrument whose concentric circle is closer to the desired corner 'A'. Thus we could use the above framework to select the appropriate policy instrument that could be used to satisfy the principles that we aim to achieve namely; efficiency, equity, and acceptability. The economic instruments that are considered are discussed in the next section.

4. CHOICE OF ECONOMIC INSTRUMENTS IN MANAGING MIGRATORY BLUE FIN TUNA

There are many fisheries management measures that can be considered by a government (Department of Primary Industry, 1986). For the purpose of our discussion, three principal management mechanisms listed bellow will be examined in this section as they could easily be applied to the southern blue fin tuna fishery in Australia. These measures are namely:

- Limited entry
- Catch quotas (open or individual)
- Financial controls

LIMITED ENTRY

A limited entry system enables the achievement of economic efficiency in the fisheries sector (Christy, 1976) in the long run, by controlling all dimensions of effort so as to achieve the optimal level of effort. This will prevent dissipation of rent.

Limited entry involves the setting of a maximum limit on the number of boats allowed to participate. Limited entry system prevents the dissipation of economic rents in fisheries. Limited entry in its simplest form does not impose any restrictions on boat size; gear type etc. except for setting limits on the number of tuna boats. Therefore, some form of licensing of tuna boats is required to restrict this number.

Economic theory predicts that in the absence of zero elasticity of substitution between the restricted and the unrestricted dimensions of effort, the unrestricted dimensions of effort will be substituted for the restricted ones. This substitution will be possible only for the rich fishermen because of the high cost of the unrestricted dimensions of effort. Therefore, this policy will be regressive in terms of equity.

Pearce and Willen (1979); and Kailis (1982) document examples of restrictive licensing of just a few effort components resulting in the expansion of other components such that the least cost combination is not achieved. Therefore this fails in the cost minimisation aspects as well. . Furthermore, restricting all dimensions of effort through licensing will hinder technical progress in the fishing industry in the long-run and therefore will not be efficient.

CATCH QUOTAS

Catch quotas may be either open quotas or individual transferable quotas. Either type of quota can be affective in achieving the biological goal of stock protection. However, with a migratory species such as blue fin tuna that breeds in Western Australia and migrates through South Australia, New South Wales and goes up to Japanese cost, protection of stock levels is only possible with a concerted united joint action by all countries that fish for southern blue fin tuna in this region.

With open quotas individual fishermen tend to increase their effort in order to take a larger share of the total allowable catch. This in turn will result in over capitalisation of tuna boats and the resulting under-utilisation of fishing boats. Therefore, the use of open quotas in managing the blue fin tuna fishery will not be considered.

With individual transferable quotas, individual quotas are allocated as a share of the total catch. Therefore, it is left to the individual fishermen to determine the most profitable way of harvesting the fish. This will satisfy the cost minimisation strategy. Therefore, such a policy will satisfy all three objectives of our 'cubic' model.

FINANCIAL CONTROLS

Management by financial controls involves providing access to all subject to the payment of an appropriate tax. This financial control could be of two forms

- Tax on inputs
- Tax on catch

TAX ON INPUTS

This is based on the fact that a tax on effort will increase the cost of fishing, which in turn will reduce the total effort by removing those fishermen who are unwilling or unable to pay the tax. But "tax on effort is likely to induce changes in the method of production, leading to higher total costs for society" (Anderson and Wilson, 1977 p.711). This will result in regulation induced inefficiency. Furthermore, tax on inputs will be successful only if it is possible to prevent alternative non-taxed inputs being used by the fishermen to increase their effort or when tax is applied to all dimensions of effort.

There are two problems with the latter approach. First problem is that such a measure will not encourage technological progress that may reduce the cost of fishing. Good management schemes should also allow for technical improvements, which can be reflected as a net gain to the society. The other problem is that effort is difficult to define and measure (Treschev, 1978), especially because it is subjected to continuous revision as technology changes. Since this management measure fails to satisfy the efficiency and the acceptability criteria, it is not recommended as a management measure for the blue fin tuna fishery.

TAX BASED ON CATCH

The tax on catch is oriented towards economic efficiency. The economic effect of imposing a tax on catch is to increase the cost of fishing or reduce profitability. This increased cost or decreased revenue deters the marginal fishing fleet from fishing and therefore will result reducing the size of effort to the most efficient level. . In Figure 2 it will shift the equilibrium effort level to E_1 from E_0. That is achieving the maximum economic yield level of effort.

Tax on catch satisfies all three faces in our 'cubic' model, namely efficiency, equity and acceptability. Of all the alternatives, other than individual transferable catch quota that were discussed, tax on catch is the only policy instrument that satisfies all the three policy objectives. It also allows for technological progress in the long-run.

To estimate the tax on catch we have to select an appropriate model that represents the relationship between catch and effort. There are three possible models that may be used to test this relationship. They are (a) Schafer model, (b0 Fox model and (c) production function threshold model (see Sathiendrakumar and Tisdell (1987).

The Schafer model and the Fox model are based on the steady-state relationship between stock size, fishing effort, and yield; sustainable yield is a function of total effort and stock size; stock size is a function of effort. Therefore, both the Schafer model and Fox model, which relate catch or sustainableyoield to effort, can be interpreted as a production relationship in whicvh effort is input and catch is the output.

In the Schafer model, the catch-fishing relationship is

$$C_t = af_t - bf_t^2 \quad (1)$$

Where C_t = total landing of fish at time t, ft = fishing effort at time t, and b are parameters. Equation 1 implies that the fishery can be fished to extinction. But extinction of species is not possible with a migratory species such as the southern blue fin tuna, especially when you take into consideration only the fishing in the Australian territorial waters. Therefore this model may be inappropriate to use.

In the Fox model the catch-effort relationship is

$$C_t = f_t(Ae^{(-bf_t)}) \quad (2)$$

Where A and b are constants. Therefore,

$$Ln(C_t/f_t) = Ln\ A - bf_t \quad (3)$$

Even though the Fox model does not imply that the fishery can be fished to extinction, both this model and the Schafer model suggest that increased effort will lead to a decline in the stock of breeding tuna.

Therefore the model that may be of use will be the production function threshold model. This model will be similar to what Sathidrakumar and Tisdell used in their 1987 paper. Where the relationship can be represented by the mathematical form:

$$C_t = A - Be^{(-kf_t)} \quad (4)$$

Rearranging

$$A - C_t = Be^{(-kf_t)} \quad (5)$$

Therefore:

$$Ln(A - C_t) = Ln\ B - kf_t \quad (6)$$

A, B and k are parameters. In practice, A may correspond to the abundance of fish in the area being fished and in principle could be estimated by population sampling procedure. Using the price of blue fin tuna we should be able to estimate the revenue function. Likewise using the capital cost and the operating cost in the blue fin tuna industry in Australia we can estimate the cost functions for the blue fin tuna in Australia.

The optimal economic yield level of effort will be where the marginal revenue per unit of effort which is obtained by differentiating total revenue by effort is equal to the marginal cost per unit of effort which is obtained by differentiating the total cost of blue fin tuna operation by unit of effort. The difference between the total revenue and the total cost will be the appropriate tax on catch that should be enforced to harvest this optimal equilibrium of effort, which will prevent the dissipation of rent from the southern blue fin tuna in Australia.

5. CONCLUSION

To give the blue fin tuna fishermen some incentive to conserve the fishery resource in a manner, which will not dissipate rent and also will not lead to crowding externalities, some form of quasi property rights have to be given. This is only possible by some sort of political/administrative mechanism. Such a mechanism will prevent the over-exploitation and diminishing returns to the society that is associated with the open-access to the fishery. In other words, a good fisheries management tool should prevent the destructive pattern of competition among fishermen for a share of the limited fishery resource.

At present biological overfishing leading to extinction of blue fin tuna may not a problem . Therefore the management policy should be to control economic over-fishing. In the context of blue fin tuna fishery only two management policies are feasible, namely tax on catch and transferable catch quotas that satisfies all the three policy objectives that were specified in the model. Furthermore, a tax on fish catch as well as individual transferable quotas also has the added advantage of not limiting technical progress in the future, unlike a tax on effort. Also this revenue from tax on catch, as well as generating money by auctioning the individual transferable quotas will provide the opportunity to generate funds that may be used to defray the cost of management. The revenue generated from this southern blue fin tuna fishery by the government should be only utilised to improve the living condition of any fishermen that may be displaced from the fishery or to improve the standard of living in the fishing community.

References

Anderson, R.C. and J.A. Wilson (1977), "Economic Dimension of Fees and Access Control under the Fishery Conservation and Management Act of 1976", *Washington Law Review*, 52: 701-745.

Christy, F.T. Jr. (1976), "The Fishery Conservation and Management Act of 1976: Management Objectives and the Distribution of Benefits and costs", *Washington Law Review*, 42: 657-680.

Crutchfield, J.A. (1986), "Fishery Management: A Time of Change". In T.J.A. Hundloe (ed), *Fisheries management*, Griffith University Press, Australia.

Department of Primary Industry (1986), *Management of the East Coast Tuna Fishery Options and Considerations*, Fisheries Paper No. 86-10, Australian Fisheries Services, Canberra.

Kailis, T.G. (1982), "Limited entry–an industry view, p. 77-86". In N.H. Sturgess and T.F. Meany (eds), *Policy and practice in fisheries management*, Australian Government Publishing Service, Canberra, Australia.

Pearce, P.H. and J.E. Wilen (1979), “Impact of Canada’s Pacific salmon fleet control program”, *J. Fish. Res. Board Can*, 36: 754-763.

Sathiendrakumar, R. and Tisdell, C.A. (1987), Optimal Economic Fishery Effort in the Maldivian Tuna Fishery: An Appropriate Model”, *Marine Resource Economics* 1987, Volume 4 Number 1, pp. 15–44.

Sathiendrakumar, R. (1996), “Sustainable Development: Passing Fad or Potential Reality?”, *International Journal of Social Economics*, Vol. 23, Nos. 4/5/6, pp. 151-163.

Tisdell, C.A. (1983), “Economic Problems in Managing Australia’s Marine Resources”, *Economic Analysis and Policy*, 13 (2): pp. 113-141.

Treschev, A.I. (1978), “Application of the Fished Volume Method of Measuring Fishing effort”, *Co-operative Research Report 79*, International Council for the Exploration of the Sea, Copenhagen.

AMARTYA SEN'S PUBLIC ACTION AND THE SMITHIAN DILEMMA

Ratan Lal Basu
Reader in Economics, Bhairab Ganguly College, Kolkata

The new millennium emerged with the most scintillating achievement of the human race in the form of communication revolution which has enabled the process of globalization to climax into turning the entire world into a global village. Thus the most luminous gem has been added to the crown of our material achievements ever since the dawn of civilization. Unfortunately the magnificent edifice of our material glories has caste a stark shadow in the form of poverty, inequality, deprivation, exploitation, unemployment and all other forms of social injustice. In fact, the entire history of human civilization has been checkered with glorious achievements and abject injustice. All the negative aspects associated with our material progress may be summarized as poverty and deprivation. The term poverty may be looked upon in both absolute and relative sense. Both have been in existence ever since the emergence of private property and have gone on snowballing along with material progress. Absolute poverty in primitive clan societies was caused undoubtedly by lack of productive power of the clans, i.e. lack of adequate scientific and technological knowledge to exploit nature to meet their basic requirements. But this argument cannot by any means be put forward to explain the existence of poverty since the beginning of civilization and it is more so for the modern era with unbelievable achievements in the arena of industrial production. So the real cause of poverty could hardly be associated with undeveloped productive capability of the human race. It is to be sought elsewhere, viz. the heinous psychosis of the minor property owner class to exploit and enslave the majority. From this standpoint the most coherent explanation of poverty and injustice is to be found in the works of Karl Marx and Frederick Engels. They have used immaculate logic to associate poverty and injustice with private property, division of labour, exchange, competition, family and the State. So, according to the Marxian approach, poverty and injustice could be eliminated only in a social situation (Communism according to Marx and Engels) where the above six basic causes of poverty are completely nonexistent. The first step towards the progress to Communism is establishment of Socialism through proletarian revolution.

However, the crumbling of most of the so called socialist regimes during the late 1980s and early 1990s has raised doubt about the feasibility of the Marxian solution. The desirability of the Communistic society has also been challenged even by many staunch adherents of the Marxian doctrine. There has been a widespread frustration among the communists and adherents of the concept of socialistic pattern of society in the so called mixed economies like pre-globalization India. The consequence has been a complete about turn, blind worship of uncontrolled market economy, i.e. the so called capitalistic system. This paradigm shift has resulted in unbelievable material progress since the late 1980s but with the dawning of the new millennium the horror of increasing poverty and deprivation has been haunting the conscientious minds. The most prominent voice that has raised protests against blind adherence to free market mechanism is that of Amartya Sen who has emphasized that to contain the maladies associated with material progress in the era of globalization, public action is essential. He has considered pluralistic democracy as the most desirable form of government which could ensure growth with social justice along with human freedom. Although better than authoritarian forms of governing in many respects, political party based democracies are overburdened with widespread corruption based on criminal-trade union-politician alliance. Sen emphasizes the role of the mass media and awareness of the common people to break through this vicious circle and make the politicians, running the governments, work in a desirable fashion.

Unfortunately this optimistic note of Sen has come up against a serious hurdle pointed out by Adam Smith long ago. According to Smith a psychosis common to most of the people, whatever be their own positions, is that they admire the powerful and the rich (whatever be the means of their achievements) instead of the really worthy ones, viz. the honest and virtuous who has fail to achieve power and wealth. This has, in fact, spelt out a gloomy prospect for the human race. In this article we endeavour to take up these issues. Accordingly, in the rest of this article, we are going to take up in detail the following topics: Poverty Concepts, Marxian Approach, Sen's Approach and Smithian Dilemma.

POVERTY CONCEPTS

In modern economic literature as the phenomenon of poverty has posed the most serious challenge to development efforts in the new millennium. This primeval malady is the source of many other serious maladies. In modern economic literature the question of absolute poverty has justifiably been considered as the most primary issue, although attention has also been drawn to the question of inequality, both intra-nation and inter-nation.

At present, the most pressing problem, of the third world countries comprising the overwhelming majority of world-population, has been the precarious situation generated by absolute poverty in its extreme form and, therefore, at least on the theoretical plain, the major concern of economic policy of the government of each of these countries has been to devise appropriate and fruitful means to reduce the intensity of the problem of absolute poverty. The question has also been a matter of deep concern for the developed countries, but for completely different reasons. Continuation of abject poverty in the third world countries generates enough provocation for the poor of these countries to resort to violence, organized or anarchic. Thus poverty in LDCs has both direct and indirect adverse consequences – directly by material deprivation of the majority and indirectly by paving the way for violent discontent.

Now as we turn to the question of removal of poverty, we immediately come upon the tricky question of quantitative measurement, without which it is hardly possible to frame any realistic target-oriented poverty removal policy. To this end the crudest approach considers income as the criterion of defining poverty and attempts to measure poverty by the Head Count Ratio (HCR). In this measure at first the minimum income necessary for provision of subsistence requirements is determined. This threshold income is called the Poverty Line. At the next step, data on the number of persons with income below this critical level are collected. At the final stage this figure is expressed as a percentage of the total population of the country under consideration.

The most important question in connection with the HCR is the definition of the critical income level pertaining to the poverty line. The critical poverty line income differs from country to country depending on the variability of per capita income, structure of national income, ethnic and cultural factors that make a world of difference in the concept of subsistence requirement. Generally the poverty line income for a poor country is less than that for a relatively opulent country.

Not withstanding these inter-country differences, the World Bank has defined a general Poverty Line for the world as $1 per person per day at purchasing power parity. Although this may enable the World Bank to have a rough idea about overall poverty in the world, for policy framing of the LDCs, the standard may seem too high and for the highly developed nations, too low. The third world countries afflicted with abject poverty are compelled to set a much lower margin of income for the Poverty Line and device policies to raise income of the poor in relation to this critical level. For example, the official Poverty Line in Indian, based on minimum calorie requirements for sustenance of life, is much below this World Bank standard.

Apart from this conceptual limitation, the HCR has revealed limitations from the policy stand point as the measure fails to quantify the income gap of the poor from the Poverty Line. Thus it does not provide any guideline as to the magnitude of the total income gap to be covered if a country wants to remove poverty of a targeted segment of the poor. Moreover this measure is also a poor instrument of inter-country comparison of poverty.

The poverty gap measures have been devised to take into income shortfall of the poor from the Poverty Line. There have been various indices of this category to take into account specific aspects of poverty gap. The details of all these measures and the mathematical formulas are irrelevant for this study. [for details see EPW Research Foundation 1993, Sen 1981, Sinha and Sen, Raj Kumar (eds.) 2000, pp. 193-265].

Amartya Sen has criticized the income-based poverty measures as they fail to take account of deprivations in terms of basic amenities of life (literacy, healthcare, safe drinking water, pollution-free atmosphere etc.). So he has defined poverty indices based on these aspects of human living, popularly known as capability-based indices (Sen, Amartya 1984, 1993). In this connection, the Human Poverty indices of UNDP are worth mentioning (UNDP, HDR 2003, pp. 342-43). Sen's approach would be taken up in a subsequent section.

INEQUALITY

In modern economic literature, attention has also been drawn to various aspects of relative poverty or inequality both in terms of income and in terms of basic amenities. The common statistical measure to quantify inequality is the Gini Coefficient derived from the Lorenz Curve[1].

All surveys to quantify inequality in terms of this approach have revealed widespread inequality in terms of income, basic amenities and human development in most of the countries (irrespective of the level of economic development). Research works have also revealed wide differences in the degree of inequality in various regions of the same country. If we look into the world scenario and compare different nations on the basis of per capita income and Human Development Index wide disparities among nations would become apparent. Time series data from the World Development Report and Human Development Report reveals widening disparities among nations over time negating all the nicely constructed growth models indicating convergence (WDR, HDR various issues).

POVERTY REMOVAL MEASURES IN LDCS

So far as the LDCs are concerned, inequality and low level of development have combined to assign such a grave significance to absolute poverty that poverty removal has been the most crucial policy issue for all sensible governments, especially in the LDCs. The two major theoretical approaches in this direction are:

(i) Trickledown Approach and

(ii) Direct Approach

The distinctions between these two approaches may be clarified with examples from India.

At the initial stage of planning in India it was expected that economic growth would automatically trickle down to remove the intensity of poverty at the lower strata of income. But this did not happen as most of the fruits of planned economic development had been cornered by the well to do minority magnifying the intensity of poverty and inequality. So since the Fifth Five Year Plan (1974-79) the 'trickledown approach' was abandoned and emphasis was laid on direct poverty removal measures. Since then innumerable special poverty removal programmes (like IRDP, SFDA, ILDDPAP, TADP, MNP etc) have been in operation (Hiraway 1986).

No doubt, this direct attack on poverty has produced some positive results, but they have been quite inadequate considering the magnitude of poverty in this highly populated country (World Bank 1997, 1998, 1999, Muqtada 1990).

Since the 1990s it has been emphasized that a combination of growth and direct programme would be the best measure for poverty removal in India (Hanumantha Rao 1992). This may be the experience of many other third world countries. The drives of the world institutions like the UNO, IMF and the World Bank have also been in this direction. This is obvious from the exhortations in all the recent issues of the World Development Report, the Human Development Report and all other publications by the world bodies.

MARXIAN APPROACH

Marxian theory of the historical process of development of the human society gives an excellent account of the genesis of poverty and inequality. From economic standpoint Marx divides the process of development of human society till his time into four major stages: primitive communism, slave society, feudalism and capitalism. He predicts that capitalism would be replaced by socialism, which again will ultimately dissolve into the utopian state of Communism.

At the first stage, during primitive communism, poverty in the modern sense did not exist (poverty in the modern sense is meaningful only when its opposite, viz. opulence, exists). It was simply limitation of amenities, applicable to all members of a clan, because of limited knowledge to explore natural resources to meet human demand. These clan societies were characterized by equality. To quote:

> "The household was communistic, comprising several, and often many, families. Whatever was produced and used in common was common property: the house, the garden, the long boat." (Engels 1884, Ch-IX, P.155)

Man-nature conflict gradually led to improvement in methods of production – man gradually having more and more command over Nature with its increasing knowledge. With acceleration of this process by increasing social division of labour, surplus over and above consumption requirements started emerging. And at the same time human values pertaining to fellow feeling and equality started degenerating into slavery – oppression of one class of people by another. To quote:

> "The increase of production in all branches–cattle breeding, agriculture, domestic handicrafts–enabled human labour power to produce more than was necessary for its maintenance. At the same time, it increased the amount of work that daily fell to the lot of every member of the gens or household community or single family. The addition of more labour power became desirable. This was furnished by war; captives were made slaves. Under the given general historical conditions, the first great division of labour, by increasing the productivity of labour, that is, wealth, and enlarging the field of production, necessarily carried slavery in its wake. Out of the first great social division of labour arose the first great division of society into two classes: masters and slaves, exploiters and exploited." (*Ibid.* P. 157).

"The continued increase of production and with it the increased productivity of labour enhanced the value of human labour power. Slavery, which had been a nascent and sporadic factor in the preceding stage, now became an essential part of the social system." (*Ibid.* P. 159)

"The distinction between rich and poor was added to that between freemen and slaves–with the new division of labour came a new division of society into classes." (*Ibid.* P. 160).

With the emergence of money as the most convenient medium of exchange and the emergence of the parasitic merchant class, the process of property ownership and accumulation of wealth by a few and the consequent poverty and inequality were further crystallized. To quote:

> "Here a class appears for the first time which, without taking any part in production, captures the management of production as a whole and economically subjugates the producers to its rule: a class that makes itself the indispensable intermediary between any two producers and exploits them both." (*Ibid.* P. 162).

"The commodity of commodities, which conceals within itself all other commodities, was discovered; the charm that can transform itself at will into anything desirable and desired. Whoever possessed it ruled the world of production; and who had it above all others? The merchants." (*Ibid.* P. 163)

"Besides wealth in commodities and slaves, besides money wealth, wealth in the form of land came into being." (*Ibid.* P. 163).

Continued material progress, made possible by increasing command over Nature, ultimately paved the way for the Industrial Revolution, which ushered in the capitalistic or bourgeois society. Capitalism enhanced the pace of materialistic development but at the same time it generated more ruthless exploitation of the labour class turning them into proletariats. To quote:

> "With slavery, which reached its fullest development in civilization, came the first great split of society into an exploiting and an exploited class. This split has continued during the whole period of civilization. Slavery was the first form of exploitation, peculiar to the world of antiquity; it was followed by serfdom in the Middle Ages, and by wage labour in modern times. These are three great forms of servitude, characteristic of the three great epochs of civilization; open, and, latterly, disguised slavery, are its steady companions." (*Ibid.* P. 172).

"The bourgeoisie, during its rule of scarce one hundred years, has created more massive and more colossal productive forces than have all preceding generations together. Subjection of Nature's forces to man, machinery, application of chemistry to industry and agriculture, steam navigation, railways, electric telegraphy, clearing of whole continents for cultivation, canalization of rivers, whole population conjured out of the ground – what earlier century had even a presentiment such productive forces slumbered in the lap of social labour?" (Marx and Engels 1848, Ch-1, P. 48).

"In proportion as the bourgeoisie, i.e., capital, is developed, in the same proportion is the proletariat, the modern working class, developed–a class of labourers, who live only so long as they find work, and who find work only so long as their labour increases capital. These labourers, who must sell themselves piecemeal, are a commodity, like every other article of competition, to all the fluctuations of market." (Ibid. Ch-1, P. 51).

According to Marx and Engels the basic causes of oppression, exploitation, and increasing poverty and inequality along with material progress were class society and the institution of private property with the associated vices like division of labour, exchange, family, competition and the State. Let us have a brief glimpse of the Marxian view regarding these factors.

PRIVATE PROPERTY

According to Marxian world outlook, private property is the basic cause of all maladies in human society. So the task of the communists is to abolish all private property. The *Primeval Sin* (downfall of Adam and Eve from the Eden of

Primitive Communism) begins from the emergence of 'Alienated' or 'Estranged' labour (for detail see Marx 1974, pp. 61-74) which is both cause and consequence of private property. To quote:

> "True, it is as a result of the *movement of private property* that we have obtained the concept of *alienated labour* (*of alienated life*) in political economy. But on analysis of this concept it becomes clear that though private property appears to be the reason, the cause of alienated labour, it is rather its consequence" (Ibid. p.72).

"Only at the culmination of the development of private property does this, its secret, appear again, namely, that on the one hand it is the *product* of alienated labour, and that on the other it is the *means* by which labour alienates itself, *the realsation of this alienation*." (*Ibid.* p. 72).

The corrupting influence of private property on every aspect of human living has been clearly stated by Marx. To quote:

> "Private property has made us so stupid and one-sided that an object is only *ours* when we have it–when it exists for us as capital, or when it is directly possessed, eaten, drunk, worn, inhabited, etc.,–in short, when it is *used* by us. Although private property itself again conceives all these direct realisations of possession only as *means of life*, and the life which they serve as means is the *life of private property*– labour and conversion into capital.

In the place of *all* physical and mental senses there has therefore come the sheer estrangement of *all* these senses, the sense of having. The human being had to be reduced to this absolute poverty in order that he might yield his inner wealth to the outer world.

The transcendence of private property is therefore the complete *emancipation* of all human senses and qualities, but it is this emancipation precisely because these senses and attributes have become, subjectively and objectively, *human*." (*Ibid.* p. 94).

"Under private property their significance is reversed: every person speculates on creating a *new* need in another, so as to drive him to a fresh sacrifice, to place him in a new dependence and to seduce him into a new mode of *enjoyment* and therefore economic ruin. Each tries to establish over the other an *alien* power, so as thereby to find satisfaction of his own selfish need. The increase in the quantity of objects is therefore accompanied by an extension of the realm of the alien powers to which man is subjected, and every new product represents a new *potentiality* of mutual swindling and mutual plundering. Man becomes ever poorer as man, his need for *money* becomes ever greater if he wants to overpower hostile being. The power of his *money* declines in inverse proportion to the increase in the volume of production: that is, his neediness grows as the *power* of money increases." (*Ibid.* p. 101).

So the process of human development, according to Marx, calls for complete abolition of private property. To quote:

> "In this sense, the theory of the Communists may be summed up in the single sentence: Abolition of private property" (Marx and Engels 1848, p. 63).

"When, therefore, capital is converted into common property, into the property of all members of society, personal property is not thereby transformed into social property. It is only the social character of the property that is changed. It loses its class character." (*Ibid.* p. 64).

"From the relationship of estranged labour to private property it follows further that the emancipation of society from private property, etc., from servitude, is expressed in the *political* form of the *emancipation of the workers*; not that *their* emancipation alone is at stake, but because the emancipation of the workers contains universal human emancipation–and it contains this, because the whole of human servitude is involved in the relation of the workers to production, and all relations of servitude are but modifications and consequences of this relation." (Marx 1974, p.73).

"In order to abolish the *idea* of private property, the *idea* of communism is quite sufficient. It takes *actual* communist action to abolish actual private property. History will lead to it; and this movement, which *in theory* we already know to be a self-transcending movement, will constitute in actual fact a very rough and protracted process. But we must regard it as a real advance to have at the outset gained a consciousness of the limited character as well as of the goal of this historical movement–and a consciousness which reaches out beyond it." (*Ibid.* p. 108-09).

"In fact, the abolition of private property is, doubtless, the shortest and most significant way to characterize the revolution in the whole social order which has been made necessary by the development of industry – and for this reason it is rightly advanced by communists as their main demand." (Engels 1969, p. 89).

Division of labour, competition, exchange, family and all other corrupting elements of society, according to Marx, have originated from the *Primeval Sin*, viz. Private Property and Estranged Labour. To quote:

> "Just as we have derived the concept of *private property* from the concept of *estranged, alienated* labour by *analysis*, so we can develop every category of political economy with the help of these two factors; and we shall find again in each category, e.g., trade, competition, capital, money, only a *particular* and *developed expression* of these first elements." (Marx 1974, p. 73).

"This *material*, immediately *perceptible* private property is the material perceptible expression of *estranged human* life. Its movement–production and consumption–is the *perceptible* revelation of the movement of all production until now, i.e., the realisation of the reality of man. Religion, family, state, law, morality, science, art, etc., are only *particular* modes of production, and fall under its general law." (*Ibid.* p. 91).

DIVISION OF LABOUR AND EXCHANGE

Marx and Engels describe how division of labour and exchange mechanism originates from private property. To quote:

> "But, slowly, division of labour crept into this process of production. It undermined the collective nature of production and appropriation, it made appropriation by individuals the largely prevailing rule, and thus gave rise to exchange between individuals..." (Engels 1884, p. 171).

"The *division of labour* is the economic expression of the *social character of labour* within the estrangement. Or, since *labour* is only an expression of human activity within alienation, of the manifestation of life as the alienation of life, the *division of labour*, too, is therefore nothing else but the *estranged, alienated* positing of human activity as a *real activity of the species* or as *activity of man as a species-being*." (Marx 1974, p. 113).

"The whole of modern political economy agrees, however, that division of labour and wealth of production, division of labour and accumulation of capital, mutually determine each other; just as it agrees that only private property which is *at liberty* to follow its own course can produce the most useful comprehensive division of labour." (*Ibid.* p. 116).

"To assert that *division of labour* and *exchange* rest on *private property* is nothing but asserting that *labour* is the essence of private property – an assertion which the political economist cannot prove and which we wish to prove for him. Precisely in the fact that *division of labour* and *exchange* are aspects of private property lies in the twofold proof, on the one hand that *human* life required *private property* for its realisation, and on the other hand that it now requires the supersession of private property." (*Ibid.* p. 117).

Marx and Engels describe clearly the adverse consequences of division of labour and exchange for the human society. To quote:

> "Whilst the division of labour raises the productive power of labour and increases the wealth and refinement of society, it impoverishes the worker and reduces him to a machine." (Ibid. p. 26-27).

"*Division of labour* and *exchange* are the two *phenomena* which lead the political economist to boast of the social character of his science, while in the same breath he gives unconscious expression to the contradiction in his science–the motivation of society by unsocial, particular interests." (*Ibid.* p. 117).

"What characteises the division of labour inside modern society is that it engenders specialised functions, specialists, and with them craft-idiocy." (Marx 1966, p. 125).

So division of labour, which is one of the major causes of class division of the society is to be abolished. To quote:

> "The existence of classes originated in the division of labor, and the division of labor, as it has been known up to the present, will completely disappear." (Engels 1969, p.93).

"Education will enable young people quickly to familiarize themselves with the whole system of production and to pass from one branch of production to another in response to the needs of society or their own inclinations. It will, therefore, free them from the one-sided character which the present-day division of labor impresses upon every individual. Communist society will, in this way, make it possible for its members to put their comprehensively developed faculties to full use." (*Ibid.* p. 94).

FAMILY

Marx considers family to be one of the evils generated from private property relations and evolved through various stages of economic advancement. To quote:

> "On what foundation is the present family, the bourgeois family, based? On capital, on private gain. In its completely developed form this family exists only among the bourgeoisie. But this state of things finds its complement in the practical absence of the family among the proletarians, and in public prostitution." (Marx and Engels 1848, p. 68).

"The bourgeois sees in his wife a mere instrument of production. He hears that the instruments of production are to be exploited in common, and naturally, can come to no other conclusion than that the lot of being common to all will likewise fall to the women." (*Ibid.* p. 70).

"For the rest, nothing is more ridiculous than the virtuous indignation of our bourgeois at the community of women which, they pretend, is to be openly and officially established by the Communists. The Communists have no need to introduce community of women; it has existed almost from time immemorial." (*Ibid.* p. 70).

Marx and Engels opine that family will perish automatically as soon as private property is abolished. To quote:

> "For the rest, it is self-evident that the abolition of the present system of production must bring with it the abolition of the community of women springing from that system, i.e., of prostitution both public and private." (Ibid. p. 71).

"The bourgeois family will vanish as a matter of course when its complement vanishes, and both will vanish with the vanishing of capital." (*Ibid.* p. 68).

"It will transform the relations between the sexes into a purely private matter which concerns only the persons involved and into which society has no occasion to intervene. It can do this since it does away with private property and educates children on a communal basis, and in this way removes the two bases of traditional marriage–the dependence rooted in private property, of the women on the man, and of the children on the parents." (Engels 1969, p.94)

COMPETITION

According to Marxian view, competition, another consequence of private property, has been the propelling force as well as the cause of disorder of bourgeois society. To quote:

> "Competition has penetrated all the relationships of our life and completed the reciprocal bondage in which men now hold themselves. Competition is the great mainspring which again and again jerks into activity our ageing and withering social order, or rather disorder; but with each new exertion it also saps a part of this order's waning strength." [Marx 1974, p. 177 (Appendix)]

"It must be carefully noted that competition always becomes the more destructive for bourgeois *relations* in proportion as it urges on a feverish creation of new productive forces, that is, of the material conditions of a new society. In this respect at least, the bad side of competition would have its good points." (Marx 1966, p. 130-31)

Marx opines that competition and monopoly are but two sides of the same coin. To quote:

> "In practical life we find not only competition, monopoly and the antagonism between them, but also the synthesis of the two, which is not a formula, but a movement.

> Monopoly produces competition, competition produces monopoly. Monopolists are made from competition; competitors become monopolists. If the monopolists restrict their mutual competition by means of partial associations, competition increases among the workers; and the more the mass of the proletarians grow as against the monopolists of one nation, the more desperate competition becomes between the monopolists of different nations. The synthesis is of such a character that monopoly can only maintain itself by continually entering into the struggle of competition." (*Ibid.* p. 132).

"Monopoly produces free competition, and the latter, in turn, produces monopoly. Therefore, both must fall, and these difficulties must be resolved through the transcendence of the principle which gives rise to them." [Marx 1974, p. 177 (Appendix)]

Abolition of competition is one of the major tasks of the Communists. To quote:

> "It will, in other words, abolish competition and replace it with association. Moreover, since the management of industry by individuals necessarily implies private property, and since competition is in reality merely the manner and form in which the control of industry by private property owners expresses itself, it follows that private property cannot be separated from competition and the individual management of industry. Private property must, therefore, be abolished and in its place must come the common utilization of all instruments of production and the distribution of all products according to common agreement – in a word, what is called the communal ownership of goods." (Engels 1969, p. 89)

THE STATE

According to Marxian view, the Sate is an institution developed solely to protect the interests of the exploiter minority against that of the exploited majority and to facilitate the process of exploitation. To quote:

> "The state is, therefore, by no means a power forced on society from without; just as little is it "the reality of the ethical idea," "the image and reality of reason," as Hegel maintains. Rather, it is the product of society at a certain stage of development; it is the admission that this society has become entangled in an insoluble contradiction with itself, that it has split into irreconcilable antagonisms which it is powerless to dispel. But in order that these antagonisms, classes with conflicting economic interests, might not consume themselves and society in fruitless struggle, it becomes necessary to have a power seemingly standing above society that would alleviate the conflict, and keep it within the bounds of "order"; and this power, arisen out of society, but placing itself above it, and alienating itself more and more from it, is the state." (Engels 1972, p. 166)

"Because the state arose from the need to hold class antagonisms in check, but because it arose, at the same time, in the midst of the conflict of these classes, it is, as a rule, the state of the most powerful, economically dominant class, which, through the medium of the state, becomes also the politically dominant class, and thus acquires new means of holding down and exploiting the oppressed class." (*Ibid.* p. 168).

"In most of the historical states, the rights of citizens are, besides, apportioned according to their wealth, thus directly expressing the fact that the state is an organization of the possessing class for its protection against the non-possessing class." (*Ibid.* p. 169).

Ultimately with the end of class antagonism, the necessity of the State would vanish and so the State would also disappear. To quote:

> "The state, then, has not existed from all eternity. There have been societies that did without it, that had no idea of the state and state power. At a certain stage of economic development, which was necessarily bound up with the split of society into classes, the state became a necessity owing to this split. We are now rapidly approaching a stage in the development of production at which the existence of these classes not only will have ceased to be a necessity, but will become a positive hindrance to production. They will fall as inevitably as they arose at an earlier stage. Along with them the state will inevitably fall. Society, which will reorganize production on the basis of a free and equal association of the producers, will put the whole machinery of state where it will then belong: into the museum of antiquities, by the side of the spinning-wheel and the bronze axe," (*Ibid.* p. 170).

TRANSITION

Although human society, according to Marx, would automatically bring about Communism by the inherent contradictions, but it may take a very long time. So he opines that this process of transition towards the ultimate goal is to be hastened by means of deliberate efforts. Capitalism has already generated the force, viz. the proletariats, which can play a crucial role in accelerating this pace by overthrowing the bourgeois Sate and establish Socialistic State under the dictatorship of the proletariat and thereby pave the path towards Communism. The weapon of the proletariat is the same class struggle which has been the driving force of human history ever since the emergence of private property.

CLASS STRUGGLE

According Marxian view, the driving force of human civilization has been class struggle, the relentless war between the exploiters and the exploited. This class struggle would ultimately lead to overthrow of the bourgeois State by the proletariat to bring about Socialism and ultimately pave the way to Communism, the blissful state. Thus Marxian human development consists in generating class consciousness of the proletariats and hastening the pace of relentless class struggle by deliberate efforts of the Communist Party. To quote:

> "The history of all hitherto existing society is the history of class struggles.

Freeman and slave, patrician and plebeian, lord and serf, guild-master and journeyman, in a word, oppressor and oppressed, stood in constant opposition to one another, carried on an uninterrupted, now hidden, now open fight, a fight that each time ended, either in a revolutionary re-constitution of society at large, or in the common ruin of the contending classes" (Marx and Engels 1848, pp. 40-41).

"Our epoch, the epoch of the bourgeoisie, possesses, however, this distinctive feature: it has simplified the class antagonisms. Society as a whole is more and more splitting up into two great hostile camps, into two great classes directly facing each other: Bourgeoisie and Proletariat" (*Ibid.* p. 41).

"The weapons with which the bourgeoisie felled feudalism to the ground are now turned against the bourgeoisie itself." (*Ibid.* p. 50).

"But not only has the bourgeoisie forged the weapons that bring death to itself; it has also called into existence the men who are to wield those weapons –the modern working class – the proletarians." (*Ibid.* p. 51).

"The proletariat is that class in society which lives entirely from the sale of its labor and does not draw profit from any kind of capital; whose weal and woe, whose life and death, whose sole existence depends on the demand for labor–hence, on the changing state of business, on the vagaries of unbridled competition. The proletariat, or the class of proletarians, is, in a word, the working class of the 19th century." (Engels 1969, p. 81).

"In proportion as the bourgeoisie, i.e., capital, is developed, in the same proportion is the proletariat, the modern working class, developed–a class of labourers, who live only so long as they find work, and who find work only so long as their labour increases capital. These labourers, who must sell themselves piecemeal, are a commodity, like every other article of commerce, and are consequently exposed to all the vicissitudes of competition, to all the fluctuations of the market" (Marx and Engels 1975, p. 51).

So the first step is to organize the proletariats under the Communist Party and inspire them to overthrow the Bourgeois State and replace it by Socialistic State under the advanced detachment of the proletariat. This aspect of the Communist party vividly explained in the following excerpt:

> "The party must be, first of all, the *advanced* detachment of the working class. The party must absorb all the best elements of the working class, their experience, their revolutionary spirit, their selfless devotion to the cause of the proletariat." (Stalin 1970, p. 103).

"The proletariat seizes the public power, and by means of this transforms the socialised means of production, slipping from the hands of the bourgeoisie, into public property." (Engels 1975, pp. 326-27).

The ultimate goal of Marxian human development process is, however, to achieve Communism, which is completely free from private property, division of labour, exchange, family and the State. But the transition, after takeover of State-power by the proletariats and replacement of Bourgeois State by Socialist State, would take a long historical process. To this end the initial steps to be undertaken have been described in detail. (Marx and Engels 1848, pp. 74-75).

The ultimate process may be like this:

> "When, in the course of development, class distinctions have disappeared, and all production has been concentrated in the hands of a vast association of the whole nation, the public power will lose its political character. Political power, properly so called, is merely the organised power of one class for oppressing another. If the proletariat during its contest with the bourgeoisie is compelled, by the force of circumstances, to organise itself as a class, if, by means of a revolution, it makes itself the ruling class, and, as such, sweeps away by force the old conditions of production, then it will, along with these conditions have swept away the conditions for the existence of class antagonisms and of classes generally, and will thereby have abolished its own supremacy as a class.

In place of the old bourgeois society, with its classes and class antagonisms, we shall have an association, in which the free development of each is the condition for the free development of all." (*Ibid.* p. 76).

Marx failed to realize (because of either superficial observation or myopic view or parochial attachments) that causes of poverty, inequality, exploitation and similar maladies do not lie in private property, family relations, the state or any other visible phenomenon, but it lies deep in human nature, in the unethical elements like greed, pride, jealousy etc. So, eradication of the maladies, if at all possible, is to be accomplished by some process that would reduce the prevalence of these basic vices in human mind.

Occasionally, however, Marx and Engels come down to the real causes of the maladies, e.g.:

> "The only wheels which political economy sets in motion are *greed* and the *war amongst the greedy–competition*." (Marx 1974, p. 62).

"General *envy* constituting itself as a power is the disguise in which *greed* re-establishes itself and satisfies itself, only in *another* way. The thought of every piece of private property as such is *at least* turned against *wealthier* private property in the form of envy and the urge to reduce things to a common level, so that this envy and urge even constitute the essence of competition." (*Ibid.* p. 88).

> "With this constitution as its foundation civilization has accomplished things with which the old gentile society was totally unable to cope. But it accomplished them by playing on the most sordid instincts and passions of man, and by developing them at the expense of all his other faculties. Naked greed has been the moving spirit of civilization from the first day of its existence to the present time; wealth, more wealth and wealth again; wealth, not of society, but of this shabby individual was its sole and determining aim." (Engels 1884, p. 173).

But these fleeting moments of digression to reality soon dissolve into the preaching of their invented doctrine.

The Marxian weapon to overthrow the bourgeois State is the proletariat class, the labour class forced down to the level of bare subsistence. To quote:

> "Eventually wages, which have already been reduced to a minimum, must be reduced yet further, to meet the new competition. This then necessarily leads to revolution." (Marx 1974, p. 61).

This cannot, however, be denied that such proletariat class had real existence in all the nascent capitalist countries during the time of Marx (the nineteenth century). But with technological advancement during the twentieth century, the scenario changed radically. The size of the proletarian class, 'who had nothing to lose but chains', in the capitalist countries, gradually diminished in size in course of technological progress during the twentieth century and almost vanished with the onset of the new millennium. The relatively better paid labourers of the modern capitalist countries could hardly be inspired to raise arms against the capitalists, unlike their proletariat brethren a century ago. Moreover, class composition in the modern capitalist countries has become extremely complex with the swelling of various grades of the middle class. This has belied the Marxian conviction that under capitalism the society would be polarized into two distinct classes: capitalists and labourers.

Unfortunately, because of his myopic vision and too much pre-occupation with invented doctrines, Marx failed to grasp the future world that is to be ushered in by capitalism. So, ultimately, in the real world, Marxism degenerated into Leninism and Maoism, aiming at overthrowing the State by organizing the poverty stricken masses of the feudal and semi-feudal countries. Marx and Engels, however, had dubbed this sort of endeavour as utopian socialism. To quote:

> "To the crude conditions of capitalist production and the crude class conditions corresponded crude theories. The solution of the social problems, which as yet lay hidden in undeveloped economic conditions, the utopians attempted to evolve out of the human brain. ....It was necessary, then, to discover a new and more perfect system of social order and to impose this upon society from without by propaganda, and, wherever it was possible, by the example of model experiments. These new social systems were foredoomed as utopian; the more completely they were worked out in detail, the more they could not avoid drifting off into pure fantasies." (Engels 1975 p. 293).

"The utopians, we saw, were utopians because they could be nothing else at a time when capitalist production was as yet so little developed." (*Ibid.* p. 303).

Marx and Engels strongly asserted that their concepts had been derived from historical facts rather than invention. To quote:

> "The theoretical conclusions of the Communists are in no way based on ideas or principles that have been invented, or discovered, by this or that would be universal reformer.

They merely express, in general terms, actual relations springing from an existing class struggle, from a historical movement going on under our very eyes." (Marx and Engels op. cit. Ch-2, P. 62).

Now think of the so called proletarian philosophy. The depth of knowledge and introspection required to grasp the essence of the Marxian world outlook can hardly be found among the wage-earning class. Thus it is simply a world outlook invented by the speculative faculty of a highly intelligent and well read middleclass intellectual like Karl Marx who claimed it to be springing from the historical experience of the labour class. Nothing could be more ridiculous than this.

Later Marxists were well aware of this fact and therefore felt the necessity of re-educating the labourers with Marxian theories. To quote:

> "The Party cannot be a real party if it limits itself to registering what the masses of the working class feel and think, if it drags at the tail of the spontaneous movement, if it is unable to overcome the inertia and the political indifference of the spontaneous movement, if it is unable to rise above the momentary interests of the proletariat, if it is unable to raise the masses to the level of understanding the class interests of the proletariat. The party must stand at the head of the working class; it must see farther than the working class; it must lead the proletariat, and not drag at the tail of the spontaneous movement." (Stalin 1970, p. 103).

Now let us look closely into the ultimate goal of Marx, i.e. Communism. In such a stage of human history, there would be no private property, no family, no State, no competition, no division of labour, and no exchange. To quote:

> "The positive transcendence of *private property*, as the appropriation of *human* life, is therefore the positive transcendence of all estrangement – that is to say, the return of man from religion, family, state, etc., to his *human*, i.e., *social*, existence." (Marx 1974, p. 91)

Men would lose their individual entity in such a stage and exist only as part of the species being (the humans) just like the trees in a forest. What a pathetic future for men has been targeted by Marx! Is it not brutal sadism to eke out such a horrible future for the human race?.

SEN'S APPROACH

In recent years Amartya Sen's contributions have assigned a new dimension to the 'economics of poverty', especially its ethical aspects. Sen's major contributions in revitalizing the non-conventional economic thought have been remarkable. He gave a new lease of life to normative economics then languishing in 'Arrow's Impossibility' theorem (Arrow 1951, Sen 1970). He also played an important role in reviving the development economics (moribund under the onslaught of aggressive neo-classicism, reemerging with renewed vigour with the up tide of the process of globalization) by redefining economic development in terms of entitlements and capabilities[2](Sen 1984) and freedom (Sen 2000). To quote:

> "The process of economic development can be seen as a process of expanding the capabilities of people. Given the functional relation between entitlements of persons over goods and their capabilities, a useful – though derivative – characterization of economic development is in terms of expansion of entitlements." (Sen 1984, P.497)

Capabilities depend, besides exchange entitlement, on provision of public goods (market failure results in no private supply)–health, education, longevity, pollution-free environment, safe drinking water etc.

"But when it comes to health, or education, or social equality, or self respect, or freedom from social harassment, income is miles off the target." (Ibid. pp.499-500).

Mahabub Ul Haq's remarkable contribution was in the arena of human development. He was the first economist to device the quantitative measurement of human development. (Haq 1997). The Human Development Indices published by the UNDP are constructed on the basis of ideas conceived by Haq.

In some of his major works, Sen and his followers have bought to the fore the role of State Policy and public action in preventing the acute manifestation of poverty, viz. famine. (Drèze and *Sen* 1989, Drèze, Sen and Hussain 1995, Sen 1981). Their general observation in this regard is that many famines occurring in India during the British period (including the horrible Bengal Famine of 1943, vividly presented in novels by two great Bengali Authors) and elsewhere in modern age were mainly due to 'Entitlement-Failure' and negative State policy and/or lack of political will. Nehru, the first Prime minister of India also subscribed to this view (Nehru 1981, p. 497).

Sen appreciates the role of the present government of India in tackling famines by suitable public action and appropriate policies. In this regard he emphasizes the role of freedom of mass media and public opinion in a democratic polity as in independent India (which is absent in dictatorial states like China). To quote:

> "The distinction between the 'collaborative' and 'adversarial' roles of the public has some relevance to this dichotomy between the advantages of political commitment vis-à-vis those of political pluralism. While a leadership committed to radical social change can often inspire more public collaboration, having a committed leadership is not adequate for–and may even be hostile to–the exercise of the adversarial role of the public. Since both the roles have value in combating deprivation, it is natural to look for the possibility of combining the advantages of committed leadership with those of pluralist tolerance. Whether combination is possible, especially in the circumstances that rule in most developing countries, remains a challenging question. There is no reason, in principle, why a political system that allows, encourages and helps the public to be active (both adversarially as well as collaboratively) cannot also lead to governments that provide bold initiatives and inspiring leadership. But it is obvious that in practice the actual possibilities are much constrained by social, political and economic circumstances, and the 'ideal combinations' are hard to realize, as history of the world has shown again and again." (Drèze and *Sen* 1989, pp. 278-79).

Sen, however, admits that dictatorial China has a better record so far as tackling chronic poverty is concerned. To quote:

> "On the other hand, there is no such relief for the third of the Indian rural population who go to bed hungry every night and who lead a live ravaged by regular deprivation. The quiet presence of non acute, endemic hunger leads to no newspaper turmoil, no political agitation, no riots in the Indian parliament. The system takes it in its stride." (Sen 1984 p.500)

"Finally, it is important to note that the protection that the Indian poor get from the active news distribution system and powerful opposition parties has very severe limitations. The deprivation has to be dramatic to be 'newsworthy' and politically exploitable. .... The Indian political system may prevent famines but, unlike the Chinese system, it seems unable to deal effectively with endemic malnutrition. In a normal year when things are running smooth, both in India and China, the Indian poor is in a much more deprived general state than his or her Chinese counterpart." (*Ibid.* p. 503).

Now, Sen hints at the possibility of combining the advantages of these two contrasting political systems. To quote:

> "Whether the disparate advantages of the contrasting systems can be effectively combined is a challenging issue of political economy that requires attention. Much is at stake." (Ibid. p.504)

In this connection it would be worthwhile to look into the merits of various major forms of political systems as regards ensuring social justice by minimizing poverty, inequality and deprivation. Here the main contenders are centrally control systems (Dictatorship, Monarchy and Socialism) and Democracy.

Dictatorship: Historical experience of all forms of non-socialist dictatorial regimes (in the past and the present) has unraveled their overwhelmingly oppressive features[3]. So we rule out this form.

Monarchy: Ancient Indian Texts (especially Manusmriti and Arthaúâstra of Kautilya[4]) (Basu 2005) have laid down detailed rules and procedures to make an ideal king. Unfortunately, in the recorded history, except Aœoka (Thapar 1961; Sastri 1967, pp.201-48; Kosambi 1981, pp.157-65), there is no evidence of the existence of another ideal king. The great Greek philosopher Plato conceived of a Philosopher King (Plato 1901, pp.215-40). As regards his concept of 'Philosopher King' Immanuel Kant made an interesting comment. To quote:

> "That 'kings will philosophize or philosophers become kings,' is not to be expected. Nor indeed is it to be desired, because the possession of power inevitably corrupts the free judgment of reason. But kings or king-like nations, who govern themselves according to laws of equality, should not allow the philosophers as a class to disappear, or to be silenced; rather should they be allowed to speak forth their maxims publicly. Nay, this is even indispensable to both for the mutual enlightenment of their functions. Nor should this process of communicating enlightenment be jealously regarded as a kind of Propagandism, because as a class the philosophers are by their nature incapable of combining into political clubs and factions." (Kant 1795, Second Supplement: Secret Article Relating to Perpetual Peace). Plato later on abandoned this idea after a bitter experience[5]. So monarchy is ruled out.

Socialism: Like the Indian concept of Ideal King or Plato's Philosopher King, socialism is also a utopian concept. It differs in one respect, viz. unlike the former two concepts the means to achieve its goal is the violent 'class struggle'. This is the basic reason that compelled the USSR, the first and the most powerful socialist state, to revert back to capitalistic path. (Basu 1999).

Democracy: Now we are left with democracy, which, from the standpoint of human freedom, is the best conceivable form of government. We have already touched upon Amartya Sen's views about the role of public opinion and the mass media in ensuring positive changes in the society. We, also rest our ultimate hope on this form of government. But the present state of democracy in the world and the global trends are not at all encouraging. The Neoclassical view, based on 'perfect competition' and '*laissez faire*' doctrine and playing the ideological basis of economic policies in the modern democratic countries till the early twentieth century, revealed its serious vulnerability during the 'Great Depression' of the 1930s. Keynesian economics emerging out of the bitter experiences of the Great Depression led to an abandonment of the *laissez faire* doctrine permitting state-intervention in the free-market economies, although to a limited scale. In the newly independent democratic countries like India during the post-war era, pervasive state-intervention in the form of comprehensive planning, control of the private enterprises, pioneering role of the state sector in strategic fields, price control, public distribution system for food and mass consumption commodities etc., became necessary both to break through the vicious circle of backwardness and to ensure social justice. But because of the inefficiency and corruption of the political parties and the government officials, both planning and public sector enterprises in these so called 'mixed economies' came up against serious hurdles, ultimately forcing them to move towards free market economies.

During the late 20th century, there was strong opinion among economists for revival of the free-market economy, completely devoid of state-interventions (Friedman 1980). In the meantime debacles of the socialist countries and planned mixed economies prepared grounds for the revival of Neoclassicism. The process of reversal got momentum with the spectacular communication revolution and ultimately the so called era of 'globalization' emerged.

With this background let us look into the efficacy of the democracies in ensuring social justice with progressive reduction in poverty, inequality and deprivations in the new era.

We have already mentioned that Amartya Sen has strongly appreciated the role of public opinion and free mass media in ensuring social justice in the democratic countries.

But Sen,s hopes, placed on the masses and the medias to make democracy really meaningful, come up against the Smithian Dilemma.

SMITHIAN DILEMMA

Adam Smith unequivocally explained why material achievements in the form of economic power is conceived as the best server of self interest of an individual in spite of all personal hazards associated with it. Here Smith goes deep into basic human psychology and puts forward his findings from empirical observations in this regard. An inherent nature of any human being, whatever his own position, is to praise and worship the successful and rich people, whatever immoral be the means by which this opulence has been achieved. Moreover, most people nurture in their subconscious, the hidden desire to achieve opulence and fame so as to get the praise and approbation of all and sundry. To quote:

> "This disposition to admire, and almost to worship, the rich and the powerful, and to despise, or, at least, to neglect persons of poor and mean condition, though necessary both to establish and to maintain the distinction of ranks and the order of society, is, at the same time, the great and most universal cause of the corruption of our moral sentiments. That wealth and greatness are often regarded with the respect and admiration which are due only to wisdom and virtue; and that the contempt, of which vice and folly are the only proper objects, is often most unjustly bestowed upon poverty and weakness, has been the complaint of moralists in all ages." (Smith, Adam 1759, I.III. 28).

"We desire both to be respectable and to be respected. We dread both to be contemptible and to be condemned. But, upon coming into the world, we soon find that wisdom and virtue are by no means the sole objects of respect; nor vice and folly, of contempt. We frequently see the respectful attentions of the world more strongly directed towards the rich and the great, than towards the wise and the virtuous. We see frequently the vices and follies of the powerful much less despised than the poverty and weakness of the innocent. To deserve, to acquire, and to enjoy the respect and admiration of mankind, are the great objects of ambition and emulation. Two different roads are presented to us, equally leading to the attainment of this so much desired object; the one, by the study of wisdom and the practice of virtue; the other, by the acquisition of wealth and greatness. Two different characters are presented to our emulation; the one, of proud ambition and ostentatious avidity. The other, of humble modesty and equitable justice. Two different models, two different pictures, are held out to us, according to which we may fashion our own character and behaviour; the one more gaudy and glittering in its colouring; the other more correct and more exquisitely beautiful in its outline: the one forcing itself upon the notice of every wandering eye; the other, attracting the attention of scarce any body but the most studious and careful observer. They are the wise and the virtuous chiefly, a select, though, I am afraid, but a small party, who are the real and steady admirers of wisdom and virtue. The great mob of mankind are the admirers and worshippers, and, what may seem more extraordinary, most frequently the disinterested admirers and worshippers, of wealth and greatness." (*Ibid.* I.III. 29).

"In equal degrees of merit there is scarce any man who does not respect more the rich and the great, than the poor and the humble. With most men the presumption and vanity of the former are much more admired, than the real and solid merit of the latter." (*Ibid.* I.III.31).

This undeniable nature of masses belies all hopes to bring back the corrupt politicians to the path of ethics and virtue. The inner discipline of all the major political parties makes it impossible for the ordinary members to protest against the mischief of the leaders. Moreover "leader worship" for Smithian psychosis makes the cadres, members and supporters of political parties to ignore the heinous activities of the leaders. The corrupt politicians also inculcate the inherent corrupt mentality of the common people. Thus the politicians get absolute freedom to do whatever best serves their personal interest even at the cost of the society and the masses. This belies all our hopes to eradicate poverty and social injustice through the democratic system, the last conceivable place of hope.

Notes

1. For various measures of inequality and the problems associated with them see Sen, 1973, 1982.
2. "Entitlement refers to the set of alternative commodity bundles that a person can command in a society using the totality of rights and opportunities that he or she faces............ On the basis of this entitlement, a person can acquire some capabilities, i.e. the ability to do this or that (e.g. be well nourished), and fail to acquire some other capabilities." (Sen, 1984, p. 497).
3. See Black 1986, Fitch and Lowenthal (eds.) 1986 for the heinous roles of dictatorial regimes in Latin America; Amitav Ghosh's novel "The Glass Place" (Ghosh 2001) portrays a vivid account of the oppressive dictatorial regime in Myanmar (Burma).
4. See Manusmriti: chapter-7, œlokas: 30-49, 58, 79, 142-47, 221-26 (*Sacred Books of the East*, Vol. XXV, edited by F. Max Müller, Oxford Clarendon Press, 1888) and Arthaśāstra of Kautilya: Book-I: ch-5/7-17; Ch-6/1-10; ch-7/1-8; ch-9/6-25; ch-19/9-11 (Kangle 1986).
5. According to the Greek author Diogenes Laertius, Plato received an invitation from Dionysius, the king of Syracuse to turn his kingdom into Utopia and Plato readily accepted the invitation. But when Plato suggested the king either to become a philosopher himself or to relinquish power for some philosopher in order to make his kingdom an utopia, the king got infuriated with Plato and sold him as a slave. Fortunately Plato's disciple Anniceris appeared in time as a rescuer by repurchasing Plato from the slave trader. This disillusioned Plato. (Laertius 2001, Book-3 (XIV-XVIII).

   We are in all praise for the Sen-Haque-Drèze approach for poverty alleviation. But we also emphasize that this is but a palliative and would never remove the deep seated cause lying in human nature. On the contrary, this may make the deprived dependent on outside help and thereby get further submerged in vice and ignorance. Long ago, Rabindranath had warned against this attitude of helping the common people. At the same time he suggested how higher values could be inculcated among the masses. To quote:

"For this reason, the most urgent necessity in our country is not to place begging bowls at their hands, but to make them confident of their own strength, to make them realize that a man united with others is a complete entity, an alienated individual is but a fragment." (Tagore 1986).

References

Arrow, K. J. (1951), *Social Choice and Individual Values*, New York, Wiley 1963.

Basu, Ratan Lal (1999), "Material Progress and Ethics: a Pilgrimage Through Time" in *The Culture Mandala* (The Bulletin of the Center for East-West Cultural and Economic Studies, Bond University, Australia), Vol.4, No. 1, December 1999-January 2000. [http://www.international-relations.com].

Basu, Ratan Lal (2005), "Human Development Part 2: Ancient Kingship, Modern Politicians and the Problem of Corruption in India" in *The Culture Mandala* (The Bulletin of the Center for East-West Cultural and Economic Studies, Bond University, Australia), Vol. 7, No.1, December 2005. [http://www.international-relations.com].

Black, Jan Knippers (1986), *Sentinels of Empire: The United States and Latin American Militarism*, New York, Greenwood Press.

Drèze, Jean and Sen, Amartya (1989), *Hunger and Public Action*, New Delhi, Oxford India Paperbacks 1999.

Drèze, Jean, Sen, Amartya and Hussain, Athar (eds.) (1995), *The Political Economy of Hunger*, New Delhi, Oxford India Paperbacks 1999.

Economic and Political Weekly (EPW) Research Foundation (1993), "Poverty Levels in India: Norms, Estimates and Trends", *EPW*, Vol. XXVIII, No.38, August 31, Mumbai.

Engels, Frederick (1969), "The Principles of Communism", *Marx-Engels Selected Works*, Volume-I, p. 81-97, Moscow, Progress Publishers.

Engels, Frederick (1975), *Anti-Dühring*, Moscow, Progress Publishers.

Engels, Frederick (1884), *The Origin of the Family, Private Property and the State*, Moscow, Progress Publishers, 1972.

Fitch, J. Samuel and Abraham F. Lowenthal (eds.) (1986) *Armies and Politics in Latin America*, New York, Holmes & Meier.

Friedman, Milton and Rose (1980), *Free to Choose*, London, Penguin.

Ghosh, Amitav (2001), *The Glass Palace*, HarperCollins.

Hanumantha Rao, C. H. (1992), "Integrating Poverty Alleviation Programmes with Development Strategies" *Economic and Political Weekly*, Vol. XXVII, No. 48, November 28, Mumbai.

Haq, Mahbub Ul (1997), *Human Development in South Asia*, New Delhi, Oxford University Press.

Hiraway, Indira (1986), *Abolition of Poverty in India*, New Delhi, Vikash Publishing House.

Kangle, R. P. (1986): *Kautīliya Arthaśāstra*, Part-II [English translation], Delhi, Motilal Banarasidass.

Kant, Immanuel (1795): "Perpetual Peace", in Kant's Principles of Politics, including his essay on Perpetual Peace, A Contribution to Political Science, trans. W. Hastie, Edinburgh, Clark 1891.

Kosambi, D. D. (1981), *The Culture and Civilization of Ancient India*, New Delhi, Vikas Publishing House.

Laertius, Diogenes (2001), *Lives of Eminent Philosophers*, Vol. I, translated by R.D. Hicks, Harvard University Press.

Marx and Engels (1848), *Manifesto of the Communist Party*, Moscow, Progress Publishers 1975.

Marx, Karl (1966), *The Poverty of Philosophy*, Moscow, Progress Publishers.

Marx, Karl (1974), *Economic and Philosophic Manuscript of 1848*, Moscow, Progress Publishers.

Muqtada, M. (1990), *The Elusive Target: An Evaluation of Target Group Approaches to Employment Creation in Rural Asia*, ILO.

Nehru, Jawaharlal (1981), *The Discovery of India*, New Delhi, Oxford University Press.

Plato (1901), *The Republic*, edited and translated by Benjamin Jowett, New York, P. F. Collier & Son.

Sastri, K. A. Nilakanta (ed.) (1967), *Age of the Nandas and Mauryas*, Delhi, Motilal Banarasidass.

Sen, Amartya (1970), *Collective Choice and Social Welfare*, Amsterdam, North-Holland 1979.

Sen, Amartya (1981), *Poverty and Famines*, New Delhi, Oxford India Paperbacks 1999.

Sen, Amartya (1984), *Resources, Values and Development*, New Delhi, Oxford India Paperbacks 1999.

Sen, Amartya (1993), "Capability and Well-Being" in Martha C. Nussbaum and Amartya Sen (eds.) *The Quality of Life*, New York, Oxford University Press.

Sen, Amartya (2000), *Development as Freedom*, New Delhi, Oxford India Paperbacks.

Sinha, Ajit Kumar and Sen, Raj Kumar (eds.) (2000), *Economics of Amartya Sen*, New Delhi, Deep and Deep Publications Pvt. Ltd.

Smith, Adam (1759), *The Theory of Moral Sentiments*, London, A. Millar, Sixth edition, 1790.

Stalin, Joseph (1970), *The Foundations of Leninism*, Peking, Foreign Languages Press.

Tagore, Rabindranath (1986), "Samabaya Nîti", in *Rabindra Rachanavali*, 125th Anniversary Edition, Vol. 14, P. 313, Calcutta, Visva-Bharati Publishers (translated from Bengali by the author of this article).

Thapar, Romila (1961), *Asoka and the Decline of the Mauryas*, New Delhi, Oxford University Press.

UNDP: *Human Development Report*, Various Issues.

World Bank: *World Development Report*, Various issues.

World Bank (1997) *India: Achievements and Challenges in Reducing Poverty*.

SUBSTANCE AND SYMBOLISM:
The 2005 G8 Summit at Gleneagles, Scotland

Ismail Shariff, Elizabeth B. & Philip J. Hendrickson
Professor of Business \ Professor, Urban and Regional Studies
University of Wisconsin-Green Bay, Green Bay, Wisconsin

On the back cover of the World Development Report 2000/2001, whose subtitle was "Attacking Poverty," stated the following: At the start of a new century poverty remains a global problem of huge proportions. Of the world's 6 billion people, 2.8 billion live on less than $2 a day and 1.2 billion on less than $1 a day. Eight of every 100 infants do not live to see their fifth birthday. Nine of every 100 boys and 16 of every 100 girls who reach school age do not attend school. Poverty is also evident in poor people's lack of political power and voice and in their extreme vulnerability to ill health, economic dislocation, personal violence, and natural disasters, and the scourge of HIV/AIDS. These litany expresses and suggests the plight of African countries more than any other countries of the globe. Therefore, this year's G8 Summit agenda rightfully focuses on eradicating poverty in Africa. In the light of this an attempt will be made in this paper to critically evaluate the outcome of G8 Summit and make some pertinent observations for future policy pronouncements.

I

On the back cover of the World Development Report 2000/2001, whose subtitle was "Attacking Poverty," stated the following: At the start of a new century poverty remains a global problem of huge proportions. Of the world's 6 billion people, 2.8 billion live on less than $2 a day and 1.2 billion on less than $1 a day. Eight of every 100 infants do not live to see their fifth birthday. Nine of every 100 boys and 16 of every 100 girls who reach school age do not attend school. Poverty is also evident in poor people's lack of political power and voice and in their extreme vulnerability to ill health, economic dislocation, personal violence, and natural disasters, and the scourge of HIV/AIDS. These litany expresses and suggests the plight of African countries more than any other countries of the globe. Therefore, this year's G8 Summit agenda rightfully focuses on eradicating poverty in Africa. In the light of this an attempt will be made in this paper to critically evaluate the outcome of G8 Summit and make some pertinent observations for future policy pronouncements.

II

In international discourse there is no doubt that this is Africa's year. Many powerful leaders of all persuasion are pushing for more aid and debt relief to the highly indebted poor countries (HIPC) of Africa. This line of thinking seems to be an extension of the proposal of the United Nations Millennium Development Goals (MDG's) adopted in 2000. Also, the African Commission, headed by British Prime Minister Tony Blair, aims to achieve the millennium development goals by guaranteeing to double aid over the next ten years. In the same vain the group of rich countries called as G8 (Great Britain, United States, Canada, France, Germany, Russia, Japan, and Italy) have concluded in their summit at Gleneagles, Scotland on July 6 and 7 with a promise of a package of measures including:

(1) a $50 billion boost to aid, and a debt-cancellation off the debts of Africa's 18 poorer countries (although African nations had called for the debt of all Africa to be cancelled);
(2) debt forgiveness must be applied by all creditors including (multi-national, bilateral and commercial) including African Development Banks;
(3) the abolition of subsidies to agricultural commodities by the rich countries that hitherto stood as a barrier to fair trade and an adoption of the time-frame as calendar for the abolition of such subsidies and;
(4) to press for two permanent seats on the United Nations' Security Council.

Looking at the above points of resolution, no one in the right frame of mind can take issue with these recommendations. For example, most of the sub-Saharan Africa is in the World Bank's lowest income category of less than $765 Gross National Income (GNI) per person per year. Ethiopia and Brundi are the worst off with just $90 GNI per person. Also, it is a fact that elsewhere, even the poorest people have gotten healthier and wealthier over the past 30 years. But in sub-Saharan Africa, life expectancy has declined, malaria and AIDS run rampant and economic conditions have plummeted. In 1975, Africa had a gross domestic product per capita that was twice as high as East Asia's. But since then, Africa's GDP per capita has declined from $1,800 to $1,500, while East Asia's has risen from $800 to $4,000. It is in the face of these realities Tony Blair rightfully asserts that "African poverty, for sure." "There is no greater problem in the world economy today." Furthermore, to deal with this problem he believes in dispensing an additional $25 billion in aid per year will help pull Africa out of stagnation.

No one with a heart or with cognitive perception can argue that to increase aid to poor countries along with accumulated debt cancellation by the rich countries is not a plus in our quest for global economic equity. All the debt forgiveness really needs is an eraser. For money has recycled back to the donor countries and is long gone. The poor countries, in the state of financial situation they are in, there is no hope that any of this debt is collectible by the rich countries in the foreseeable future. Therefore, it is best not only for the rich countries, but also for all international financial institutions (IFIs) to close the books and move on to a new life as donors. United Kingdom Chancellor, Gordon Brown, has put forward a bold plan to tackle both poverty and debt relief to the countries in Africa. He has called for a doubling of European aid by 2010 as well as a 100 per cent debt relief, as well as an end to many trade subsidies. UK is one of six European nations who have pledged to increase their aid to target of 0.7 per cent (a figure originally recommended by the Brand Commission as far back as 1987) of GDP, a figure which only five countries have managed to reach. So far, U.S. treasury spokesman as recently as July 3, 2005, reiterated that "the problem looking at targets of 0.7 per cent of GDP is that when people focus on numbers like that they don't know what they are talking about in nominal terms." In other words, U.S. is not in support of such an increase in her commitment.

As for the 100 per cent debt relief, to accomplish this, Gordon Brown has proposed an establishment of an International Finance Facility (IFF) for development aid to Africa in order to pay for education and medical programs like mass immunization. Towards this end he has pledged that U.K. would double its own aid to $800 billion by 2010. But the U.S. remains concerned about the nature of the U.K.'s proposal that debt forgiveness plans should be financed in part by selling gold reserves held by the International Monetary Fund (IMF). It is true that the surge in the price of gold in the last five years has boosted the value of the reserves, and the U.K. wants to use the extra cash to erase the outstanding uncollectible debt from the HIPC. The U.S., along with some other countries, including Japan, Germany, Italy, has never been keen on the idea of selling IMF gold.

Washington has also raised questions over the setup of IFF, which would allow developing countries in general, and HIPC in particular, to borrow against future aid pledges. President Bush, commenting on it said on July 3, 2005, in Scotland, that IFF for Africa "doesn't fit our budgetary process."

So, given the above uncertainty, it stands to doubt the realization of both doubling of aid to Africa by 2010 and also a 100 per cent debt relief. What is feasible is the possibility of realizing the pledge of $50 billion in aid (a doubling from its current aid level) agreed to at the G8 Summit. Here also one has to be cautious to note if past experiences are a guide to the future, there may be less to these pledges than meets the eye. After all, the world's rich countries have made such pledges before, and aid has actually been falling for a number of years.

Furthermore, there are questions about the quality of additional aid that may be provided. Poor countries are warned that it will be pledged with strict conditions, for example, requiring them to open their markets to foreign investment. They are also warned that much of the aid may be tied to the purchase of goods and services in the country offering the aid. These two aspects of aid apply to U.S. which (perhaps surprisingly) has pledged $8.8 billion per year, following another big increase in 2002. For example, much of U.S. aid is in the form of food aid, which is spent on U.S. farmers. The U.S. has set up a special body of its own, the Millennium Challenge Corporation (MCC), to administer U.S. aid to Africa. It has put in place tough conditions, like anti-corruption measures and good governance. As a result, only $400,000 of U.S. aid has actually reached the sub-Saharan Africa so far, and only four countries have fully qualified.

In direct contrast to the above restrictions and slow flow of aid, the Poverty-Lobby for Africa wants more aid, spent more quickly, than the G8 leaders are likely to offer, and they want debt relief extended from the 18 countries currently eligible to 62 poor countries. Also, for the world to meet the United Nations Millennium Development Goals (MDGs) there needs to be a massive and continuing increase in aid flows–an additional $50 billion a year from now (2005/06), rising to an additional $100 billion per year by 2010–which would continue until 2015. That would see rich countries achieve the goal of spending 0.7 per cent of GDP on aid by 1010. So far, the G8 leaders are trying to reach a deal which would double aid by 2010, and they have already pledged half of that, or $25 billion, to be spent in Africa by 1010. But the aid lobby says that much of that $25 billion is not new money, but re-announcements. The U.S. pledge to double its aid to Africa to $8.5 billion a year by 2010 came after intense pressure in June of 2005, on President Bush by Tony Blair, and is unlikely to increase further. And the EU pledge to reach a collective aid target of 0.56 per cent of GDP by 2010, and 0.7 per cent by 2015, is also unlikely to be revised upwards, given the several budget problems in many EU countries. Since four of G8 countries are members of the EU, that would leave Canada, Russia and Japan as the only countries who could fund the additional increase. But Japan has already promised to double aid from $1 billion to $2.5 billion, and neither Canada nor Russia could make up the shortfall.

The massive sums owed by poor countries is another key issue for both campaigners and the G8 leaders. Finance ministers from the G8 countries agreed on a deal two weeks before the G8 summit, which extended a $40 billion debt relief to 18 countries. But campaigners would like the deal to extend to more countries with fewer conditions and faster disbursements. The campaigners are of the view that G8 should agree to write off more than $500 billion in debt. In particular, they are unhappy with the debt deal agreed with–Nigeria, Africa's biggest debtor, which saw it agree to repay Western countries $12 billion from oil revenues in return for cancellation of other long-term debts. As a matter of fact, Nigeria owes the rest of the world $35 billion out of which $25 billion is owed to members of the 19-nation-strong Paris Club. It has not received any new loans since 1992, but repaid $8.5 billion debt since then. Part of Nigeria's case in asking for a total debt relief has been that most of the money it received was lent to corrupt military dictators, a fact that Nigeria says was well known by foreign banks and governments.

The biggest shift in focus for campaigners in recent years has been from aid to trade–proven to be the contentious issue for both the G8 leaders and the poverty lobby, which fueled demonstrations before and during the G8 Summit in Gleneagles, Scotland.

Trade is a far more potent force than financial assistance for aiding general economic development in Africa–and the decline of Africa's economy can partly be traced to its declining share of world trade. Africa is loosing out because it mainly sells primary products like coffee, cotton and extractive raw materials, whose prices are falling, and is not able to produce high-value exports like airplanes, computers and any other manufactured products of any significant value. Its agricultural sector is also hurt by the huge $300 billion subsidies given to the Western farmers in the U.S. and EU. Each cow in EU receives more aid than each person in Africa. The developing countries bone of contention revolves around the fact that they need a breathing space, when they are still able to produce their own economies but are unable to sell their foods more easily in Western markets. But EU and the U.S. negotiators, instead of honoring the plight of the developing countries, are demanding that these countries open their own market first, before they themselves take any action to open their markets to these countries. As a result of this unfair trade practices, it is estimated that it is costing the developing countries $700 billion a year, far more than the total aid flows to these countries. In spite of these facts, the campaigners in favor of the developing countries know how to resolve the agricultural subsidies issue, the real battle over this will take place in Hong Kong, at world trade talks in December 2005 and they are already making preparations to campaign there. In general, the campaigners are pleased that they have mobilized world opinion on an unprecedented level and pledge to fight on, even if Gleneagles is a disappointment. Mr. Kumi Waidoo, head of the Global Call for Action against poverty, in his website, has reiterated the fact that "we should take heart from the fact that without the massive mobilization of like-minded people around the world, the world would not have achieved so much in such a short time." He further went on to state that "we will keep up the pressure, and we never thought the G8 Summit at Gleneagles would be a "one-shot solution."

III

Looking back at the Gleneagles Summit and its measure to make poverty history, we can say that the G8 leaders at least on the surface appeared to be unsurprisingly reassuring. No one can claim the G8 Summit, which concluded on Friday, July 22, 2005, saved the world. No one can claim that the G8 failed to act. However, though G8 made progress on debt relief and aid, but the deal got nowhere on the issue of trade. It is also true that if one were to analyze carefully, we will find the debt relief package cost so little–maybe $1.5 billion a year across all the G8 countries–normally that that amount of money was not worth reporting. Nonetheless, the G8 love to make their modest step sound like giant steps. They are adept at getting big headlines for little money.

Now the question staring at us as to whether this year's G8 Summit was a success? The answer to this pertinent question depends on the standard one uses to measure it. Certainly by the standards of previous G8 Summits this one has achieved a great deal despite the disruption caused by the bombing in London. Debt relief was in fact first agreed in 1996, at the G8 Summit in Birmingham, UK eight years ago. The fact that it has taken so long to get agreement on the multi-lateral deal is a reflection of the deep disagreements among the major industrial countries. Japan, Germany and France have always been reluctant to agree to a complete write-off of debts, preferring to have greater leverage over the behavior of the HIPC countries by offering to pay off their debt service cost instead. Despite this reservation, it is unprecedented at this year's G8 meetings to reach substantive deals–such as $50 billion African aid boost and debt cancellation for the 18 HIPC countries (Benin, Bolivia, Burkina,

Faso, Ethiopia, Ghana, Guyana, Honduras, Madagascar, Mali, Mauritania, Mozambique, Tanzania, Uganda, and Zambia) who have qualified under the HIPC initiative.

The G8 Summit also agreed to renew efforts to forge a trade deal, pledged $36 billion for the Palestinian authority, and said it would increase access to Aids treatment. Also, the G8 Summit broke ground by bringing poverty campaigners and leaders from developing countries face to face with the world's eight most powerful leaders. In the words of Britain's Prime Minister, Tony Blair, the chairman of the G8 Summit, "It isn't the end of poverty in Africa, but it is the hope that it can be ended. It is not all everyone wanted but it is progress –real and achievable progress." And Bob Geldof, the former rock star and Live 8 organizer just days before the G8 Summit, paraphrased words first uttered by Winston Churchill–"I would not say this is the end of extreme poverty, but it is the beginning of the end." He further said, "Of course, the various deals fall far short of what many campaigners wanted. But they have set an important precedent which could lead to further developments over the course of the year, when other key negotiating meetings are taking place in the course of this year." Professor John Kirton, director of the University of Toronto G8 research group, commenting on the outcome of this year's G8 Summit, said, "This is the single most successful summit in the 30-year history of the event." He further asserted that "the so-called 'Sherpas' who plan the Summit met civil society–representatives or non governmental organizations (NGOs) and were offered a constructive role to play at the Summit." He added that "they made poverty history and Live 8 campaign played the most important part as far as any G8 Summit in showing how NGOs can exert real pressure and influence the agenda and outcome." But from now on, given their constructive role, it will be hard for other G8 Summits to exclude these groups in the way they were excluded from the Sea Island Summit hosted by President George Bush in 2004. Moreover, this G8 Summit continued and strengthened the trend to involve developing countries in the negotiations process. The leaders of the seven African nations attended the Summit, as did the leaders of the five leading "emerging market" countries like China, India, Brazil, Mexico, and South Africa. Therefore, it will be hard not to invite them in the future G8 meetings as they are playing an increasingly important role in the world economy and trade negotiations. Of course, this year's G8 Summit did not solve all the world's problems. But there are two key meetings later this year where campaigners and others will be able to test the G8's real resolve. In September, the U.N. meets in special session in New York to consider reforms and strategies toward reaching the MDGs. Will the major powers pledge the same increase in aid ($25 billion) for non-African countries that is requested to lift their poor out of poverty by 2015? In December, the trade issue will be confronted head-on, as the world trade talks resume in Hong Kong in a last ditch effort to reach a deal after four years of wrangling.

IV

After all is said and done, one thing to jump up is the fact that the G8 perception of eradicating world poverty, either through increasing aid or through the cancellation of outstanding debts, begs the question–Are these two measures sufficient to eradicate world poverty? Historically speaking, the answer is a flat no. For example, since World War II, the Western countries have channeled more than $500 billion towards development aid, but with exception of a few East Asian countries, a great majority of them have regressed backward; and are far from being self-sufficient. Except for the fact that the total debt amassed by the world's poorest countries shot up from $25 billion in 1970 to $523 billion in 2005, resulting in endless poverty as many as half of these economies spiraled out of control. Despite the cash injections provided by the loans over the years, no indebted African country has sincerely prospered. As such, according to some observers the very fact of easy access to loans and grants from the developed countries have made them not only dependent on this kind of aid, but also have suppressed any desire to act on their own to better their economic plight. Therefore, the key to helping these countries to become proactive is not to provide more aid but to help create the necessary institutional arrangements to further themselves. The key to eradicate poverty in the HIPC is not through more aid, but through wealth creation and we can only create wealth through the private sector, through investment in job creation. Tony Blair, at the G8 Summit, reiterated the fact that "the private sector is the engine for growth." He further stated that "Your investment, expertise, and practical ideas are essential to helping Africa share in the benefits of the global economy." Also, the Summit chairman, Sir Mark Moody-Stuart, who is also the chairman of South African mining giant, Anglo American, said "the summit would be an opportunity for a diverse set of businesses with shared objectives for Africa to come together to speak with one voice, and act with one purpose." Companies from both Africa and the G8 countries are members of the Business Action for Africa Coalition. This coalition aims to influence the policies of the international community and African governments to beat back poverty and promote economic growth. There will only be sustainable development in Africa if the increase in Western governments' aid flow is complemented by not only resurgence of enterprise, but also transparency in all African government operations to enforce total elimination of the menace of corruption entwined in the African countries. In a way, just as Pascal Dozie, chief executive of Nigeria's Diamond Bank, has rightly reiterated the fact that "to thrive, Africa's private sector needs help to grow, including protection of property rights, the enforcement of the rules of laws, and establishment on a sound footing, stable and democratic governments."

In addition to the above course of action, one has to take into account various factors responsible for the current status of the African countries. They are: (1) colonial legacy; (2) dependence on extractive industry; and 3) rampant corruption.

Professor Sir Nicholas Stern, former director of policy and research at the Commission for Africa, speaks about why Africa's colonial past remains a burden, and about what should be done to secure a prosperous future for this poverty-stricken confinement. On a relative basis it is a very different colonial legacy in Africa than it is in India. In case of India, something like 40 per cent of the agricultural land being irrigated and we see a much better and efficient system of railways, roads, etc. No doubt, since independence of the African countries, they are partly to be blamed for not building up the infrastructure and transport links which are essential for a dynamic economy. During the colonial rule, the only development of infrastructure such as rails and roads are limited solely to trunk roads linking production location to the hinterland connecting to port facilities, and as such total lack of any other meaningful development of serviceable transportation infrastructures.

In Africa, it is fair to say the colonial system was particularly focused on exploiting and extracting the continent's natural resources, and infrastructure was built to export the copper, diamonds, timber, oil, gold, or whatever. So part of the infrastructure story is historical legacy, part is lack of investment, part is the fragmentation of the continent into several independent countries. Where the sub-continent of India has been divided into three independent states, there are 48 sub-Saharan countries in Africa and political frontiers become economic barriers.

In addition, Africa is still reliant to a large degree on mining, whereas India has grown, because it has invested in not only infrastructure, but also in education and manufacturing, especially for exports. It costs about twice as much to take goods out of Africa relative to other countries–that means taking goods from village to town, town to capital city, capital city to port, and port to ultimate destination. It is as such, more costly in Africa for reasons of the weakness of the governance, so these basic problems of actually getting business done are much more severe. That is why the Commission for Africa is so strong in its recommendations in investing in its capacity to trade.

Finally, let's recognize that there is corruption in most of the African countries, but let us also recognize the degree of corruption varies across countries and it has been quite severe in Africa. The really terrible 20 years or so in Africa were the mid-70s to mid-90s, when corruption was rampant across the length and breadth of government bureaucracies. During this period, according to my own experiences working as a United Nations Economic Advisor to one of these African countries, and other reliable firsthand sources, no public project was sanctioned unless the minister in charge of the particular project is assured of a 10 per cent deposit of the total value of the project in his bank account in Western countries before he finally approves the project by affixing his signature. But since the mid 90s, one can see that Africa has started to change itself in getting to grips with this cancerous type of problem. But still, the problem remains and demands a total commitment on the part of the new generation of democratically elected leaders in the African countries to eliminate the menace of this problem inflicting a heavy toll on the well-being of their masses.

V

In the final analysis through the terrorist attack on London on the eve of the 2005 G8 Summit at Gleneagles, Scotland cast a pall over the meeting of the heads of states. The bombings instantly overshadowed the Summit's scheduled talks, an intrusion of history–in all its barbarianism and mayhem, into what would otherwise have been a carefully managed and choreographed summit. But what is important, was the immediate response of the leaders of the G8 to the attacks was an impressive display of resolve and solidarity. The joint declaration also underscored the profound, frequently overlooked, resolve about the nature of the G8 as an international institution. This is not necessarily a bad thing in confronting the war on terror and shaping the global balance of power and economic equity.

One widely circulated criticism leveled at the G8, concerns the absence of "action forcing" commitments and the lack of continuity from summit to summit. This year Tony Blair wanted to talk about African poverty and climate change. Last year, George W. Bush put the Middle East democracy at the top of the agenda, and next year with Russia at the helm of the G8's rotating presidency, Vladimir Putkin may push his own set of agenda items to the front. Thus, by its very structure, it may lack continuity of purpose. Admittedly, there is a great deal of truth to this criticism, but in the words of Vance Serchuk of the American Economic Institute, it misses the more important and immutable reality about the G8. Unlike other international institutions, the G8 is an activity, not an organization. There is no G8 secretariat, no G8 headquarters, no G8 diplomats with immunity from parking tickets. Rather, G8 is and should remain as a grand salon, an informal talk shop for global leaders to focus on solving world problems, maybe one at a time.

LINKAGES AMONG FOREIGN DIRECT INVESTMENT, R&D EXPENDITURE, EXPORT PERFORMANCE, AND ECONOMIC GROWTH: The Cases of Brazil and Chile

Drs. Mazhar M. Islam, Halima A. Qureshi & Eric Rahimian
Department of Economics & Finance, School of Business
Alabama A&M University, USA

This paper investigates the long run relationship among GDP, FDI, R&D and current account for Brazil and Chile using time series data from 1974 to 2004. ADF test shows the time series variables in our study are non-stationary in levels. However most of the variables are found to be stationary at the first difference level. Next we apply Johansen (1991) cointegration test to determine the long run relationship. For both countries, we find one to two cointegration equations suggesting there is long run relationship among the variables. We have applied autoregressive procedure to test the direction of causality among the variables of interest in our paper. We find strong evidence of export-led growth in both countries. We also find Granger causality running from GDP to FDI indicating that a growing economy attracts FDI. While for Chile we find higher GDP leads to higher R&D expenditure, we find no such relationship between GDP and R&D expenditures for Brazil.

I. INTRODUCTION

Research on economic growth in the past few decades has identified several factors as sources of economic development. Among them, Foreign Direct Investment (FDI) and Research and Development (R&D) Expenditures are shown to be two important factors for promoting economic growth. Several researchers such as Zhang (2001), Sun and Parikh (2001), Barell and Pain (1997), and others, have shown that increased FDI has also been associated with higher economic growth in the host countries. According to their research, FDI, which can serve as a substitute for domestic investment as well as a source of foreign technology spill-over, can stimulate the engine of growth in an economy.

Previous research has also shown that R&D expenditures can be an important source for economic development. R&D based growth models have been presented by Uzawa (1965), Shell (1973), Lucas (1988), Romer (1990), Grossmand and Helpman (1991), Aghion and Howitt (1992), and others. Their work supports the view that growth depends on technological progress which arises from intentional investment in R&D sectors by profit maximizing agents. The extent of R&D expenditures in a country also has important bearing on trade performance of an economy. R&D plays an important role by creating technological innovations that reduces the domestic relative price of a good, thus enhancing exports and reducing imports. Studies by Gruber *et al.* (1967), Kessing (1967), Mansfield *et al.* (1979), and Franke (1989) conclude that R&D intensity is a good predictor of corporate growth, which in turn is a primary engine for increasing market share in the global economy. Thus, the previous studies suggest that R&D expenditures can directly promote economic growth through technological progress in an economy and by improving trade performance (i.e., export-led growth).

Though there are several studies which investigate the impact of FDI and R&D expenditures on economic growth, these studies are far from complete. First, the past studies attempted to analyze the impact of these two variables on economic growth separately. Since FDI and R&D expenditures are important sources of economic development, we propose to study them jointly. Secondly, the role of R&D was mostly examined from micro level perspective. At the macro level, the studies are mainly based on Western developed countries, or on East Asian developing economies. We fill in the gap by providing a macro level analysis of impact of R&D expenditures by using data from two Latin American countries, Brazil and Chile.

The organization of the paper is as follows: Section I – Introduction, Section II-Methodology and Hypotheses, Section III - Empirical Findings, and finally, Section IV-Conclusion.

II. METHODOLOGY

Augmented Dickey Fuller (ADF) Unit Root

ADF requires running a regression of the first difference of the series against the series lagged once, lagged difference terms, and a constant with a time trend such as

$$\Delta X_t = \lambda_0 + \lambda_1 X_{t-1} + \lambda_2 T + \Sigma\, \lambda_i \Delta X_{t-i} + \varepsilon_t$$
$$i = 1, \ldots\ldots\ldots\ldots, k$$

where Δ is the first difference operator, ε_t is an error term, and k is the number of lagged first differenced term and is determined such that ε_t is approaching white noise. The H_0 hypothesis that X_t is non-stationary time series translates into H_0: $\lambda_1 = 0$. The output of the ADF test consists of the i(tau)-statistic on estimated coefficient of the lagged variable (λ_1) and the critical values for the test of a zero coefficient. If the estimated ADF statistic is larger (in absolute) than its critical value then the null hypothesis is rejected, suggesting that the series is stationary (i.e., the H_0 is rejected if λ_1 is significantly negative).

Cointegration

A set of time-series variables are said to be cointegrated if they are integrated of the same order and a linear combination of them is stationary. Such linear combination would then point to the existence of a long-term relationship among the variables. If we have k endogenous variables, each of which is first-order integrated, there can be from 0 to k-1 linearly independent cointegrating vectors. If there are none, the conventional time series analysis such as vector autoregressive (VAR) applies to the first differences of the data. The Johansen (1991) test can be applied to determine the number of cointegrating equations (cointegrating rank). If there are k cointegrating equations, it means none of the series is actually integrated, and the VAR can be reformulated in terms of the levels of all of the series. Taking a VAR model, Johansen (1991) and Johansen and Juselius (1990) derived a maximum likelihood approach for estimation and testing the number of cointegrating relationships among components of a k-vector of x_i variables by trace test.

Granger Causality

The Granger (1969) approach provides a formal test for the direction of causality between *x* and *y*. The idea is to see how much of the current *y* can be explained by past values of *y* and to find whether adding lagged values of *x* as an explanatory variable can improve the explanation. *y* is said to be Granger-caused by *x* if *x* helps in the prediction of *y*, or equivalently if the coefficients on the lagged values of *x* are statistically significant. Similarly, the statement (2) below is used to see if *x* is Granger caused by *y*. For the following models:

$$Y_t = \alpha_{10} + \Sigma\, \alpha_{1i} X_{t-i} + \Sigma\, \beta_{1j} Y_{t-j} + \varepsilon_{1t} \quad (1)$$

$$X_t = \alpha_{20} + \Sigma\, \alpha_{2i} X_{t-i} + \Sigma\, \beta_{2j} Y_{t-j} + \varepsilon_{2t} \quad (2)$$

We can distinguish the following cases:

(i) If $[\alpha_{11,} \alpha_{12,} \ldots\ldots\ldots, \alpha_{1p}] \neq 0$ and $[\beta_{21}, \beta_{22,\ldots\ldots\ldots\ldots}, \beta_{2q}] = 0$, there exists a unidirectional causality from X_t to $Y_{t,}$ denoted as $X \rightarrow Y$.

(ii) If $[\alpha_{11}, \alpha_{12,} \ldots\ldots\ldots, \alpha_{1p}] = 0$ and $[\beta_{21}, \beta_{22,\ldots\ldots\ldots\ldots}, \beta_{2q}] \neq 0$, there exists a unidirectional causality from $Y_{t,}$ to X_t, denoted as $Y \rightarrow X$.

(iii) If $[\alpha_{11}, \alpha_{12,} \ldots\ldots\ldots, \alpha_{1p}] \neq 0$ and $[\beta_{21}, \beta_{22,\ldots\ldots\ldots\ldots}, \beta_{2q}] \neq 0$, there exists a bidirectional causality between X_t to $Y_{t,}$ denoted as $X \rightarrow Y$.

III. EMPIRICAL RESULTS

The empirical analysis focuses on investigating the long run relationship between GDP, FDI, R&D Expenditures and Export performance for Brazil and Chile. We test these relationships by using the 1974-2004 time series data collected from International Financial Statistics and World Development Report. The first step in our empirical analysis involves testing whether the time series variables used in our study are stationary. The ADF test procedure is used to test for a unit root. Table 1 summarizes the ADF Tests. We find all the variables in our study have unit root, i.e., are non stationary. We also find that all the variables are stationary at the first difference. Since applying OLS to non-stationary variables in levels may produce spurious results, we use cointegration test the long-run relationship among the variables in our study. We tested the long-run relationships among the variables employing Johansen's (1990) cointegration technique.[1] The cointegration estimation results are reported in Table 2 and Table 3. For Chili both the trace test and Maximum Eigenvalue test indicates two cointegration equations. For Brazil, the trace test indicates one cointegration equation while Maximum Eigenvalue test indicates two

Table 1
Summary of ADF Unit Root Tests

Country Variables	*ADF Coefficient in levels*	*MacKinnon critical value*	*ADF Coefficient in first difference*	*MacKinnon critical value*
	τ_m	τ_t	τ_μ	τ_t
Brazil				
GDP	–0.811	–3.63	–4.01**	–2.64
FDI	–0.854	–3.75	–4.56**	–2.66
EX	1.520	–3.71	–6.70**	–1.95
R&D	–1.995		–6.42**	
Chile				
GDP	0.728	–3.67	–2.38*	–1.95
FDI	1.32	–2.67	–3.05**	–2.67
EX	–0.55	–2.65	–4.51**	–2.68
R&D	2.707		–6.49**	

Note: ** and * indicate rejection of null hypothesis of unit root (non-stationary) at the 1% and 5% levels of significance, respectively. Mackinnon critical value for rejection of hypothesis of a unit root has been applied at the 1% and 5% levels. Optimum lag structures are determined by the Akaike and Schwarz information criteria.

Table 2
Cointegration Test: Brazil

Sample (adjusted): 1977-2000
Trend assumption: Linear deterministic trend
Series: EX, FDI, GDP, and R&D
Lags interval (in first differences): 1 to 1
Unrestricted Cointegration Rank Test (Trace)

Hypothesized No. of CE(s)	*Eigenvalue*	*Trace Statistic*	*0.05 Critical Value*	*Prob.***
None *	0.848301	73.99625	47.85613	0.0000
At most 1	0.634050	28.73562	29.79707	0.0659
At most 2	0.171054	4.609410	15.49471	0.8488
At most 3	0.004449	0.107011	3.841466	0.7436

Trace test indicates one cointegrating equation at the 0.05 level
* denotes rejection of the hypothesis at the 0.05 level
**MacKinnon-Haug-Michelis (1999) p-values

Unrestricted Cointegration Rank Test (Maximum Eigenvalue)

Hypothesized No. of CE(s)	*Eigenvalue*	*Max-Eigen Statistic*	*0.05 Critical Value*	*Prob.***
None *	0.848301	45.26063	27.58434	0.0001
At most 1 *	0.634050	24.12621	21.13162	0.0184
At most 2	0.171054	4.502399	14.26460	0.8029
At most 3	0.004449	0.107011	3.841466	0.7436

Max-Eigenvalue test indicates two cointegrating equations at the 0.05 level
* denotes rejection of the hypothesis at the 0.05 level
**MacKinnon-Haug-Michelis (1999) p-values

Table 3
Cointegration Test: Chile

Sample (adjusted): 1977-2000

Trend assumption: Linear deterministic trend
Series: R&D, GDP, FDI, and EX
Lags interval (in first differences): 1 to 1

Unrestricted Cointegration Rank Test (Trace)

Hypothesized No. of CE(s)	*Eigenvalue*	*Trace Statistic*	*0.05 Critical Value*	*Prob.***
None *	0.884446	98.54065	47.85613	0.0000
At most 1 *	0.796323	46.74825	29.79707	0.0002
At most 2	0.261567	8.558917	15.49471	0.4077
At most 3	0.051997	1.281533	3.841466	0.2576

Trace test indicates two cointegrating equations at the 0.05 level

* denotes rejection of the hypothesis at the 0.05 level

**MacKinnon-Haug-Michelis (1999) p-values

Unrestricted Cointegration Rank Test (Maximum Eigenvalue)

Hypothesized No. of CE(s)	*Eigenvalue*	*Max-Eigen Statistic*	*0.05 Critical Value*	*Prob.***
None *	0.884446	51.79241	27.58434	0.0000
At most 1 *	0.796323	38.18933	21.13162	0.0001
At most 2	0.261567	7.277384	14.26460	0.4568
At most 3	0.051997	1.281533	3.841466	0.2576

Max-Eigenvalue test indicates 2 cointegrating equations at the 0.05 level

* denotes rejection of the hypothesis at the 0.05 level

**MacKinnon-Haug-Michelis (1999) p-values

cointegration equations. Cointegration test, therefore, reveals that there is long run relationship among the variables in our study.

Having found the long run relationship among the variables in our study, next, we assess the direction of causality among GDP, FDI, R&D Expenditures and Export performance by applying a vector autoregressive approach. The estimated F-statistic for block exogeniety is used to determine Granger causality. The results of the Granger causality tests are reported in Table 4 and Table 5. For both Chile and Brazil, we find the direction of causality running from GDP to FDI implying a growing economy attract FDI.

Investigating the relationship between GDP and Export Expenditures, we find some evidence of unidirectional causality from Export Expenditures to GDP growth for both countries. Therefore, our investigation strongly supports the theory of export-led growth. For Chile, we find direction of causality running from GDP to R&D implying higher GDP is a source of higher R&D expenditure. No causal relationship is found between GDP and R&D Expenditures for Brazil.

When investigating the relationship between Export and FDI, for Brazil and Chile we find bidirectional relationship, which implies FDI and Export performance reinforce each other.

Table 4
Pair-Wise Granger Causality Tests: Brazil

Sample: 1970 - 2004
Lags: 2

Null Hypothesis:	Obs.	F-Statistic	Probability
GDP does not Granger cause FDI	28	20.9070	6.7E-06
FDI does not Granger cause GDP		1.27397	0.29873
GDP does not Granger cause EX	28	0.68406	0.51454
EX does not Granger cause GDP		3.27528	0.05602
R&D does not Granger cause GDP	29	0.07109	0.93157
GDP does not Granger cause R&D		1.11444	0.34449
FDI does not Granger cause EX	28	3.90398	0.03469
EX does not Granger cause FDI		2.75585	0.08455
R&D does not Granger cause FDI	24	0.14726	0.86404
FDI does not Granger cause R&D		0.67617	0.52038
R&D does not Granger Cause EX	23	2.89106	0.06777
EX does not Granger Cause R&D		0.90801	0.45905

Table 5
Pair-Wise Granger Causality Tests: Chile

Sample: 1974-2004
Lags: 2

Null Hypothesis:	Obs	F-Statistic	Probability
FDI does not Granger Cause GDP	28	0.80583	0.45893
GDP does not Granger Cause FDI		11.3916	0.00036
EX does not Granger Cause GDP	28	2.55971	0.09915
GDP does not Granger Cause EX		2.18510	0.13526
R&D does not Granger Cause GDP	25	0.05567	0.94599
GDP does not Granger Cause R&D		6.18107	0.00813
FDI does not Granger Cause EX	28	6.48902	0.00583
EX does not Granger Cause FDI		6.41075	0.00613
R&D does not Granger Cause FDI	24	5.53041	0.01280
FDI does not Granger Cause R&D		5.29784	0.01484
EX does not Granger Cause R&D	24	10.3827	0.00090
R&D does not Granger Cause EX		0.82432	0.45362

Empirical results presented in Table 5 show that for Chile, there is bidirectional relationship between FDI and R&D expenditures which implies these two variables complement each other since they are sources of technological improvement. However, no causal relationship between FDI and R&D expenditures are found for Brazil.

Lastly, in investigating the relationship between Export Performance and R&D Expenditures, our results show that for Brazil higher R&D Expenditures causes Export to go up which support the view that R&D Expenditures by lowering price of exported goods would improve Export Performance. However, for Chile we find the direction of causality running from Export Performance to R&D expenditures.

IV. CONCLUSION

This paper investigates the long run relationship between GDP, FDI, R&D and trade performance for Brazil and Chile using time series data from 1974 to 2004. ADF test shows the time series variables in our study are non-stationary at the level. However most of the variables are found to be stationary at the first difference level. Next, we apply Johansen (1991) cointegration test to determine the long run relationship. For both countries, we find one to two cointegration equations suggesting there is long run relationship among the variables. A vector autoregressive procedure is applied to test the direction of causality among the variables of interest in our paper. We find strong evidence of export led growth in both countries. We also find Ganger causality running from GDP to FDI indicating that a growing economy attracts FDI. While for Chile we find higher GDP leads to higher R&D expenditure, we find no such relationship between GDP and R&D expenditures for Brazil.

Notes

1. The cointegration analysis is conducted with an assumption of a linear deterministic trend with an intercept.

References

Aghion, P. and P. Howitt (1992), "A Model of Growth Through Creative Destruction," *Econometrica*, Vol. 60, pp. 323-351.

Barrell, Ray and Nigel Pain (1997), "Foreign Direct Investment, Technological Change, and Economic Growth Within Europe," *The Economic Journal*, Vol. 107, Issue 445, pp. 1770-1786.

Borensztein, E., J. De-Gregorio and J.W. Lee (1998), "How Does Foreign Direct Investment Affect Economic Growth?" *Journal of International Economics,* Vol. 45, Issue 1, pp. 115-135.

Dickey, D. A. and W. A. Fuller (1979), "Distribution for the Estimators for Autoregressive Time Series with a Unit Root," *Journal of the American Statistical Association*, Vol. 74, pp. 427-431.

Engle, R. F., and Granger, C. (1987), "Cointegration and Error Correction: Representation, Estimation and Testing," Econometrica, 55: 251-276.

Franko, I. G. (1989), "Global Corporate Competition: Who's winning, Who's Losing, and the R&D Factor as one reason Why," *Strategic Management Journal*., 10, 449-474.

Granger, C. (1986), "Developments in the Study of Cointegrated Random Variables," Oxford Bulletin of Economics and Statistics, 68:213-228.

Granger, C. (1988), "Some Developments in a Concept of Causality," *Journal of Econometrics*, 39: 199-211.

Grossmand, Gene M., Elhanan Helpman (1989), "Product Development and International Trade," *The Journal of Political Economy*, Vol. 97, Issue 6, pp. 1261-1283.

Gruber, W., Mehta, D., and Vernon, R., H. G. (1967), "The R&D Factor in International Trade and International Investment of the United States Industries", *Journal of Political Economy*, 75, 20-37.

Johansen, S. (1989), "Estimation and Hypothesis Testing of Cointegration Vectors in Gaussian Vector Autoregressive Models". Econometrica.

Johansen, S. and Juselius, K. (1990), "Maximum Likelihood Estimation and Inference on Cointegration—with Applications to the Demand for Money." *Oxford Bulletin of Economics and Statistics*, 52, 169-210.

Keesing, D. (1967), "The Impact of R&D on U.S. Trade," *Journal of Political Economy*, 75, 38-48.

Lucas, R. E. (1988), "On The Mechanics of Monitory Economics," Vol. 22, pp. 3-42.

Mansfield, E., Romeo, A. and Wagner, S. (1979), "Foreign Trade and U.S. Research and Development," *The Review of Economics and Statistics*, LXI, 49-57.

Romer, Paul M. (1990), "Endogenous Technological Change," *The Journal of Political Economy*, Vol. 98, Issue 5, Part 2, pp. 71-102.

Shell, K. "Inventive activity, Industrial Organization and Economic Growth", In Modules of Economic Growth, J. A. Mirrlees and N.H. Stern eds., (London: Macmillan,1973).

Sun, Haishan and Ashok Parikh (2001), "Export, Inward Foreign Direct Investment (FDI) and Regional Economic Growth in China," Regional Studies, Vol. 35.3, pp. 187-196.

Uzawa, H. (1965), "Optimum Technical Change in an Aggregative Model of Economic Growth," *International Economic Review*, Vol. 6.

Zhang, Kevin Honglin (2001), "Does Foreign Direct Investment Promote Economic Growth? Evidence From East Asia and Latin America," Contemporary Economic Policy, Vol. 19, No. 2, pp. 175-185.

ECONOMIC GROWTH AND UNEMPLOYMENT IN MALAYSIA: An Empirical Note

Raja Nazrin
University of Malaya

Eu Chye Tan*
Faculty of Economics & Administration
University of Malaya, Malaysia

The aim of this paper is to assess the relationship between economic growth and unemployment in Malaysia based upon Okun's concept. The Ordinary Least Squares (OLS) technique is applied to detrended data series. Both the Hodrick-Prescott filter and the band-pass filter of Baxter and King are interchangeably used for the detrending. The OLS estimates suggest that a one percentage point rise in the unemployment rate could precipitate a decline in the real gross domestic product by about 1.3 or 1.6 percent, with the impact of any movement in the unemployment rate on the economy being fully realized within a year. Structural changes experienced in the economy have not undermined the stability of the estimated relations.

JEL Classification: E 24 O40

Keywords: Growth, Unemployment

1. INTRODUCTION

The purpose of this paper is to explore the relationship between economic growth and unemployment in Malaysia in the context of Okun's theory. Annual data from 1975 to 2005 are mobilized in the study and the choice of the sample period and its data frequency is dictated by data availability. The study has important macroeconomic policy implications as Malaysia being a developing nation with a young multi-ethnic population is always conscious of the need to generate sufficient employment opportunities. Access to gainful employment is sine qua non for her socioeconomic and political stability. Indeed, the link between unemployment and economic growth is constantly a matter of political and economic concern. By identifying the magnitude and direction of the relationship between unemployment and economic growth, fiscal and monetary authorities could then target economic growth in order to induce a certain rate of employment growth, thus maintaining a certain socially acceptable or optimal rate of unemployment.

---

* Corresponding Author: *tanec@um.edu.my*

Generally, Okun's famous theory states that excess capacity or a lack of aggregate demand is a cause of unemployment (Okun, 1962). The theory postulates a simple relationship between unemployment and output growth. When referred to specifically, the theory is referred to as a law that maintains that an increase by 1% in the unemployment rate would contribute to a decline of about 3% in the growth of real GNP in the U.S. In other words, a one-percentage point reduction in the unemployment rate would generate approximately 3% more output. The theory has often been deployed in conjunction with the Phillips curve amongst economists and policy-makers to understand the labor and commodity market implications of economic policy measures (Knoester, 1986; Apergis & Rezitis, 2003). Okun's law has continued to be a useful and stable empirical relationship between output and unemployment (Weber & West, 1996).

Moreover, this study could contribute to the development economics literature as it sheds light on the relationship between economic growth and unemployment in a developing economy such as Malaysia. Malaysia is being widely acclaimed including by the World Bank as a model which other developing nations could possibly follow. The bulk of previous empirical studies are concentrated around advanced economies such as the United States, United Kingdom, Australia, Greece, Germany, France, Italy, Japan and Canada (Gordon, 1984; Motley, 1984; Knoester, 1986; Kaufman, 1988; Nguyen and Siriwardana, 1988; Adams and Coe, 1989; Holloway, 1989; Watts and Mitchell, 1991; Prachowny, 1993; Weber, 1995; Weber and West, 1996; Moosa, 1997; Attfield and Silverstone, 1997 & 1998; Apergis & Rezitis, 2003). The major point of contention amongst these studies is with regard to the magnitude of the Okun's coefficient.

The rest of the paper is configured as follows. Section 2 dwells upon the empirical framework while the empirical results are reported and discussed in Section 3. Concluding remarks are made in Section 4.

2. THE EMPIRICAL FRAMEWORK

The Okun's notion of the relationship between unemployment and output is commonly represented in mathematical terms as follows:

$$y - y^* = -\beta\,(u - u^*) \qquad (1)$$

where y refers to the natural logarithm of output and u to the unemployment rate. The terms, y^* and u^* are their corresponding equilibrium values defined as potential output and the natural unemployment rate respectively. The left-hand side of the equation defines the output gap while the right captures the unemployment gap with β being the Okun's coefficient. In the absence of unemployment gap, actual output would approach potential output

However, Okun's inference on the relationship between unemployment and output growth is based on the assumption that other factors would change pari passu with the unemployment rate and in fact the coefficient of three is supposed to capture the combined effect of all influences on output. The other influences may include expansion of the labor force, longer average weekly hours and higher productivity. Thus the Okun's coefficient in (1) above should be interpreted as mutatis mutandis and not ceteris paribus.

Apart from relying upon equation (1), this study also attempts to estimate the relationship between unemployment and output based upon an equation derived from the Cobb-Douglas production function broadly though not strictly along the lines of Prachowny (1993). In natural logarithms, the production function may be written as

$$y = \alpha k + \beta e + \tau \tag{2}$$

where y, k, e and τ represent output, capital, total employment and the disembodied technology factor respectively. Potential output (y^*) is assumed to be generated also by the same production function, with capital and labor inputs being at their long-run sustainable levels, i.e. k^* and e^*. Hence, the output-gap at any instance is simply

$$y - y^* = \alpha(k - k^*) + \beta(e - e^*) + (\tau - \tau^*) \tag{3}$$

Letting l be the natural log of the total labor force, the unemployment rate can then be defined as $u = l - e$ with a natural rate, u^*. Assuming that $\tau = \tau^*$ and substituting u and u^* in (3), an alternative estimating equation is arrived at as follows:

$$y - y^* = \alpha(k - k^*) + \beta[(l - l^*) - (u - u^*)] \tag{4}$$

Thus empirical estimation of equation (4) would merely involve augmentation of equation (1) by $k - k^*$ and $l - l^*$ with the coefficient of the latter constrained to be equal to that of $u - u^*$ in absolute value terms. Under this alternative formulation, an output gap could prevail even in the absence of unemployment gap.

To capture the possible importance of dynamics, a one-period lagged output gap may be incorporated into equations (1) and (4) to curb any problem of serial correlation associated with static equations. Output may not respond instantaneously to changes in capital and labor market conditions due to adjustment inertias.

Two alternative techniques are mobilized for the determination of the equilibrium values of variables and thus their gaps, namely the Hodrick-Prescott filter (Hodrick and Prescott, 1997) and the band-pass filter attributable to Baxter and King (1995). They generally involve decomposing variables into trend and cyclical components. With respect to the application of the band-pass filter, the range of durations to pass through is set at 2 to 8 years in line with the recommendations of Baxter and King. As for the Hodrick-Prescott filter, the smoothing parameter is set at 7.

All the data are drawn from various issues of the Central Bank of Malaysia's Monthly Economic Bulletin and Malaysia's Ministry of Finance Economic Report. Real gross domestic product is adopted as a proxy for output while capital stock series is derived via the perpetual inventory method from annual real investment figures.

3. EMPIRICAL RESULTS AND ANALYSES

Tables 1 and 2 present the OLS estimates of equations (1) and (4) and their dynamic versions based upon the Hodrick-Prescott(H-P) and the band-pass (B-K) filtered series respectively. All the estimated equations could withstand a battery of diagnostic tests for autocorrelation, functional form misspecification, normality of residuals and heteroskedasticity, thus satisfying the classical assumptions. This warrants an evaluation of the statistical significance of the individual estimated coefficients.

Table 1
OLS Estimates (Based upon Hodrick-Prescott Filtered Series)

	1.1	*1.2*	*4.1*	*4.2*
Constant	0.000	0.0004	0.000	-0.0003
		[0.909]		[0.909]
u-u*	-2.863	-2.782		
	[0.003]	[0.005]		
k-k*			0.298	0.340
			[0.090]	[0.147]
(l-l*)-(u-u*)			1.261	1.307
			[0.000]	[0.000]
Lagged (y-y*)		0.125		-0.088
		[0.450]		[0.552]
Adjusted R^2	0.236	0.222	0.609	0.599
F	10.265	5.127	24.365	15.420
	[0.003]	[0.013]	[0.000]	[0.000]
S.E. Regression	0.020	0.020	0.014	0.015
D.W.	1.906		1.877	
Durbin's h		-0.130		1.617
		[0.897]		[0.106]
LM (χ^2) tests for				
(i) serial correlation	0.049	0.036	0.108	0.826
	[0.825]	[0.850]	[0.742]	[0.364]
(ii) functional form	0.625	0.980	0.582	0.117
	[0.429]	[0.322]	[0.446]	[0.732]
(iii) normality	1.191	0.694	5.577	3.475
	[0.551]	[0.707]	[0.062]	[0.176]
(iv) heteroskedasticity	0.059	0.048	0.0003	0.177
	[0.808]	[0.827]	[0.987]	[0.674]

Notes: Figures in [ ] refer to marginal significance levels
Diagnostic test results based upon F-statistics do not differ in terms of conclusion from those of LM tests.

Based upon the original specification of Okun's equation, the Okun's coefficient is estimated as being highly significant statistically at -2.86 and -3.06 depending upon whether the H-P or the B-K series is used (equations 1.1 & 1.1A). Such estimates are well within the -3 region publicized by Okun. Lagged output appears to be hardly significant statistically and its inclusion merely contributes to a decline in the adjusted R^2 (equations 1.2 & 1.2A).

However the production function approach would yield lower estimates for the Okun's coefficient. The H-P filtered series provide an estimate of -1.26 while the B-K filtered series place it at -1.56 (equations 4.1 and 4.1A). Nevertheless, this is very consistent with other previous empirical studies that report

Table 2
OLS Estimates (Based upon Baxter & King Filtered Series)

	1.1A	*1.2A*	*4.1A*	*4.2A*
Constant	0.0002 [0.960]	0.00004 [0.992]	0.0009 [0.790]	0.0007 [0.838]
u-u*	-3.064 [0.006]	-3.014 [0.008]		
k-k*			0.177 [0.393]	0.256 [0.330]
(l-l*)-(u-u*)			1.560 [0.000]	1.536 [0.000]
Lagged (y-y*)		0.106 [0.564]		-0.082 [0.609]
Adjusted R^2	0.255	0.233	0.642	0.630
F	9.193 [0.006]	4.637 [0.021]	22.528 [0.000]	14.609 [0.000]
S.E. Regression	0.022	0.022	0.015	0.015
D.W.	1.953		2.009	
Durbin's h		-0.430 [0.667]		0.523 [0.601]
LM (χ^2) tests for				
(i) serial correlation	0.00002 [0.996]	0.305 [0.581]	0.001 [0.972]	0.157 [0.692]
(ii) functional form	1.055 [0.304]	1.629 [0.202]	0.451 [0.502]	0.254 [0.614]
(iii) normality	0.654 [0.721]	0.146 [0.930]	2.441 [0.295]	2.780 [0.249]
(iv) heteroskedasticity	0.056 [0.814]	0.027 [0.870]	0.180 [0.672]	0.124 [0.725]

Notes: Figures in [ ] refer to marginal significance levels
Diagnostic test results based upon F-statistics do not differ in terms of conclusion from those of LM tests.

significantly lower estimates for the coefficient than the much publicized -3. As in the earlier set of estimates, lagged output is not statistically significant and tends to reduce the adjusted R^2 of the estimating equation (equations 4.2 and 4.2A).

Equation (4) seems to be a better estimating equation than equation (1) since it yields considerably higher adjusted R^2 to the order of 0.6 against 0.2 and lower standard errors of regression. Thus equations 4.1 and 4.1A should be the preferred equations for making policy inferences. Moreover, they do satisfy the structural stability condition to be meaningful. Stability of estimated coefficients and their consistency with a priori expectations may be a more important model selection criterion than the adjusted R^2 (Maddala, 1977). Table 3 furnishes the outcomes of the Chow's first and second tests for structural breaks in respect of estimated equations 4.1 and 4.1A. Three possible breakpoints are identified, viz. 1987, 1989 and 1990 that correspond with the timing of the significant deregulatory reform undertaken on the Malaysian economy. Notwithstanding the reform, the F-statistics invariably uphold the null hypothesis of no structural breaks.

Table 3
Chow Test Statistics (F)

Type	*Break Point*	*Equation 4.1*	*Equation 4.1A*
First	1987	1.261 [0.309]	0.131 [0.940]
	1989	1.020 [0.401]	0.069 [0.976]
	1990	1.163 [0.344]	0.254 [0.857]
Second	1987	0.631 [0.811]	0.414 [0.928]
	1989	0.747 [0.712]	0.569 [0.828]
	1990	0.853 [0.620]	0.680 [0.740]

Note: Figures in [ ] refer to marginal significance levels.

As a supplementary verification for structural stability, the cumulative sum (CUSUM) and the CUSUM of squares (CUSUMSQ) tests attributable to Brown, et.al (1975) are conducted. The CUSUM test is suitable for detecting systematic changes in the regression coefficients, whilst the CUSUMSQ test is appropriate when there are haphazard and sudden changes in the coefficients. Figures 1 and 1A are plots of the CUSUM recursive residuals with a pair of straight lines drawn at the 5 per cent statistical significance level in respect of estimated equations 4.1 and 4.1A respectively. The corresponding CUSUMSQ residuals are plotted in Figures 2 and 2A. It is interesting to note that these tests do corroborate the results of the Chow tests that suggest structural stability as the residuals fall well within the 5 per cent band.

4. CONCLUDING REMARKS

This paper estimates the relationship between economic growth and unemployment in Malaysia in the spirit of Okun's theory by applying the Ordinary Least Squares (OLS) technique to filtered data series. Both the Hodrick-Prescott filter and the band-pass filter of Baxter and King are interchangeably employed for the filtering. The OLS estimates suggest that a one percentage point increase in the unemployment rate can be associated with

Figure 1
Based upon Equation (4.1)

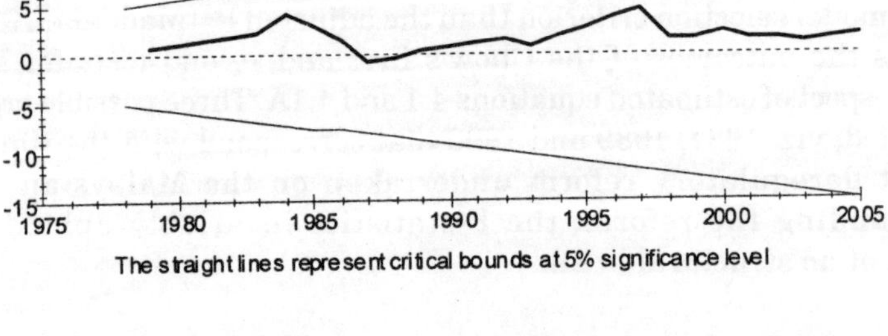

Figure 1A
Based upon Equation (4.1A)

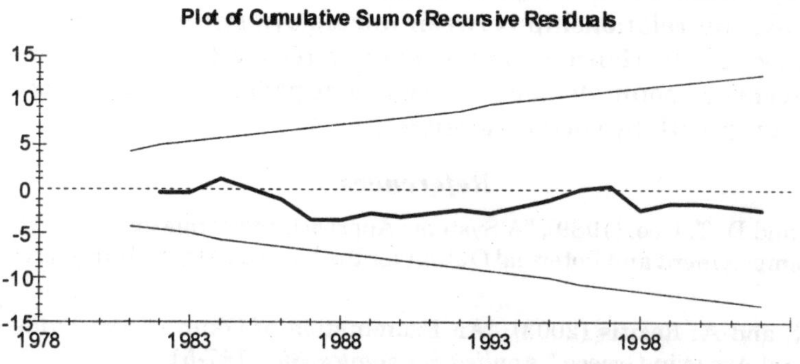

The straight lines represent critical bounds at 5% significance level

Figure 2
Based upon Equation (4.1)

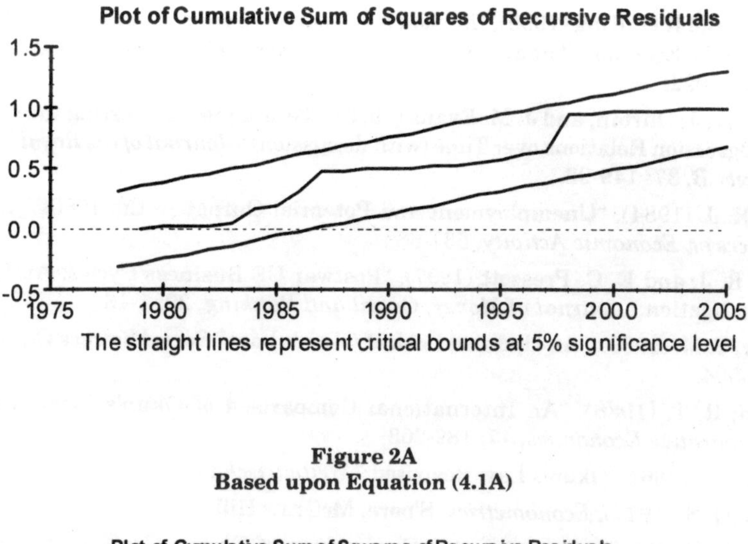

The straight lines represent critical bounds at 5% significance level

Figure 2A
Based upon Equation (4.1A)

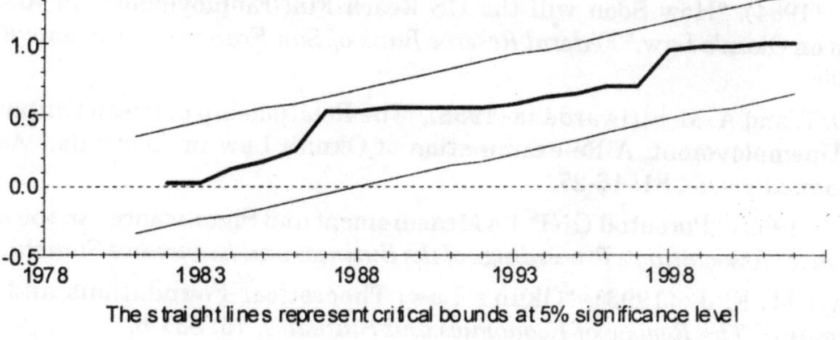

The straight lines represent critical bounds at 5% significance level

about 1.3 or 1.6 percent decline in the real gross domestic product of Malaysia, with the impact of any movement in the unemployment rate being felt fully by the economy within a year. Despite structural changes that have taken place in the economy, the relationship between unemployment and economic growth has remained intact. Hence by implication, to reduce the unemployment rate by one percentage point, demand management policies in the country have to target output growth by such magnitudes.

References

Adams, C. and D. T. Coe. (1989), "A Systems Approach to Estimating the Natural Rate of Unemployment and Potential Output for the United States." IMF Working Paper 89/89.

Apergis, N. and A. Rezitis (2003), "An Examination of Okun's Law: Evidence from Regional Areas in Greece." *Applied Economics*, 35: 1147-51.

Attfield, C. L. F. and B. Silverstone (1997), "Okun's Coefficient: A Comment." *Review of Economics and Statistics*, 79: 326-9.

——(1998), "Okun's Law, Cointegration and Gap Variables." *Journal of Macroeconomics*, 20: 625-37.

Baxter, M. and R.G. King (1995), "Measuring Business Cycles: Approximate Band-pass Filters for Economic Time Series." National Bureau of Economic Research Working Paper 5022.

Brown, R. L., J. Durbin, and J. M. Evans (1975), "Techniques for Testing the Constancy of Regression Relations over Time (with discussion)." *Journal of the Royal Statistical Society B*, 37: 149-92.

Gordon, R. J. (1984), "Unemployment and Potential Output in the 1980s." *Brookings Papers on Economic Activity*, 537-68.

Hodrick, R. J. and E. C. Prescott (1997), "Postwar US Business Cycles: An Empirical Investigation." *Journal of Money, Credit and Banking*, 29: 1-16.

Holloway, T. M. (1989), "An Updated Look at Okun's Law." *Social Science Quarterly*, 70: 497-504.

Kaufman, R. T. (1988), "An International Comparison of Okun's Law." *Journal of Comparative Economics*, 17: 182-203.

Knoester, A. (1986), "Okun's Law Revisited." *Weltwirtschaftliches Archiv*, 122: 657-65.

Maddala, G. S. (1977), *Econometrics*. S'pore: McGraw Hill.

Moosa, I.A. (1997), "A Cross-country Comparison of Okun's Coefficient." *Journal of Comparative Economics*, 24: 335-56.

Motley, B. (1984), "How Soon will the US Reach Full Employment? An Assessment based on Okun's Law." *Federal Reserve Bank of San Francisco Economic Review*, 3: 26-39.

Nguyen, D. T. and A. M. Siriwardana (1988), "The Relationship between Output Growth and Unemployment: A Re-examination of Okun's Law in Australia." *Australian Economic Review*, 81: 16-27.

Okun, A. M. (1962), "Potential GNP: Its Measurement and Significance." in the *American Statistical Association's Proceedings of the Business and Economics Statistics Section*.

Prachowny, M. F. J. (1993), "Okun's Law: Theoretical Foundations and Revised Estimates." *The Review of Economics and Statistics*, 75: 331-6.

Watts, M. and W. Mitchell (1991), "Alleged Instability of the Okun's Relationship in Australia: An Empirical Analysis." *Applied Economics*, 23: 1829-38.

Weber, C. E. (1995), "Cyclical Output, Cyclical Unemployment and Okun's Coefficient: A New Approach." *Journal of Applied Economics*, 10: 433-45.

Weber, C. E. and J. E. West (1996), "Functional Forms in Regression Models of Okun's Law." *Applied Economics Letters*, 3: 607-9.

COMPARATIVE ANALYSIS OF DOMESTIC AND FOREIGN BANK OPERATIONS IN BANGLADESH

Abdus Samad

Department of Finance and Economics
Utah Valley State College, Orem, Utah

This paper compares the performance of domestic and foreign banks with the development processes of the Bangladesh economy. The application of Student's t and Kruskal-Wallis tests to the major balance sheet and income statement items of domestic and foreign banks in Bangladesh during the period 2000-2001 were performed and suggests that compared to domestic banks, foreign banks are not exposed to a greater risk and are less interested in providing inventory industrial loans for economic development. However, the tests indicated that there is no difference in profit performance. The policy implications of these findings are discussed.

JEL Classified numbers: *F21, G20, and G21.*

Key words: *Banks, Profits, Comparative performance, Bangladesh.*

INTRODUCTION

When Bangladesh got independence in 1971, its banking sector was entirely owned and controlled by the government. The entry of foreign banks was limited to only two banks. In the 1990s, Bangladesh witnessed significant changes in the economic and banking structure that had been established. Tremendous emphasize was placed on the privatization of industrial and banking sector. As a result, all public sector banks have been denationalized, except for four banks. Today, there are thirty-five privately owned banks operating in Bangladesh.

The entry of foreign banks has always been encouraged. Anticipating that the presence of foreign banks would enhance the financial competition and improve the performance of domestic banks, as well as the process of industrialization, was a key factor to encourage foreign banks to come to Bangladesh. The most important expectation of the foreign banks was that their presence in Bangladesh would improve the speed of economic development through their involvement in the process of industrialization. Today, the operation of foreign banks is not limited to only two banks. The physical presence of foreign banks has increased in both relative and absolute terms. There are as many as12 foreign banks in operation in Bangladesh. The entry of foreign banks

Corresponding Author: *samadab@uvsc.edu*

has been almost entirely through the *de novo* establishing of branches rather than the acquisition of existing banks.

After the entry and operation of foreign banks, there had been no studies regarding their performance. Bankers and policy makers are concerned that foreign banks are not supporting the enhancement of the industrialization process and also are not sensitive to the needs of the local market. Foreign banks, as found in other documents, are 'just cherry-pick up the domestic clients'. It is assumed that foreign banks are only interested in providing loans to foreign companies.

This type of concern or allegation is not uncommon in the operation of foreign banks in any country. Foreign banks in most countries are located in big metropolitan areas and are usually involved in export and import trade financing and foreign currency activities. They are rarely engaged in retail banking. It is not surprising that banks behave similarly in Bangladesh.

In some countries, policy makers and regulators are worried that foreign banks do not serve the credit and deposit needs of domestic customers. The banks do not like to undertake more risks than domestic banks are taking. Many developing countries assert that foreign banks do not take part in the industrial and agricultural development process by providing long and short term loans.

To what extent such concerns are valid in the experience of Bangladesh, is the underlying motivation of this study. A study in this area is helpful to bankers, policy makers, regulators, and academia. The purpose of this paper is to compare the performance of domestic and foreign banks operations in Bangladesh and to see whether, and to what extent, the operational differences are to the disadvantageous of domestic economy.

The paper is structured as follows: Section II briefly describes the development of Bangladesh banking and the reforms underway. Section III provides the survey of bank performance in literature. The performance measures and data are outlined in Section IV. Section V contains empirical results and conclusions

SECTION II: DEVELOPMENT AND REFORMS IN BANGLADESH BANKING

Period from 1971-1981

The banking system of Bangladesh is branch banking. Bangladesh, previously known as East Pakistan, inherited this developed banking system from Pakistan. With the independence of Bangladesh in 1971, the banking system of Bangladesh was nationalized including all private banks. Banks were now controlled by the government. The then government's love for socialism and the spirit of nationalism were the driving force behind the nationalization of banks. Another factor that added to the nationalization of banks was that owners of most banks were non-Bengali and they left during the liberation period of Bangladesh. After liberation, owners were absent. The government of Bangladesh simply owned these banks without paying any compensation. The operation and management of banks were placed under autonomous corporation. During the period when banks and industries were nationalized, the total number of banks was nine, including two foreign banks.

Period from 1982-1990

The reform in the banking sector at this time was long over due. The performance of nationalized banks was very poor. Banks were losing millions of TK every year. Non-performance outstanding loans were unprecedented and were increasing on a daily basis. The problem was because loans were allocated to politically connected elites and banks nonperformance loans increased.

Due to a lack of competition, banking services deteriorated significantly. The concept that 'customer is the king' was not present in bank management serving customers. All parties—government, bankers, and public—realized the necessity of banking reforms.

The government of Bangladesh, under president Satter, took steps to denationalize banks in 1982. The first bank that was sold to the private enterprise was the Pubali Bank. During 1982-1990, few banks were privatized. At the same time, the establishment of private banks was encouraged. There was a great response from bankers who were waiting for the opening of the economy for private enterprises. Currently, there are 32 privately owned domestic banks operating in Bangladesh, in addition to four nationalized banks.

Period from 1990-2001

In order to increase banking competition in the banking sector and attract foreign capital in the process of the country's economic development, the entry of foreign banks was encouraged. Repatriation of bank profits and capitals, a major concern of foreign bankers, was ensured. To date, there are 12 foreign banks operating in Bangladesh. The entry of these foreign banks is mostly through the de novo establishment of branches.

Thus, the commercial banking of Bangladesh witnesses a three-tier banking system—nationalized commercial banks, privately owned domestic commercial banks, and foreign commercial banks.

SECTION III: SURVEY OF BANK PERFORMANCE LITERATURES

There is extensive literature on the performance of commercial banks. Most of these studies have focused on describing the factor(s) that determine the performance of banks. Heggestad mad Mingo (1977), Rhodes (1982), Gilber (1984), and William and Molyneux (1992) have supported the traditional structure conduct performance (SCP) hypothesis. Their studies found that the concentration of three or four dominant firms is the major factor in determining profitability. In other words, there is a monotonic relationship between a firm concentration and superior performance.

There are others like Domsetz (1973), Carter (1978), Smirlock (1985), and Evanoff and Frontier (1988) who support an alternative hypothesis that a firm's expanded efficiency enables the firm to reduce costs and increase the market share, resulting in higher performance and greater profitability. Thus, according to the efficiency performance (EP) hypothesis—an increased market share and an increased profitability of firms—was a dominant factor for increasing profits in the United States banking industry.

Comparative studies of bank performances include Meinster and Elyasiani (1988), Sabi (1996), Samad (1999), Samad and Hassan (2001) and, Akhigbe and McNulty (2003).

Meinster and Elyasiani examined the performance between foreign and domestic owned banks in the U.S. and found no difference between them.

Sabi compared the performance of foreign and domestic bank operation in Hungary and found that compared to domestic banks, foreign banks are more profitable, not exposed to credit risk, and hesitant to providing loan term loans.

Samad (2004) studied interest free Islamic banks and interest based conventional banks of Bahrain and found that there were differences in some measures. Islamic banks were found to have greater liquidity reserves than conventional banks. A similar result was found in Samad (1999 and 2001).

Akhigbe and McNulty investigated the proficiency of small U.S. banks. Given that small and large banks use the same production technology, they found that small banks are more profit efficient than large banks.

SECTION IV: PERFORMANCE MEASURES AND DATA

Performance Measures

There are financial management theories that provide many indicators for assessing a bank's performance. According to rational expectation and efficient market hypotheses, the best indicator of bank performance is the behavior of bank's stock price. Since most bank stocks are not publicly traded in Bangladesh, this method cannot be used. There is an internal factor method which uses various ratios. This method is widely used in measuring a bank's performance. This study uses internal factors, the factors which are related to items of balance sheet and income statement of banks as well as within the control of the bank management. After examining the income statements and balance sheets of a bank, this study utilizes eight financial ratios for comparing the domestic and foreign bank performances in Bangladesh. These financial ratios are placed under three categories.

Profitability Performance

This study uses the following two indicators for measuring a bank's profitability performance:

1. Return on Assets (ROA) = net profit/total assets. ROA is a good indicator of a bank's financial performance and managerial efficiency. It shows how competent the management is in allocating assets into net profit. The higher the ROA, the higher the profitability performance of a bank.

2. Return on equity, (ROE) = net profits/equity. ROE shows a rate return on base capital, i.e. equity capital. From an investor's point of view, ROE is the best indicator of a bank performance. An investor can evaluate return on his/her equity. The higher the ROE, the higher the profit performance of a bank.

Credit and Liquidity Risk

Credit risk measures the quality of loans. The higher the amount of the loan and/or interest in default, the greater the credit of a bank. Similarly, the higher the amount of a loan, long term in particular, the greater the liquidity risk. A bank may fail to meet the liquidity needs of customers. This paper uses the following indicators:

1. **Non-performance loans ratio (NONPL)** = Non-performance loans/ total loans. The higher the NONPRL, the greater the credit risk of a bank. A higher ratio of non-performance loan is an indication of poor loan quality.

2. **Short-term industrial loan ratio (SRINDL)** = Short term industrial loans, i.e. inventory loans/ total loans. The short term industrial loan has two implications. First, the higher the short term industrial loan, the lower the credit and liquidity risk. Second, the higher is the amount of the short term industrial loans, the greater the participation of domestic economic development.

Commitment to Domestic Development

The following three indicators are used measure a bank's commitment to domestic economic development:

1. **Total loan to assets ratio (LTA)** = Total loans/total asset. The higher the LTA ratio, the greater the commitment to consumer lending.

2. **Industrial loan ratio (INDUSL)** = Total industrial loans/total loans. The higher the INDUSL ratio, the greater the commitment to industrialization.

3. **Large and Medium industry loan ratio (LMEDIL)** = Loans to large and medium industry/total loans. The higher the LMEDIL ratio, the greater the bank's participation in economic development.

Statistical Methodology for Comparison

This paper uses two statistical methods—Kruskal-Wallis *K* and student's *t* tests—for the comparison of operational performances. The *t* tests produce strong results due to the non-normal distribution of ratios. This problem is overcome by the non-parametric, Kruskal-Wallis K test. The Kruskal-Wallis K tests do not restrict to normality assumption. The *K* statistics H" follows X^2 distribution with c–1 degrees of freedom where c = number of groups.

The paper tests two hypotheses:

Null hypothesis, $H_{0:}\ \mu_{fbk} = \mu_{dbk}$: There is no difference between the mean of foreign and domestic banks, in particular, both have the same.

Alternative hypothesis, $H_a : \mu_{fbk} \neq \mu_{fbk}$: There is a difference between foreign and domestic banks, in particular, they have different means.

Where μ_{fbk} = Mean of foreignbanks, μ_{dbk} = mean of domestic banks.

Secondly, in order to see the impact of ownership—foreign and domestic—on the domestic development of Bangladesh, binary variable is utilized: 1 for foreign bank and 0 for domestic bank. One dependent variable is industrial loan to total loans with ownership as independent variable. The coefficient for ownership is expected to be positive. Results are provided in Table 3.

Data

Data for this study are obtained from the Ministry of Finance and the Statistical Year Book of Bangladesh, Government of Bangladesh. Financial Institutions Statistics book provides some income and balance sheet information for 32 domestic and 13 foreign banks 2000-2001. Out of 32 domestic and 13 foreign banks, relevant data are available for 27 domestic and 12 foreign banks. The data for various ratios are calculated by the author.

This study uses yearly non-performance data. The yearly nonperformance loan accounts for loans that are one year over due. The yearly nonperformance loan is the best indicator of a bank's credit risk. It is even better than measures such as loan loss reserve ratio. The banks reserve is kept against expected loan losses. It does not truly represent actual the bank credit risk.

SECTION V: EMPIRICAL RESULTS AND CONCLUSION

Empirical Results

Table 1 shows descriptive statistics, means, and standard deviations for the selected balance sheet and income items for a sample of 27 domestic and 12 foreign banks. It is clear from the table that domestic banks in Bangladesh have a much wider scale of operations than foreign banks. The larger scale of domestic bank operations is reflected by the increased number of branches and bankstaffs. The higher *t* values of the student's *t* test for branches and staffs suggest that there are significant differences between domestic and foreign bank operations. Domestic banks have an extensive network of branches and staff.

The larger scale of domestic bank operations is also reflected in loans and deposits due to their extensive network of branches and staff. The domestic bank mean loans and assets TK9852.96 million and TK13055.41 million respectively are significantly larger than those of foreign banks mean loans and deposit TK3633.41 million and TK5319.66 million respectively. This is substantiated by higher t-values (and low p-values).

Similar differences are observed in industrial loans. Domestic bank mean industrial loans TK 2530.63 million is significantly larger than that of foreign bank mean industrial loans TK1021.83 million.

However, no significant differences are found in net profits and assets between domestic and foreign banks. This is substantiated by low t-values.

Table 1
Descriptive Statistics for Performance Measures[1]

	Domestic Banks		*Foreign Banks*			
Variables	*Mean*	*SD*	*Mean*	*SD*	*t-values*	*P-values**
Loans	9852.96	8255.73	3633.41	5239.47	2.39	0.02
Deposits	13055.41	9862.84	5319.66	6409.48	2.48	0.01
Net Profits	418.55	381.33	346.00	523.01	0.48	0.6
Total assets	48805.85	164408.5	16496.42	26339.33	0.67	0.5
Industrial Loans	2530.63	2453.56	1021.83	872.84	2.06	0.04
Branches	49	74	3	3.4	2.12	0.04
Bank-staffs	1028	1181	142	144	2.56	0.01

* P- values provide confidence level/level of significance.

Table 2 presents the comparative performance measured in terms of eight financial ratios placed which are placed under three categories and discussed above. The advantage of the ratio analysis is that it compensates bank disparity created by bank assets sizes.

Both *t* and Kruskal-Wallis *K* statistics for ROA in Table 2 indicate that there is no significant difference in profit performance between foreign and domestic banks. This indicates that there is strong competition in the Bangladesh bank market. The private banks of Bangladesh are managerially as efficient as the foreign banks. The significant difference on ROE supported by the Kruskal-Wallis *K* statistics should not mislead us, but it should be interpreted cautiously. The difference between foreign and domestic bank ROE is spurious. This is because almost half of the foreign banks did not have information for paidup capital. As a result, foreign bank ROE is significantly lower than that of a domestic bank.

However, both *t* and Kruskal-Wallis *K* statistics in Table 2 indicate that the differences between foreign and domestic banks in almost all measures of credit-liquidity and commitment to industrialization and economic development are significant.

The Kruskal-Wallis *K* and *t* statistics for credit and liquidity measures indicate that differences between foreign and domestic banks are significant. The mean of domestic bank NONPL (0.38) is significantly higher than the foreign bank mean of 0.09. The higher domestic bank mean of NONPL suggests that domestic banks are more aggressive and subject to a higher credit risk compared to foreign banks. The lower NONPL of foreign banks supports the claim that foreign bank loans are 'cherry pick up client'. They are cautious and picky in loan advancement.

Both *t* and Kruskal-Wallis *K* statistic for liquidity measure (SRINDL) indicate that there are significant differences between foreign and domestic bank operations. Foreign bank SRINDL mean 2.04 is significantly higher than domestic bank SRINDL 0.24. The higher percentage of a foreign bank short term industrial loans compared to that of a domestic loan suggests that foreign banks are more liquid than domestic banks. The short term industrial loans are generally inventory loans and are quickly recoverable. Therefore, SRINDL are less risky. On the other hand, the higher percentage of SRINDL suggests higher involvement of foreign banks in Bangladesh industrialization.

Both Kruskal-Wallis *K* and *t* statistics in Table 2 indicate that differences between foreign and domestic banks for commitment to domestic development are highly significant. Although foreign bank involvements in industrialization (indicated by SRINDL) are significant, their participation in economic development (measured by LMEDIL) is significantly lower than that of domestic banks. Domestic bank LMEDIL mean 0.52 is significantly higher than foreign bank LMEDIL mean 0.24.

Foreign bank percentage of total industrial loan, INDUSL is significantly higher than that of domestic banks. The higher INDUDL of foreign banks suggests that foreign banks are involved in the process ofindustrialization. This result refutes the concern that foreign banks do not participate in domestic industrialization.

Kruskal-Wallis *K* statistics for LTA indicates the difference between foreign and domestic banks in meeting domestic customer credit needs are highly significant. Foreign bank mean LTA is significantly lower than that of domestic bank mean LTA. The foreign bank lower LTA supports policy maker concerns that foreign banks are less concerned wth the needs of domestic customers. This further suggests that foreign banks are highly picky (cherry pick up clients) in advancing loans. As such, foreign bank loans are less risky compared to that of domestic banks

There is no difference in the percentage of agricultural loans (shown by AGRL) between foreign and domestic banks.

Table 2
Comparative Performance between Domestic and Foreign Bank Financial Ratios

	Performance Measures	*Domestic Banks*	*Foreign Banks*	*Test Statistics* *t-values*	*Kruskal-Wallis K*
	A. Profitability Measures				
1.	ROA	0.043	0.036	0.22	2.5
2.	ROE	0.59	0.31	0.1.5	12.2***
	B. Credit and Liquidity				
3.	NONPL	-0.38	-0.09	1.96**	4.9**
4.	SRINDL	0.24	2.04	5.47***	17.8***
	C. Commitment to Domestic Development				
5.	LTA	1.16	0.23	0.89	12.24***
6.	INDUSL	0.27	0.17	3.92***	9.9***
7.	LMEDIL	0.52	0.24	4.09***	10.1***

** Difference in means: Significant at 5% level

*** Difference in means: Significant at 1% level

Table 3
Impact of ownership on Foreign Bank on the Development of Bangladesh

Variable	*Coefficient*	*t-statistic*	*probability*
Ownership	-1.80	-5.47	0.0000
Constant	2.04	7.46	0.0000

R-square= 0.44
F-statistics = 29.99
Prob (F-statistic) = 0.0000

The coefficient for the ownership variable in the above regression in Table 3 is negative suggesting that foreign banks are less interested in issuing industrial loans and is statistically significant.

CONCLUSION

This paper examined the operation of foreign and domestic banks in the process of industrialization and economic development of Bangladesh. Eight financial ratios are used to measure the operation of bank performance. The comparison of the financial ratios of foreign and domestic banks indicates that there are significant differences in operation between them. The results support the findings of Sabi (1996).

The finding of this study that there is no difference in the profitability performance between foreign and domestic banks. This finding supports the study of Murphy and Sabov (1993).

This study provides support that foreign banks are less concerned to the needs of domestic customers. This is substantiated by the lower percentage of loan advancement (LTA) of foreign banks. The lower LTA also supports a bank's view that foreign banks are 'cherry pick up clients'. Foreign banks are cautious in loan advancements. As such, foreign bank credit risks are significantly less than that of domestic banks. Foreign bank lower credit risk is shown by lower non-performance (NONPL). The finding in this paper is consistent with the findings of Sabi (1996) that foreign banks are risk averse.

This paper finds that foreign banks are actively involved in the process of industrialization, the result that contradicts common concerns. This is substantiated by the higher percentage of short-term industrial loans (SRINDL).

In regard to the commitment of economic development, this paper finds that foreign banks are significantly less committed to advancing loans to large and medium industries, the loans that characterize long-term and development loans. This result supports the findings of Sabi.

Foreign bank are less committed to customers needs and may be explained by the facts that they do not have extensive networks of branches compared to domestic banks. Secondly, they have less bank staffs compared to domestic banks. Thirdly, all of the foreign banks are located in Dhaka, the capital of Bangladesh.

Reference

Akhigbe, Aigbe and James E. McNulty (2003), "The Profit Efficiency of Small U.S. Commercial Banks", *Journal of Banking and Finance*, Vo. 28, pp. 307-325.

Carter, John. (1978), "Collusion, Efficiency, and Antitrust". *Journal of Law and Economics* 21 (October), pp. 435-444.

Demsetz, Harold. (1973), "Industry Structure, Market Rivalry, and Public Policy". *Journal of Law and Economics* 16 (April), pp. 1-9.

Evanoff, D.D., and D. I. Frontier. (1988), "Reevaluation of the Structure–conduct Performance Paradigm in Banking". *Journal of Financial Services Research I* (June), pp. 313-329.

Gilbert, R A. (1984), "Bank Market Structure and Competition". *Journal of Money, Credit and Banking* 16 (Nov), pp. 617-645.

Heggestad, A.A., J.J Mingo. (1977), "The Competitive Condition of US Banking Markets and the Impact of Structural Reform". *Journal of Finance* 32 (June), pp. 649-661.

Meinster, David and Elyasian, Elyas (1994), "An Empirical test of Test of Association between Production and Financial Performance: The case of Commercial banking industry", *Applied Financial Economics,* vol. 4. pages 55-59.

Murphy A. and Z. Sabov (1991), "Financial Institution Structure in a Developing Two-Tier Banking System: An Empirical Analysis From Eastern Eueope", *Journal of Banking Finance*, Vol. 15, No. 6, pp. 1131-142.

Pozdena, Randall J. (1986), "Structure and Performance: Some Evidence from California Banking" Economic Review, Federal Reserve Bank of San Francisco, (Winter), pp. 5-17.

Rhoades, S. (1982), "Welfare Loss, Redistribution Effects, and Restriction of Output due to Monopoly".

Sabi, Manijeh (1996), "Comparative Analysis of Foreign and Domestic Bank Operation in Hungary",*Journal of Comparative Economics*, Vol. 22, pages (179-188).

Samad, Abdus (1999), "Comparative Efficiency of the Islamic Bank Malaysia vis-à-vis conventional Banks", *IIUM Journal of Economics and Management*, Vol. 7, No. 1, pp. 1-25.

Samad, Abdus and Kabir Hasan (2001), "The performance of Malaysian Islamic Bank during 1984-1997: An Exploratory study" *International Journal of Islamic Financial Services*, October-December 1999, Vol.1, No. 3, pp. 7-26.

Samad, Abdus (2004), "The Performance of Interest-free Islamic Banks vis-à-vis Interest-based Conventional Banks of Bahrain", *IIUM Journal of Economics and Management*, vol. 12, No. 2, pp. 115-129.

Smirlock, Michael. (1985), "Evidence on the (Non) Relationship between Concentration and Profitability in Banking". *Journal of Money Credit and Banking* 17 (February), pp. 69-83.

Williams, D.M. Lloyad, Phil Molyneux, and John Thornton (1994), "Market Structure and Performance in Spanish Banking". *Journal of Banking and Finance* 18, pp. 433-443.

THE CHALLENGES OF GOVERNMENT EXPENDITURE GROWTH IN BOTSWANA

Christopher Mupimpila
Department of Economics, University of Botswana, Botswana

This paper segments the challenges of government expenditure growth in Botswana into two parts: proximate and underlying challenges. The paper analyses the proximate challenges and then gives empirical results on the determinants of government expenditure growth in Botswana. Government revenues and expenditures on social services are the significant determinants of government expenditure growth in the country. The paper also considers the underlying challenges of government expenditure growth in Botswana. This leads to the conclusion that long term sustainability in Botswana requires economic development and structural change.

JEL classification: *H110, H 500.*

Key words: *government expenditures, sustainability, structural change.*

1. INTRODUCTION

For 16 years prior to the 1998/99 fiscal year, Botswana had government budget surpluses. The 1998/99 budget deficit was followed by three years of consecutive deficits during the financial years of 2001/02, 2002/03 and 2003/04. Thus, Botswana is now in an era that demands more caution and restraint in public finances.

This paper analyses the challenges of government expenditure growth in Botswana. It adopts the approach by Perrings *et. al.* (1995), that distinguishes between proximate and underlying causes of a problem. The proximate causes focus on the symptoms while the underlying causes are the real, fundamental causes of a problem. The first section of the paper describes the pattern and debate on government expenditure growth in Botswana. It shows some of the measures the government of Botswana has adopted to gauge the amount of public expenditures devoted to capital formation. The second section of the paper presents empirical findings on the determinants of government expenditure growth in Botswana. This is followed by a summary and conclusions.

The case of Botswana shades light on other developing countries because Botswana has had rapid economic growth and a stable macroeconomic environment. However, the country's public sector has low productivity and implementation capacity. These factors are constraints to economic development.

Corresponding Author: *mupimpi@mopipi.ub.bw*

2. GOVERNMENT EXPENDITURES IN BOTSWANA

In developed and developing countries, government expenditures are usually divided into two parts; such as current and capital, ordinary and extraordinary, recurrent and non-recurrent expenditures (Mupimpila, 1981). Similarly, government expenditures in Botswana are dived into two categories: recurrent and development expenditures. Recurrent expenditure is non-investment, consumption expenditure while development expenditure is what, in some countries, called capital expenditure. As a percent of total expenditures, recurrent expenditures in Botswana have been increasingly greater than development expenditures. In 1980, recurrent expenditures comprised 58.4% of total expenditures but rose significantly over time and were 78.5% of total expenditures in 2005 (Republic of Botswana, 1985; Bank of Botswana, 2006). On the other hand, the proportion of development expenditures has fallen from 41.6% in 1980 to 21.5% of the total expenditures in 2005. It is clear that there has been a remarkable increase in recurrent expenditures as a share of total expenditures.

Appendix A depicts the components of recurrent and development expenditures in Botswana for the period 1980-2005. The data shows that social services comprise the largest percentage of both recurrent and development expenditures. Since expenditures on social services predominate in both the recurrent and development budget, it is interesting to know what constitutes recurrent and development expenditures. Just how does one define the recurrent and development aspect of social expenditure? What is the basis for double-budgets in the public sector?

Double-budgets in the public sector have their origins in corporate capital budgeting, where the practice is to separate current from capital expenditures (Burkhead, 1956; Goode and Birnbaum, 1956). In corporate budgeting, current income is expected to cover current expenditure (including depreciation on capital) while borrowing mainly finances capital expenditure. Double-budgets in government are therefore an extension of the practice in business finance. Furthermore, double-budgets in government were first instituted in Scandinavian countries; Denmark and Norway introduced the system in 1927 and Sweden in 1937. One of the most important recommendations of committees formed to resolve the economic problems of these countries was the separation of the budget into two parts: current and capital expenditure, the latter to be financed mainly by borrowing.

There are supporters and opponents of double-budgeting in government (Mupimpila, 1981). Proponents of the system maintain that financing capital expenditure by borrowing avoids frequent tax revisions. Besides, it is argued, loan finance for capital expenditure affords a better distribution of the cost of government services between present and future generations. Since many government services will be used by and benefit future generations, it is unfair to recover the whole cost of such services from the present generation. Given that amortization of loans occurs in the future, borrowing to finance capital expenditure allows a better distribution of the cost of government services among beneficiaries and taxpayers.

Opponents of the double-budget system in government say that loan finance is likely to be inflationary. This is particularly true in developing countries where borrowing from the general public is very limited, savings are low and financial institutions are not well developed. The opponents also say that this system tends to consider asset-formation from a narrowly physical point of view. It is argued, a government assets and liabilities statement may not be very useful if some expenditures are overlooked that contribute to physical capital formation (United Nations, 1958). Rather, recurrent and capital expenditures are complementary because every capital project requires recurrent expenditures.

However, the division of the government budget in recurrent and capital or development expenditure is justified because it shows the amount of public expenditures devoted to capital formation. In Botswana, the government realizes the importance of utilizing mineral reserves for investment purposes. Consequently, in 1994 the government adopted two aggregate measures designed to monitor the extent to which mineral revenues are invested productively. These measures are the Sustainable Budget Index (SBI) and the Accumulated Investment Surplus (Republic of Botswana, 1994; Wright, 1997; BIDPA, 2003; Mupimpila, 2005b). The SBI is the ratio of recurrent expenditure to recurrent revenues. As already indicated, recurrent expenditure is essentially non-investment, consumption spending while recurrent revenues are the remainder of deducting the value of asset sales, mainly mineral revenues, from total revenues.

In a given financial year, the SBI should, ideally, be less than or equal to unity. If the SBI exceeds unity, this means that some of the recurrent expenditure is being financed by non-recurrent revenues, i.e., asset sales, or by government borrowing. Thus an SBI above unity is a signal to the government that some of the mineral revenues are not being used optimally (see Figure1). On the other hand, the Accumulated Investment Surplus (AIS) deals with the un-spent revenues from asset sales. Since these revenues are productive investment, the AIS principle requires that any un-spent asset revenues should not be used later for recurrent expenditure.

Figure 1 shows the SBI from 1981 to 2001. From the trend, it is clear that the SBI was below unity during 1981-93, except for the period 1987-89 when the index was about unity. However, after 1993, the SBI has consistently been above unity. This shows that after 1993, non-recurrent revenues have financed some of the recurrent expenditure. Statistics show since 1990, there has been an exponential growth in recurrent expenditure in Botswana. As already indicated, Tables A. 1 and A. 2 show social services now comprise the largest proportion of both recurrent and development expenditures. Clearly, it is the expenditure on social services that explain the exponential growth in recurrent expenditure since 1990. Expenditure on social services also explains the growth in development expenditure. For example, health expenditure was only 2.8% in 1980 but in 2005, it was 26.7% of development expenditure. The fact the SBI has consistently been above unity since the 1990s means that government expenditure growth cannot be sustained in the long run because the nation's

Figure 1: The Sustainable Budget Index (SBI), 1981-2001

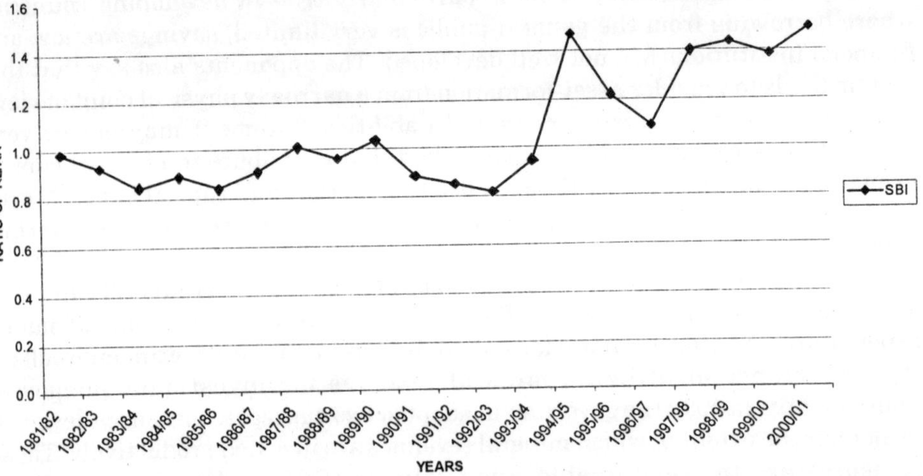

productive capital stock is being depleted faster than it is being replaced. BIDPA (2003) explores this issue in two ways. First, it defines a Broad Sustainable Budget Index (BSBI) whereby recurrent expenditures on education and health are deducted from the total recurrent expenditures. This is because some types of recurrent expenditures are investments in capital accumulation. To compute the BSBI, the recurrent expenditures on education and health are deducted from the total recurrent expenditures and recurrent revenues divide the result. Secondly, BIDPA defines a Narrow Sustainable Budget Index (NSBI), by assuming that only half of the recurrent expenditures on education and health are investment. However, even with the use of the BSBI and the NSBI, BIDPA concludes that the government budget in Botswana is now on an unsustainable path.

Specifically, there are three easily discernible issues concerning public sector in Botswana. These issues are, in this paper, called the proximate challenges of government expenditure growth in Botswana. First, there is a view that the government in Botswana has expanded beyond the three core functions it is expected to perform in a market economy, namely to; (i) allocate resources, through the provision of public goods and services, (ii) distribute income and wealth, through taxes and expenditure programmes, and (iii) stabilize the economy by such instruments as monetary and fiscal policies. It is said that the government in Botswana has expanded beyond these core functions and has therefore become very large, cumbersome and inefficient (Republic of Botswana, 2000; CIM & BIDPA, 2000; BIDPA, 2004b). In Botswana, the public sector is by far the largest formal sector employer. Central and local government, together with parastatal employment constitute 44 % of formal sector employment in Botswana (BIDPA, 2004b, p. 1). The view is that the public sector in Botswana is over-extended, should be re-oriented towards facilitation and regulation and away from direct provision of goods and services.

Secondly, there is the notion that the fault is in the manner in which public sector reforms that have so far been implemented. Public sector reforms are required because of the low productivity and implementation capacity of the sector (BIDPA, 2004b; Obuseng, 2006; Dingare, 2007; Republic of Botswana, 2000; 2007). To date, there have been some public sector reforms in Botswana, and these have centred on public administration, decentralization and privatization. The reforms have included performance management systems, productivity improvements programmes, transparency and accountability, commercialization and privatization. These reforms have been implemented by such initiatives as Work Improvement Teams (WITS), the Performance Management System (PMS), Organization and Methods (O&M) reviews, as well as Job Evaluation. The reforms have also led to the creation of such institutions as the Public Enterprises Evaluation and Privatization Agency (PEEPA), the Ombudsman, and Directorate on Corruption and Economic Crime (DCEC). According to BIDPA (2004b, p.2), what seems to lacking is "... a comprehensive policy and mechanism for coordination of the public sector reforms."

Thirdly, there is the view that down sizing or right sizing the public sector may not necessarily be a solution to the problems of low productivity and implementation capacity in Botswana. What is required is a change in values. Therefore, when they talk about public sector reforms, some analysts draw our attention to the need for change in values and norms, the work ethic. Commenting on this issue, Obuseng (2006, 14) stated:

> The focus on grand strategies is fine but they will amount to naught if our institutions remain ill-disposed to adopting governance practices that will allow Botswana to prosper. If, qualitatively, service delivery is to reach the levels society desires and the economy is to reach its target growth rates and produce durable impacts on unemployment and poverty, the culture of service in the civil service must change, and radically.

The change suggested by Obuseng is about values and norms, the work ethic in the civil service. Our beliefs form our values and norms; and it is the values and norms that drive our behaviour. To give a specific example, for some time now, Botswana has been trying to promote small micro and medium enterprises (SMMEs). However, one of the main factors stifling the growth and development of small business in Botswana is the delay by government departments to pay for goods and services they procured from SMMEs (*Business and Financial Times*, 2004). By nature, SMMEs often face liquidity problems, but they are exacerbated if the civil service delays in paying what is owed to the SMMEs. These are some of the micro foundations of macroeconomics that need to change.

The determinants of public expenditure growth in developing countries have been explored empirically in several studies (Enweze, 1973; Goffman and Mahar, 1971; Landau, 1983; Lotz, 1970; Martin and Lewis, 1956; Mogotsi and Mupimpila, 2003; Mupimpila, 2005a; Ram, 1986; Thorn, 1967). The significant factors are considered to be the expenditure on social services, the openness of the economy, and military spending. Increased expenditure on social welfare is due to urbanization, caused, among others, by rural-urban migration. An open economy is usually defined as a country that has international trade in goods and services.

Since the world is now said to be a global village, the degree of openness has an impact on government expenditure growth due in part to the demonstration effect. However, growth in military expenditures is, in some cases, the largest single source of growth in government spending. Enweze (1973) found military spending to be the most significant source of growth in government spending in developing countries. Growth in military spending is attributed to national sovereignty and destabilizing factors such as coup d'etats, civil wars, border conflicts and external aggression.

3. DATA AND VARIABLES

The study assumes that government expenditures depend on national income, the monetisation of and degree of openness of the economy, the level of inflation, government revenues and social expenditures. The econometric model estimated is:

$$GEX_t = \beta_0 + \beta_1 GDP_t + \beta_2 MON_t + \beta_3 XPT_t + \beta_4 CPI + \beta_4 GVR_t + \beta_5 SOC_t + \varepsilon_t \quad (1)$$

Where GEX is total government expenditures in real terms; GDP is gross domestic product, the measurement of national income in real terms. The variable MON is the level of monetisation in the economy and is proxied by the money supply (M_2), which is M_1 (currency outside bank & demand deposits) plus saving notice and time deposits in real terms. The degree of openness of the economy is measured by XPT, the value of the total exports in the economy in real terms. CPI is the annual percentage rate of inflation and is used to calculate the deflator employed to transform all variables into real terms (100=1980). GRV is the government total revenues, composed of non-tax and tax revenues including mineral revenue but excluding grants. The variable SOC represents expenditures on social services consisting of education; health; food and social welfare programmes; housing, urban and regional development; and other community and social services. All of the variables are in real terms. βi i=0,..., 5 are the coefficients.

It is expected that the variables GDP, MON, XPT, GVR and SOC all have a positive and significant impact on government expenditures, GEX, in Botswana. The data fitted to the empirical model, equation (1), in this study are from various issues of the Statistical Bulletin, published by the Republic of Botswana, Central Statistics Office. Estimates are for the years 1980 to 2005. The estimation was by using ordinary least squares, using the software package Econometric Views (EViews).

4. EMPIRICAL RESULTS

The empirical results of the specified model above are summarised in Table 1 while the time-series properties and other tests of the model are given in Appendix B. The results in Table 1 are the first difference of the log transformed variables. As is clear from Table 1, both the R^2 and adjusted R^2 show very high explanatory power of the model. The goodness-of-fit measures show that the regressors in the estimated equation explain a significant percentage of the variations in government expenditures during the study period, 1980-2005. The F–Statistic is significant and it indicates that all explanatory variables jointly determine government expenditures in Botswana. The computed LM test and Heteroscedasticity test lead to accept the null hypotheses that there is neither serial correlation nor presence of Heteroscedasticity problems, respectively. Furthermore, the diagnostic test performed for stability of the model using Ramsey RESET test indicates that the functional form of the model is reasonably good since we cannot reject the null hypotheses for the stability of the functional form of the model.

All the independent variables in the model have the expected signs. Asterisks in Table 1 show the significant coefficients, with one and two asterisks denoting 1% and 10% significance levels, respectively. The results show that social services (SOC) and government revenues (GRV) are the significant variables that determine government expenditure growth in Botswana. The expenditure on social services is significant at 1% while government revenues are significant at the 10% level. Therefore, statistically, expenditure on social services is the most significant determinant of expenditure growth in Botswana. These findings are in line with the observations made earlier in this paper, that social services account for the largest and rising share of recurrent expenditures in Botswana. Among the social services, expenditure on education is the largest and rising share of expenditure on social services (Table A.1 and A.2).

Table 1
Parameter Estimates of Government Expenditure (DL)

Variables	*Coefficient*	*Std. Error*	*t-Ratio*	*T-Probability*
CONSTANT	-0.0317	0.0178	-1.7797	0.0911
DLGDP	0.1387	0.1410	0.9836	0.3377
DLMON	0.0407	0.1161	0.3506	0.7297
DLXPT	0.0021	0.0792	0.0262	0.9794
DLGVR	0.2117**	0.1082	1.9566	0.0653
DLSOC	0.6832*	0.1372	4.9795	0.0001
Model Diagnostics				
R^2	0.94	Residual Sum of squares		0.077
Adjusted R^2	0.92	Akaike Information Criterion		-2.453
Durbin-Watson	1.39	LM Testc[2]		1.162366(0.295212)
F-Statistics	59.89486(0.0000)	White Heteroscedasticity test		0.75422(0.667779)
Log Likelihood	36.67	Ramsey RESER Test		1.189164(0.328569)

Note: The asterisks * and ** denote significance at the 1 and 5 percent levels.

However, these findings are in contrast to those of Mupimpila (2005), where national income (GDP), the degree of openness of the economy (XPT) and the expenditures on social services (SOC) were the significant variables that determine the growth of government expenditures in Botswana. The difference is due to two factors. First, the previous study was for the period1980-2000 while the present study covers a longer period, 1980-2005. Secondly, as already indicated, for 16 years before the 19989/99 fiscal year, Botswana enjoyed government budget surpluses. The 1998/99 deficit was followed by three years of consecutive budget deficits during the financial years of 2001/02, 2002/03 and 2003/04. Thus, after 2000, there were consecutive budget deficits, which must have induced the government to be more cautious in public finances than was previously the case.

The fact the coefficient of government revenues (GRV) is significant is in itself a sign of fiscal discipline in Botswana's budget. Government expenditures should be dictated by the availability of revenues, not just social factors, such as the need for education and better health care. Since the mineral boom began, in the 1970s, mineral revenues have become the major source of government revenues in Botswana. The government owns 50% of the diamond mining company in Botswana, Debswana. Besides the dividends from Debswana, the government also benefits through the income taxes and royalties paid by Debswana. These measures, together with the boom in diamonds, explain why mineral revenues are by far the major source of government finance in Botswana. However, the dependency on mineral revenues poses serious challenges for the country (BIDPA, 2003; Mupimpila, 2005b). First, diamonds are non-renewable resources; they are exhaustible. Diamonds are traded in a volatile world market. These factors make mineral revenues an unsustainable source of government finance in the long run. Secondly, since diamonds are exhaustible, there is need to invest the diamond windfalls in alternative future sources of income (Hartwick, 1977). Thirdly, like other developing countries, Botswana has a very narrow revenue base; with three sources accounting for much of the government revenues. The introduction of the value-added tax in 2002 was designed to broaden the revue base.

Taken together, the foregoing issues are the underlying challenges of government expenditure growth in Botswana. The issues point to the economic problem: the allocation of scarce resources among competing ends. The economic problem is about constrained optimization (Layard and Walters, 1978). Economic development and structural change loosen the constraints. Furthermore, the efficiency of the public sector is a function of the level of economic development. Botswana's economy has, in the past two decades, experienced phenomenal growth, powered by the country's rich mineral wealth. However, growth and economic development are not synonymous. Economic development implies structural change, including the value systems. Culture is dynamic, but for it to change; there must be underlying forces that induce the change.

5. SUMMARY AND CONCLUSIONS

This paper has described the proximate and underlying challenges of government expenditure growth in Botswana. The proximate challenges are about public sector reforms, down sizing or right sizing the public sector, as well as the change in norms and values. The paper alluded to some of the reforms and also described the measures adopted by the government of Botswana to gauge the amount of public expenditures devoted to capital formation. Relative statistics show that social expenditures now predominate in recurrent and development expenditures in Botswana. Empirical evidence confirms this and also shows that government revenues are a significantly related to government expenditures.

The underlying challenges of government expenditure growth in Botswana are related to the economic problem. They are about the dependency on an exhaustible resource and a very narrow revenue base. Sustainability of expenditure programmes requires economic development and structural change.

APPENDIX

Appendix A: The pattern of recurrent and development expenditures in Botswana

Table A.1 shows that social services account for the largest and rising share of recurrent expenditures. Percentage-wise, social services were 34.3% of total recurrent expenditures in 1980, 40.2% in 1995, and 47.6% in 20005. Among the social services, expenditure on education is the largest and rising share of expenditures on the social sector. Overall, education has been the largest component of the government budget in Botswana.

Table A. 2 shows the pattern of development expenditure in Botswana during 1980-2005. In this case, it is clear that economic services accounted for the largest share of development expenditure from 1980 to 2000. This trend continued to decline while social services received the second largest and rising portion of development expenditure. In recent years, social services have accounted for the largest share of total expenditures in Botswana (Tables A. 1 and A. 2). In 2005, social expenditure was 47.6% and 52% of recurrent and development expenditures respectively. This shows that, in Botswana, government expenditure is by far on socio-economic services. Through its expenditure programme, the government is creating the socio-economic infrastructure necessary for development.

Table 1
Recurrent Expenditure in Botswana (Percentage)

	1980	*1985*	*1990*	*1995*	*2000*	*2005*
General services, including defense	37.3	35.4	32.6	31.8	29.8	30.4
Social Services	34.3	31.0	34.9	40.2	45.5	47.6
Education	22.6	20.6	22.4	23.8	27.9	28.7
Health	6.1	5.2	5.8	6.4	6.3	8.2
Food & social welfare programmes	0.3	0.6	0.8	0.1	3.6	0.5
Other community & social services	3.8	3.2	4.0	7.9	5.5	6.2
Other community & social services	1.5	1.4	1.9	1.9	2.3	4.0
Economic services	18.2	17.5	15.8	11.9	10.6	12.2
Agriculture, forestry & fishing	9.2	7.2	7.0	5.5	4.5	3.9
Mining	1.0	0.9	0.7	0.5	0.6	0.6
Electricity and water supply	2.3	2.0	2.0	1.7	1.9	2.9
Roads	1.9	3.2	3.4	2.7	1.8	1.3
Others	3.8	4.2	2.7	1.6	1.8	3.5
Transfers	10.2	16.1	16.7	16.1	14.1	9.8
Interest on public debt	3.0	6.1	3.6	2.6	1.0	0.0
Deficit grants to local authorities	6.9	8.8	11.5	11.5	11.7	9.8
FAP grants	0.3	1.2	1.5	2.1	1.4	0.0

Source: Calculated from BoB Annual Reports and CSO Statistical Bulletins.

Table 2
Development Expenditure in Botswana (Percentage)

	1980	*1985*	*1990*	*1995*	*2000*	*2005*
General services, including defense	13.8	11.9	18.1	19.5	24.3	18.8
Social services	34.1	29.3	37.0	37.1	37.1	52.0
Education	14.5	8.4	10.9	19.7	15.9	10.8
Health	2.8	3.2	2.5	1.9	3.1	26.7
Food & Social welfare programmes	-	5.2	0.2	7.5	3.8	3.3
Housing, urban & regional development	15.9	11.6	23.0	7.0	9.5	8.7
Other community & social services	0.9	0.9	0.4	0.9	4.8	1.6
Economic services	52.2	56.8	44.9	43.4	38.6	29.2
Agriculture, forestry & fishing	8.1	12.4	6.1	5.5	3.2	1.6
Mining	12.1	0.9	4.4	14.5	0.9	0.9
Electricity and water supply	5.3	16.4	3.7	12.5	13.2	14.9
Roads	10.7	9.0	7.4	7.2	13.6	7.8
Others	16.0	18.1	23.3	3.7	7.9	4.0
Transfers						
Interest on public debt	0.1	2.0	0.0	0.0	0.0	0.0
Deficit grants to local authorities	-	-	-	-	-	-
FAP grants	0.1	0.2	0.0	0.0	0.0	0.0
	-	-	-	-	-	-

Source: Calculated from BoB Annual Reports and CSO Statistical Bulletins

Appendix B: Time–Series Properties, Unit Root and Cointegration Tests

Time Series Properties

Preliminary tests were carried out on the data to establish its normality and stationarity. Table B.1 shows a summary of the descriptive statistics. It is evident that the data satisfy the normality test as shown by the insignificant Jarque-Bera probality.

Table B.1
Descriptive Statistics for variables in levels

	LGEX	*LCPI*	*LGDP*	*LGRV*	*LMON*	*LSOC*	*LXPT*
Mean	8.295333	2.284614	9.166467	8.392454	7.565134	7.331508	8.474226
Median	8.151083	2.292484	8.982777	8.380633	7.477339	7.273206	8.296354
Maximum	10.34304	2.791165	11.37434	10.37972	9.892174	9.562004	10.36327
Minimum	5.567355	1.871802	6.509359	5.379904	4.642058	4.528948	5.540479
Std. Dev.	1.481488	0.244310	1.499718	1.468414	1.583288	1.597562	1.373443
Skewness	-0.238945	0.350470	-0.156975	-0.499026	-0.231454	-0.182658	-0.471388
Kurtosis	1.919535	2.662254	1.925175	2.346616	2.011680	1.840460	2.350607
Jarque-Bera	1.512098	0.655840	1.358297	1.541602	1.290315	1.601155	1.419751
Probability	0.469518	0.720421	0.507049	0.462642	0.524580	0.449070	0.491705
Observations	26	26	26	26	26	26	26

Unit Root Tests

Economic time series data may exhibit a trend or unit root(s) over time. If this happens, the time series is said to be non-stationary. Non-stationarity implies that their mean and autocovariances depend on time. Time series data is said to be stationary or mean-reverting if their mean and autocovariances are independent of time. With unit roots present, there could be spurious regressions- where results may suggest statistically significant relationships, when in reality there are no meaningful relationships between the variables. This study employed the Augmented Dickey-Fuller (ADF) unit root tests and Table B. 2 gives a summary of the results. The tests show that all the variables were non-stationary before differencing.

Table B. 2
Results of Unit Root Tests for Data Series in levels

Variable	*Calculated t-statistic*	*Critical value t-statistic (5%)*	*Inference*
LGEX	1.074817	-2.9907	Non-stationary
LCPI	-2.717510	-2.9907	Non-stationary
LGDP	1.850442	-2.9907	Non-stationary
LGRV	2.737182	-2.9907	Non-stationary
LMON	1.678732	-2.9907	Non-stationary
LSOC	1.826062	-2.9907	Non-stationary
LXPT	1.378147	-2.9907	Non-stationary

Critical values produced by EViews

Integration Tests

The Johansen cointegration technique requires that the variables be integrated of the same order. In this study the ADF tests were conducted on the differenced series in order to determine the order of integration of the variables. The results of the stationarity tests on the differenced series are shown in Table B. 3.

Table A. 3
Results of Unit Root Tests for first differenced data series

Variable in first difference	*Calculated t-statistic*	*Critical value t-statistic (5%)*	*Inference*	*Order of integration*
LGEX	-4.824472	-2.9969	Stationary	I(1)
LCPI	-4.474964	-2.9969	Stationary	I(1)
LGDP	-5.776722	-2.9969	Stationary	I(1)
LGRV	-3.088808	-2.9969	Stationary	I(1)
LMON	-5.529645	-2.9969	Stationary	I(1)
LSOC	-4.875399	-2.9969	Stationary	I(1)
LXPT	-3.986573	-2.9969	Stationary	*I(1)*

Cointegration Test

If variables are integrated of the same order, even though they may be non-stationary, their linear combinations can be stationary (Engle and Granger, 1987). Table 3 shows that the variables are I(1) which forms the basis of cointegration analysis. Cointegration analysis was conducted using the Johansen cointegration test and the results are presented in Table B. 4.

Table A.4
Johansen's Cointegration Test

Eigen Value	*Likelihood Ratio*	*5% Critical*	*1% Critical Value*	*Hypothesised No. of CE(s)*
0.996025	341.2992	124.24	133.57	None**
0.955197	208.6313	94.15	103.18	At most 1**
0.924398	134.0996	68.52	76.07	At most 2 **
0.819556	72.12507	47.21	54.45	At most 3 **
0.538382	31.02907	29.68	35.65	At most 4 *
0.325507	12.47666	15.41	20.04	At most 5
0.118445	3.025616	3.76	6.65	At most 6

*(**) denotes rejection of the hypothesis at 5% (1%) significance level.

L.R. Test indicates 5 cointegrating equations at 5% significance level.

The eigenvalue statistic rejects the null hypothesis that there are no cointegrating vectors. The results show the presence of 5 long run relationships from the 7 series, *LGEX, LCPI, LGDP, LGRV, LMON, LSOC* and *LXPT*. As such cointegration is accepted and a long run growth function is specified.

References

Bank of Botswana (2006), *Annual Report 2005*. Gaborone: Bank of Botswana.

Bank of Botswana (2003), *Annual Report 2002*. Gaborone: Bank of Botswana.

Botswana Institute for Development Policy Analysis, BIDPA (2005), *The 2005/06 Budget Briefing*. Gaborone: BIDPA.

Botswana Institute for Development Policy Analysis, BIDPA (2004a), *The 2004/05 Budget Briefing*. Gaborone: BIDPA.

Botswana Institute for Development Policy Analysis, BIDPA (2004b), *Public Sector Reforms*. Gaborone: BIDPA.

Botswana Institute for Development Policy Analysis, BIDPA (2003), *The 2003/04 Budget Briefing*, Gaborone: BIDPA.

Business and Financial Times (2004), "Ruing the Cost of Low Productivity," *Business and Financial Times*, April/May 8:3, pp. 16-17.

Burkhead, J. (1956), *Government Budgeting*. NY: John Wiley & Sons.

Burkhead, J. and Miner, J. (1974), *Public Expenditure*. Ch: Aldine Publishing Company.

Christian Michelsen Institute, CMI and Botswana Institute for Development Policy Analysis, BIDPA (2000), *Making Government Smaller and More Efficient: The Botswana Case*. Royal Norwegian Ministry of Foreign Affairs.

Dingare, M. (2007), "How Independent is Parliament from the Executive," *Mmegi/The Reporter*, 27 February, p. 6.

Enweze, C. (1973), "Structure of Public Expenditures in Selected Developing Countries: A Time Series Study" *Manchester School of Economics and Social Studies*, 41, pp. 430-463.

Goffman, I. J. and Mahar, D. J. (1971), "The Growth of Public Expenditures in Selected Developing Nations: Six Caribbean Countries, 1940-65" *Public Finance*, XXVI, p. 57-74.

Goode, R. and E. A. Birnbaum (1956), "Government Capital Budgets," *IMF Staff Papers*, V:1, pp. 23-46.

Gujarati, D. N. (2003), *Basic Econometrics*, NY: McGraw-Hill Companies.

Hartwick, J. M. (1977), "Intergenerational Equity and the Investment of Rents from Exhaustible Resources," *American Economic Review*, 67: 5, pp. 972-974.

Landau, D. (1983), "Government Expenditure and Economic Growth: A Cross-Country Study" *Southern Economic Journal*, 49, pp.783-792.

Layard, P. R. G. and A. A. Walters (1978), *Microeconomic Theory*, NY: McGraw-Hill Book Company.

Lotz, J. R. (1970), "Patterns of Government Spending in Developing Countries," *Manchester School of Economics and Social Studies*, 2, pp. 119-144.

Martin, A. and Lewis, W. A. (1956), "Patterns of Public Revenue and Expenditure," *Manchester School of Economics and Social Studies*, XXIV, pp. 203-232.

Mogotsi, I. and Mupimpila, C. (2003), "The Impact of Government Size on Economic Growth in Botswana" *The Indian Journal of Economics*, LXXXIII, pp. 331: 459-73.

Mupimpila, C. (2005a), "Determinants of Government Expenditures in Botswana," *The ICFAI Journal of Applied Economics*, IV: 4, pp. 62-73.

Mupimpila, C. (2005b), "Fiscal Systems and Policy in Botswana," in H. K. Siphambe *et. al., Economic Development of Botswana, Facets, Policies, Problems and Prospects*; Gaborone: Bay Publishing, pp. 82-101.

Mupimpila, C. (1981), *The Government Budget and Economic Development: The Experience of Zambia, 1968-1978*. Unpublished M. A. thesis, Syracuse University, U.S.A.

Musgrave, R. A. and Musgrave, P. B. (1989), *Public Finance in Theory and Practice*, NY: McGraw-Hill Book Company.

Obuseng, S. (2006), "The IMF's 2005 Article iv on Botswana: Is this the End?" *Mmegi / The Reporter*, 10 March, p.14.

Peacock, A. T. and Wiseman, J. (1979), "Approaches to the Analysis of Government Expenditure Growth," *Public Finance Quarterly*, 7, pp. 3-23.

Perrings, C. A., *et al.* (1995), *Biodiversity Conservation*, Dordrecht: Kluwer Academic Publishers.

Ram, R. (1986), "Government Size and Economic Growth: A New Framework and Some Evidence from Cross-Section and Time-Series Data," *American Economic Review*, 76:1, pp. 191-203.

Republic of Botswana (2007), *Budget Speech*, Gaborone: Government Printer.

Republic of Botswana (2006), *Budget Speech*, Gaborone: Government Printer.

Republic of Botswana (2004), *Statistical Bulletin*, 26: 4, 27:1-4, Gaborone: Central Statistics Office.

Republic of Botswana (2001), *Statistical Bulletin*, 25: 4, Gaborone: Central Statistics Office.

Republic of Botswana (2000), *Government White Paper on Privatization Policy*, Gaborone: Central Statistics Office.

Republic of Botswana (1994), *Mid-Term Review of NDP 7*, Gaborone: Ministry of Finance and Economic Development.

Republic of Botswana (1990), *Statistical Bulletin*, 15:1, Gaborone: Central Statistics Office.

Republic of Botswana (1985), *Statistical Bulletin*, 10:1, Gaborone: Central Statistics Office.

Thorn, R. C. (1967), "The Evolution of Public Finance During Economic Development," *Manchester School of Economics and Social Studies*, 35, pp. 19-51.

United Nations (1958), *Manual for Economic and Functional Classification of Government Transactions*, New York: United Nations Department of Economics and Social Affairs.

Wright, M. (1997), "Fiscal Policy in Botswana: Challenges for Public Sector Finance in the Mid-1990s" in Salkin, J. S. *et al.*, *Aspects of the Botswana Economy, Selected Papers*, pp.147-73.

COMPARATIVE ANALYSIS OF SHEEP-GOAT FARMING IN A TYPICAL GREEK ISLAND:
Economy and Environment

Fotis Chatzitheodoridis, Anastasios Michailidis & George Theodossiou
Technological Education Institution of Western Macedonia
Department of Agricultural Products Marketing and Quality Control, Greece

Animal production was one of the major activities in the Greek islands as it was completely placed into traditional management system and fallow represented a kind of care for the dry fields that demand increased protection in order to protect their fertility. The aim of this study was to investigate the structure of sheep and goat breeding in a typical Greek island for both aspects of economy and environment. Especially using comparative analysis between sheep and goat breeding farms, that are fully or part time employment, it was tried to be connected the financial results with the "friendliness" that these farms have with the environment mainly in account with the exerted grazing pressure by them. Using data, collected from 75 sheep and goat breeding farms varied in size and yields, the analysis finds that the profit gained by this employment is mainly owed to the direct payments given to the breeders by the State, while this employment imputes complemental rather and not main income.

Keywords: sheep, goat, breeding, pluriactivity, productivity, environment

JEL codes: O130, O180, Q000, Q120, R300

INTRODUCTION

Agriculture (both plant and animal production) was one of the major activities in the Aegean islands during the past. Taking into account the structure of natural environment that is characterized by the absence of plain areas the agriculture was interwoven with the continuous effort to shape and maintain upgrades at the sloping and marginal productivity's areas of the islands. Animal production was completely placed into traditional management system and fallow represented a kind of care for the dry fields that demand increased protection in order to protect their fertility (Bazin, 1986). During this period of time, primary sector worked efficiently and in harmony with the island's environment as their labour force incorporated improved methods of field's management.

Corresponding Author: *tassosm@auth.gr*

The mechanization of agriculture in country's plains created conditions of unequal competition against the islands upgrade cultivulations. Machines determined the differences at human labour and the agriculture yields. Technology substituted products and traditional techniques and thus the comparative advantages of the islands in the section of agriculture were reduced or eliminated.

The exit of human force in searching better living and working conditions resulted in collapse of the traditional agricultural management systems and a new kind of an extensive type of animal breeding began to dominate in the islands. This change in management system increased the pressure, especially on pastureland, so that both heavy grazing (Tomaselli, 1977) and fire, threaten how to devastate the ecosystems.

Agriculture was and yet remains the basic activity for the residents of the Greek islands. During the last years the importance of primary sector for the island's economy is continually reducing because of tourism development that competes agriculture in relation to human force and land. Pluriactivity is an extensive phenomenon in the islands and it is usually connected with main or secondary job in tertiary sector. This fact prevents tourism development as an exclusive activity and also prevents the abandonment of agriculture land (Chatzitheodoridis, 2004).

Some of the farms (both plant and animal production) that exist in mountainous and disadvantageous areas (islands are among them) are connected with the production of regional food production that has special characteristics of geography origin and superior quality (Parrott *et al.*, 2002). These products usually escape the "productivity sense" and touch the "sense of quality" so that work as a brand name for region as they create good thinking and associations to consumers both for the region and the product (Ilbery and Kneafsey, 1999; Ilbery and Kneafsey, 2000; Lamprianidis, 2003). Examples for such products in Aegean islands are some kinds of wine in Samos, Lemnos and Santorini and some kinds of cheese for other islands like Lesvos and Lemnos.

The aim of this study was to investigate the structure of sheep and goat breeding in Lemnos island for both aspects of economy and environment. Especially using comparative analysis between sheep and goat breeding farms that are fully or part time employment, it was tried to be connected the financial results with the "friendliness" that these farms have with the environment mainly in account with the exerted grazing pressure by them.

RESEARCH AREA

Lemnos is a typical Greek island located nearly to the centre of the northern part of Aegean sea. It is the eighth Greek island according to its size, with total area about 477 km^2 and population about 17,288 people according to 2001 census.

Sheep and goats are the only animals breaded in the island for milk production, since very early. Sheep and goat breeding farms are characterized by the small number of animals per unit, the unimproved sheep and goat races that are very good adapted to the local environment, the low milk production per animal, the extensive management system of the farm, while the feeding of animals is mainly based on grazing (Anifantakis, 1994).

There were 1,150 sheep and goat breeding farms during 1997 in Lemnos islands while the total number of animals was 82,262 for the same year. It has been noticed a continuous decrease on farm's number, an increase of total milk yield and a decrease on total meat production since 1980 until today. Milk yield was 1,842,425 litres during the year 2004, while cheese production was about 500 tones for the same year.

Cheese is mainly produced by the four cheese factories of the island, while breeders produce small cheese quantities for their own consumption. The kinds of cheese produced in Lemnos are the smooth white cheese, called "Kalathaki" and the cheese called "pheta". Lemnos Kalathaki cheese is labelled as protected sign of origin, according to 2081/1992 EU rule. This cheese is so famous, that has not absorption problems, as a great quantity of its yield is consumed in most part of Greece, besides small quantities which are exported.

Today "Kalathaki" production represents about 99% of the total island's cheese production, instead of 80% before 1997, while demands are increasing and sale price in the market is also increasing.

MATERIALS AND METHODS

Sources of primary and secondary data and several collecting techniques were used during this study. The main volume of primary data was collected through the use of two questionnaires which were applied on the selected sample. These questionnaires had been completed through personal interviews. During May, plant material was collected from 50 sampling areas (1x1 meters each one) for biomass determination. Turf was collected from these areas, dried (60°C for 48h) and then weighed for the dry matter determination of plant material (Chapman, 1976).

The farm accounting data for this empirical application were collected though a cross sectional farm management survey carried out during 1997. The size of sample that was estimated by this distribution included a total of 75 sheep and goat breeders. The first questionnaire included personal and family data of the inquired person, employment, income as well as personal thinking about the employment and the environment. The second questionnaire included questions about the structure of the farms and the financial data from the previous breeding period.

The below analysis methods were used:

- The classical technical-economical analysis with the aim of complete economic description through the productivity of sheep and goat breeding. For the determination of the economical environment the accounting method and the correlation of economical results per two were used. Productivity analysis was completed using the Cobb-Douglas production function, which provides estimates of each production factor and also estimates the measure of marginal productivity.
- The descriptive statistics and the hypothesis testing using t-student for the comparison between quality traits.

– The determination of produced biomass in order to estimate the possible feeding shortage and the grazing pressure by the farms.

MARGINAL ANALYSIS

As was observed by the results, the mean number of animals per farm was 146 and the mean milk production was 90.57 kg, while the mean meat production was 12.58 kg per animal.

It was estimated that each animal (sheep or goat) needed about 0.26 acres of land for pasture while the demands for labour force were 19.77 h per animal per year. Monthly variation of labour indicates continuous employment. Correlation between size of farm and labour per animal showed that the needed labour was negative affected by the farm size. This relationship was too strong, as it was shown by the estimated equation and the correlation coefficients of correlation and determination ($Y = 59.86$, $b = -0.34$, $r^2 = 0.78$). On the contrary it was estimated that the correlation between labour and milk production per animal was not so strong.

It was also shown that there was a small participation of variable capital (6.94%) into the total invested capital and a great participation of fixed capital (93.06%). Feeds purchased represent about 81.30% of variable capital, while the worth of pastureland represents about 77.30% of the constant capital.

Factor analysis of production expenses revealed that sheep and goat breeding is an intensive production branch mainly for its demands for capital (47.60%) and labor (40.00%) as well as variable expenses (34.20%) and family labour (33.60%). Thus both of variable expenses and family labour have high participation to the total expenses (67.80%).

Correlation between the cost of milk production and farm size showed that this cost was highly affected by the size of farm ($Y= 4.67x10^6$, $X^{-0.204}$, $r=-0.64$, $r^2=0.41$).

Finally this employment has a mean gain of about 6.88 euro per animal that was clearly owed to direct payments. This is mainly due to high constant expenses in connection with the medium production.

The agricultural income was estimated to be about 64 Euro per animal. It was the most considerable financial result and was mainly depended on milk (39.20%) and meat (21.20%) production rather than the farm size (7.70%). Family agricultural income represents about 75% of agricultural income, while the remainder 25% of this income represents mainly use of unfamiliar human labour.

Product's price was also a fundamental factor that affected the height of the financial results. Milk price is determined every year by Lemnos Union of Agricultural cooperatives while meat price is determined immediately by the market. The productivity analysis was determined using the most elementary case, the Cobb-Douglas production function. Four independent variables were used for the estimation of this relation as follow:

$$Y = 2.79 x_1^{0.076} x_2^{0.967} x_3^{0.051} x_4^{-0.044} x_5^{-0.069}$$

Where,

Y=gross output,

X_1=cost (in euros),

X_2=variable capital (in euros),

X_3=purchased feeds (in euros),

X_4=rent of land and annual expenses of buildings (in euros) and

X_5= machinery (annual expenses in euros).

The coefficient of correlation (R = 0.990) between depended and independed variables is so high that the coefficient of multiple determination suggests that the major part of the interfarm variation in output is explained by the observed production factors. The sum of elasticities indicates that farms operate under constant returns to scale and the partial elasticities indicate that the factors, which affect the gross output are labour (7.6%), livestock capital (96.7%), feed (5.1%) while land and machines have a negative effect (4.4% and 7.0%, respectively).

Marginal productivity of livestock capital was high (0.0057) in comparison to the opportunity cost (0.00337) for the total of sheep and goat breeding, as it was indicated by the relationship between marginal productivity and opportunity cost (1.69). Marginal productivity of labour, feeds, land and machinery equipment does not generally cover their utility cost as it was indicated by the relationship between marginal productivity and opportunity cost, while indicates that there is need for these factors to be limited. Generally marginal analysis of sheep and goat breeding mainly indicates that the number of productive animals must be increased while the labour must be reduced and this reduction must be extended for all the other production factors.

ECONOMY AND SIZE OF THE FARMS

The sample of 75 sheep-goat farms that were investigated in this study were classified at five categories according to their size: very small (up to 50 animals), small (from 51 to100 animals), medium (from 101 to 200 animals), large (from 201 to 300 animals) and very large (over 300 animals). According to this classification a rate of 25.3% (19 farms) belongs to very small, 24% (18 farms) to small, 26.5% (20 farms) to medium, 10.6% (8 farms) to large and 13.3 % (10 farms) to very large farms, respectively.

The farmers of small and very small units use mainly private pasturelands (80% of total), while these with large and very large units rent pasturelands at percentage of 92.8% and 92.4% respectively. Sheep-goat farming becomes more extensive with the increase of farm's size as the needs for pastureland per animal increases from 0.106 to 0.39 acres from very small to very large farms respectively. Labour that is 34.84 h per animal for the very small farms decreases to 12.83 h per animal for the very large farms. This reduction of labour per animal with the increase of farm size is a result of scale economy and has nothing to do with the use of technology, for example machine milking.

The production expenses per animal and the production cost per kg milk and meat decreases as the size of farm increases (Table 1). As a result, the increase of farm size has a positive effect both to the cost of milk and meat production, because of the sharing of fixed cost to a great number of animals. Labour cost also decreases from 66.46€ to 27.60€ per animal as the size of farm increases from very small to very large farms. Variable cost are also decrease from 41.40€ to 30.01€ per animal for small and very large farm, respectively, while annual expenses of fixed cost and mainly the rent for pastureland increases significantly from 4.92€ to 18.07€ per animal, as the farm size increases from 33 to 407 animals. This reduction of variable cost in relation to the size of farm is owed to decreased value of purchased, while the increase of fixed cost is owed to the increase of pasturelands, because of the more extensive management system of large sheep-goat farms.

Significant reduction is also shown at annual expenses of fixed cost per year in relation to farm size (Table 1). This change indicates that except economies of scale that are developed at the large sheep-goat farms, which use mainly rent pasturelands, the owners of these farms rent also mainly old stables. This fact limits them to invest in buildings and equipment.

Very small to medium farms show damages from 33.29€ to 0,094€ per animal, while large and very large farms show gain from 15.41€ to 17.91€ per animal respectively. Profit, in relation to farm size is succeeded only in farms that have at least 201 animals. There is also an impressive increase of capital efficiency until the farm size of 300 animals, although capital efficiency is low in relation to loan rate of capital (15%).

Agricultural income increases from 50.26€ to 65.64€ per animal for very small and very large farms respectively, while family agricultural income decreases as the farm size increases, from 49.26€ to 40.81€, from very small to very large farms. Mean income levels are 9.333€ and 6,931.82€ per farm for agricultural and family agricultural income, respectively.

Mean yearly expenses for buying and good per family in whole Greece for the year of this research were 10,212.765€. This number indicates that family agriculturally income for very small to medium farms of the research sample was not enough for the mean family expenses so that these farms were not profitable. On the other hand large and very large farms were viable as it was shown by the family agricultural income in comparison to the mean yearly expenses of whole Greece.

SHEEP-GOAT FARMING AND ENVIRONMENT

A percentage of 42.7% of the breeders from the investigated sample had also another employment, while 57.3% were employed only in primary sector. This investigation showed that 78.1% of pluriactivated breeders were employed in tertiary sector, 15% in secondary sector, while 6.3% were employed in all these three sectors.

A total of 46 breeders (61.3% of sample) were satisfied with the income they had from this employment. On the contrary 29 breeders (38.7% of the sample) were not satisfied with this income. All breeders recognize the significant effect of subsides to their income. When they were questioned about their acts in the case were the subsides would stopped, only one breeder answered that he would continue his employment with the stock breeding.

Table 1
Comparative Technical-Economical Analysis Per Size Categories

Technical-economical data and economical results	*Size categories of farms*				
	Up to 50 animals	*51-100 animals*	*101-200 animals*	*201-300 animals*	*Over 301 animals*
I. Technical data					
1. Number of farms	19	18	20	8	10
2. Number of herd (mean)	33	77	143	249	407
3. Labour (h/animal)	34.84	27.89	23.22	18.58	12.83
II. Gross output					
1. Milk yield (kg/animal)	87.18	91.59	92.22	90.22	89.74
2. Milk price (Euro/kg)	0.69	0.69	0.69	0.69	0.69
3. Meat yield (kg/animal)	11.38	13.94	12.85	13.38	11.73
4. Meat price (Euro/kg)	1.78	1.78	1.78	1.78	1.78
5. Subsidy (Euro/animal)	21.52	21.52	21.52	21.52	21.52
Total (Euro/animal)	102.10	109.70	108.20	107.76	104.50
III. Production expenses					
1. Rent of land (Euro/animal)	4.92	6.64	11.11	8.69	18.07
2. Labour cost "	66.46	53.20	45.99	38.86	27.60
3. Purchased "	31.88	30.86	29.64	27.51	24.68
4. Medicine "	2.47	2.00	2.16	2.12	1.90
5. Fuel-oil "	2.92	1.85	1.39	0.93	0.74
6. Machinery repairs "	1.25	0.98	0.90	0.35	0.60
7. Interest of variable capital "	2.89	2.68	2.56	2.32	2.09
8. Annual expenses of livestock capital "	8.11	8.11	8.11	8.11	8.11
9. Annual expenses of fixed capital "	14.08	8.19	6.00	3.03	2.37
10. Taxes "	0.40	0.44	0.43	0.43	0.41
Total (Euro/animal)	135.39	114.97	108.29	92.35	86.58
IV. Profit or damage (Euro/animal)	-33.29	-5.27	-0.09	15.42	17.91
V. Milk production cost (Euro/animal)	1.22	0.92	0.87	0.75	0.71
Meat production cost (Euro/animal)	3.78	2.40	2.53	2.09	2.36
VI. Agriculture income (Euro/animal)	50.26	62.14	62.82	66.39	66.43
VII. Labour income (Euro/8h)	8.71	13.97	15.83	23.37	28.90
VIII. Capital profitability (%)	-4.24	2.43	3.58	7.52	6.22

On the contrary, 39 breeders (52%) answered that they would search for another employment complementally with their formal occupancy and revealed that they would maintained all or part of their farm. On the other hand, 35 breeders (46.7%) would completely change their employment. A percentage of 52% of the breeders hoped to an improvement of their income through the increase of animal's production, 42.7% through the increase of farm size, and 5.3% through the increase of product's prices.

All the breeders of the investigated sample produce the kind of cheese called "Kalathaki". A percentage of breeders (84% of the total sample) believed that they maintain the correct methods and conditions during the cheese production, but the others recognize that these conditions are not correct and that the final product has quality problems (very salty). A percentage of 48% of the breeders dispose the cheese immediately, 29.3% use it for their own consumption, while the rest of the breeders (22.7%) store the cheese in order to sell it later. It must also be noticed that a large amount of the produced cheese is given as a rent for the use of the pasturelands.

Sheep and goat breeding development creates environmental problems such as heavy grazing, which downgrades soils. Breeders believe that fire improves pastureland's grass, so they often burn the fields (especially in areas where the main plant is *sarcopoterium spinosum*).

As it is shown in the next table 32% of the questioned breeders believe that fires have a positive effect on the long-term improvement of pastureland's grass (Table 2).

Table 2
Level of Education of Breeders According to their Opinion about the Long-term Effect of Fire on Pastureland's Grass

	First level	*%*	*Second level*	*%*	*Third level*	*%*
- Positive effect	14	27.5	6	47.4	4	80.0
- Negative effect	37	72.5	13	52.6	1	20.0
Total	51	100.0	19	100.0	5	100.0
Results of hypothesis tested:		$x^2 = 5.78$	$\alpha = 0.05$			

It is interesting to notice the statistical difference among the different educational level of breeders in relation to their opinion for the long-term effect of fires at the pastureland's flora (x^2=5.78 and a=0.05). As illustrated in Table 2, positive opinion about the long-term effects of fire in the improvement of pastureland's grass have a percentage of 27.5% from the first educational level group, 47.4% from the second level and 80% from the third level group. On the other hand 72.5%, 52.6% and 20% of the breeders from the first, second and third educational level groups respectively, believe that fires does not improve pastureland's grass in long-term. It is clear that the breeders with high educational level have different opinion from those with lower educational level in relation to their opinion about the effect of fires on pastureland's grass. Although it is not easy to justify these different opinions, it would be reasonable to suggest that breeder's education has nothing to do with their employment or that they do not have yet the necessary expertise in the breeder's job and as they must be young breeders.

The quantity of feeds (forage and others), the dry matter of feed per animal and per class size of farm, and the percentage of these feed in relation to the covering of animal's annual feed requirements are illustrated in Table 3. This study estimate that the supplied feed covers about 31% of animal's annual feed requirements and that the produced biomass covers another 37% of these requirements. So the total amount of feed (supplied and forage) covers about

68% of the annual feed requirements. It is remarked a negative feed storage according to the maximum quantity of animal's annual feed requirements. Animals will try to cover this storage with grazing of plants, which are not so easy to consume (Georgakopoulou, 1996).

Table 3
Feeding Shortage According to the Farm Size

Size of farms	*Annual feed requirements (kg d.m. / animal)*		*Supplied feed (kg d.m. / animal)*		*Forage (kg d.m. / animal)*		*Supplied feed and forage (kg d.m. / animal)*	
		%		%		%		%
- up to 50	548	100,0	195	36,0	82	15,0	277	50,0
- 51 - 100	548	100,0	189	35,0	110	20,0	299	55,0
- 101 - 200	548	100,0	182	33,0	185	34,0	367	67,0
- 201 - 300	548	100,0	168	31,0	139	25,0	307	56,0
- over 301	548	100,0	151	27,0	301	55,0	452	83,0
Mean	548	100,0	169	31,0	201	37,0	370	68,0

It can be observed that farms cover their animal's feed requirements at a percentage of 50-55 for smaller, 67% for medium, 56% for large and 83% for very large farms respectively. Feeding storage in dry matter is negative for all sizes and varies from 96 to 271 kg dry matter per animal for very small up to very large farms respectively.

It is notable that very small and small farms, as well as big farms exert the higher grazing pressure at the ecosystem of the island, because of the small areas of pasturelands per animal. Medium farms exert lower grazing pressure in comparison to the other mentioned farm, because of the larger pastureland areas, while very large farms (up to 301 animals) exert the lowest grazing pressure.

CONCLUSIONS

The sheep goat farming to the Greek islands and especially to the island of Lemnos, has a mean profit that was clearly owed to direct payments. Without these direct payments this activity has considerable damage and so, sheep goat farming completely depends on direct payments. This possibility, sheep goat farmers are intended to face, in case this happens, where they will abandon sheep goat farming, or keep this as a secondary job.

More specifically, the small up to intermediate sheep goat farmhouses, in contrary to larger in size, present damage, while the agricultural familial income of the small and intermediate farmhouses does not cover the medium necessary expenses, so that, these farmhouses are judged not viable. The members of these families, obviously turn themselves also to other activities for the satisfaction of their needs. On the contrast, the agricultural familial income of large and very large farmhouses, places these exploitations in viable conditions.

The small non profitable farms, because of their small size, are mainly connected with the breeders who are pluriactivated, as they need a second employment to have a complementally income. The mainly employed with the animal farms, are the owners of very large farms which can be characterized as more friendly to the island's environment and the degradation of the island's ecosystems.

Finally, this study estimates that smaller farms, which are the major kind of farming in the island of Lemnos, downgrade even more the already downgraded environment. This is because these farms try to keep or to increase their productivity. These farms are supposed to be partly responsible for the temporal and territorial evolution of vegetation.

References

Anifantakis, E. (1994), Rule 2081/92, Lemnos Kalathaki, Protected Sign of Origin, Agricultural University of Athens, Athens (in Greek).

Basin, G. (1986), *Quelles Perspectives pour Les Agricultures Montagnardes?*, INRA, Grignon.

Chapman, S.B. (1976), Production Ecology and Nutrient Bugets, pp. 157–228. In S.B. Chapman (edt.) *Methods in plant ecology*, Blackwell Sci. Publ., Oxford.

Chatzitheodoridis, F.C. (2004), The Relationship between Pluriactivity and Tourism Development Model in an Island of Aegean Sea: Structural Factors of Local Employment and Integrated Development, *Social Science Tribune*, 40(1): 129-148 (in Greek).

Georgakopoulou A. (1996), Management Practices of Sheep-Goat farming of Lemnos island, Aegean University, Mitilini (in Greek).

Ilbery, B. and Kneafsey, M. (1999), Niche Markets for Regional Speciality Food Products in Europe. *Environment and Planning*, 31(1): 2207-2222.

Ilbery, B. and Kneafsey, M. (2000), Producer Constructions of Quality in Regional Speciality Food Production. *Journal of Rural Studies*, 16: 217-230.

Lamprianidis, L. (2003), Local Products as a Means to Facilitate the Development of Less Favored Areas of the European countryside, *Áeihoros*, 2(1): 6-35 (in Greek).

Parrott, N., Wilson, N. and Mundoch, J. (2002), Spatialising Quality: Regional Production and the Alternative Geography of Food. *European Urban and Regional Studies*, 9(3): 241-261.

Tomaseli, R. (1977), Degradation of the Mediterranean Forests and Maquis: Ecology, Conservation and Management, UNESCO.

WERE CURRENCIES DELIBERATELY UNDERVALUED TO PROMOTE EXPORTS? AN EMPIRICAL EXAMINATION OF SELECTED ASEAN COUNTRIES (1965-1998)

Saadiah Mohamad
Universiti Teknologi MARA, Malaysia

Mahendhiran Nair
Monash University Malaysia

There has been a debate in the literature that several South-East Asian economies have deliberately undervalued their currencies in order to enhance export competitiveness prior to the 1997 Asian Financial Crisis. This paper evaluates this hypothesis using the unrestricted error correction model (Pesaran et al. 2001) to measure the misalignment between the real exchange rate (RER) and the equilibrium real exchange rate (ERER). The study was conducted for the following Association of South-East Asian Nation (ASEAN) economies: Indonesia, Malaysia, Singapore and Thailand, for the period 1965-1998. The empirical evidence suggests that only Thailand experienced sustained under-valuations not supported by economic fundamentals. The evidence also suggests that Indonesia and Thailand experienced more severe exchange rate misalignment compared to Malaysia and Singapore over the sample period. The sustained episodes and the high degree of exchange rate misalignment in Indonesia and Thailand explain why these two economies were the most severely impacted by the 1997 Asian Financial Crisis.

Keywords: *real exchange rate, exchange rate misalignment, unrestricted error correction, and bounds test.*

JEL Classification: *F21, F31, F37 and C22*

INTRODUCTION

Exchange rate movements can have significant effects on trade. Nominal exchange rate depreciations or devaluations will result in cheaper exports and more expensive imports. These are expected to boost export performance through increased price competitiveness. Hence, devaluations can be used as a policy to improve international competitiveness and encourage growth. However, the increased price in imports as a result of currency devaluations may lead to higher inflation levels. Since relative inflation rates influence the net impact of

---

Corresponding Author: *saadiah228@salam.uitm.edu.my; mahendhiran.nair@buseco.monash.edu.my*

exchange rate changes on competitiveness, a more useful measure of exchange rates would be *real exchange rates* (RER).

Exchange rate policy plays an important role in providing increased incentives for exporting. Most countries that have successfully promoted manufactured exports experienced real exchange rate (RER) depreciation, leading to a significant increase in the domestic relative price of tradables to non-tradables (Sekkat and Varoudakis 1999). Large RER depreciations in many countries in Asia have prompted debates that exchange rate has been used as a policy instrument in Asia to manage export competitiveness, resulting in rising unemployment in developed countries (Montiel 1997, and Benaroya and Janci 1999).

It is true that both the nominal exchange rates (NER) and the real exchange rates (RER) have shown depreciating trends in most of these ASEAN countries (refer to Figure 1). However, there is some uncertainty whether these trends were due to a deliberate exchange rate policy or simply that the observed exchange rates (both NER and RER) were tracking the equilibrium rates (ERER) which itself could exhibit a depreciating trend.

Figure 1: Real (RER) and Nominal (NER) Exchange Rates (1990 was with base 100)

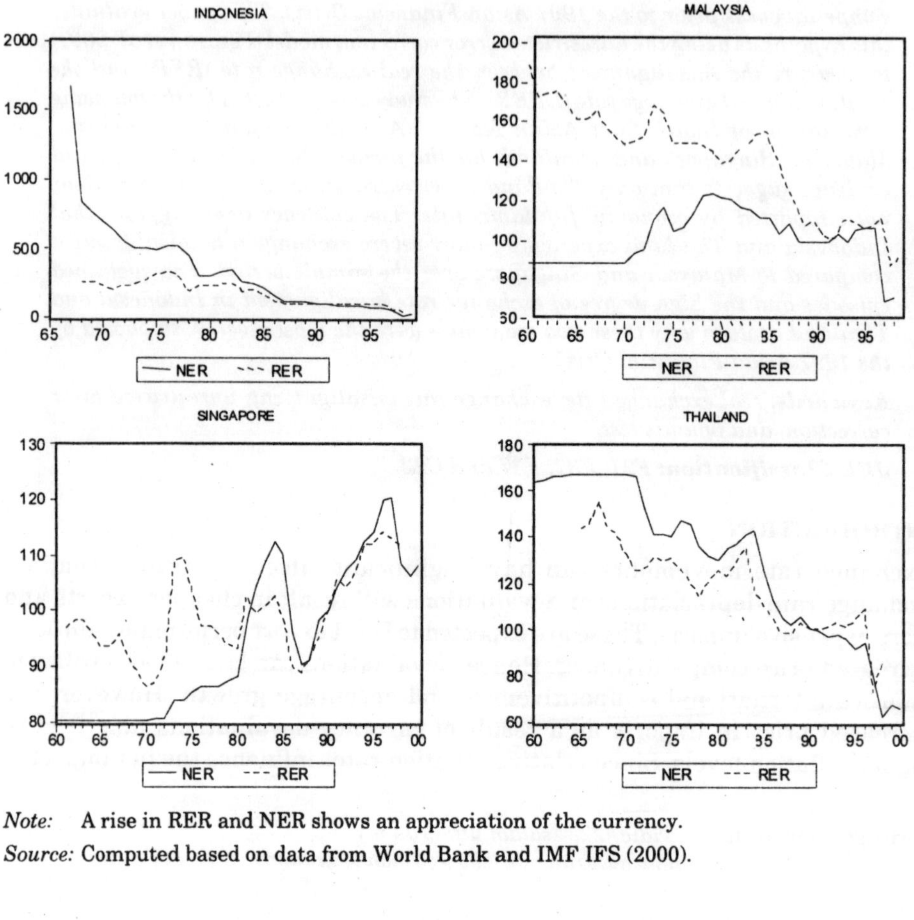

Note: A rise in RER and NER shows an appreciation of the currency.

Source: Computed based on data from World Bank and IMF IFS (2000).

The objective of this paper is to develop an empirical model to estimate the path of the ERER for the selected ASEAN economies. This will allow the measurement of the levels of misalignment between the actual RER and the ERER. Once the levels of misalignment are determined, episodes of currency undervaluation or overvaluation can then be identified. This will provide evidence if there has been a deliberate policy to keep the currencies in these countries undervalued over the period 1965-1998.

This paper is organised in the following way. In the next section the theoretical framework and econometric method are discussed. In the following sections of the paper the empirical analysis and concluding remarks are given.

THE THEORY AND EMPIRICAL METHODOLOGY

In this section, a brief description of the theoretical framework and the econometric model that captures the dynamics of the ERER for the selected ASEAN economies are given. The RER is defined as the relative price of non-tradables (P_n) to tradables (P_T) (Edwards 1989):

$$RER = \frac{P_n}{P_T} \tag{1}$$

The RER can also be written as follows:

$$RER = \frac{P_n}{P_T} = E\frac{P_n}{P_T^*}, \tag{2}$$

where, P_T is the domestic price of tradables, P_n is the domestic price of non-tradables, P_T^* is the world price of tradables and E is the nominal exchange rate defined as the price of domestic currency in terms of foreign currency (foreign currencies per unit of domestic currency).

The equilibrium real exchange (ERER) rate is defined here as (Baffes et al 1999):

$$\log q_t^* = \beta' F_t, \tag{3}$$

where, q_t^* is the ERER and F_t is the vector for the fundamental variables at period t. The vector b is the parameter of interest. The empirical analysis in this study is further motivated by the theoretical models of Edwards (1989) and Elbadawi and Soto (1997), where the RER is written as:

$$\log q_t = f\left(F_t,\ NFI_t,\ DRNK_t,\ MACRO_t,\ CNER_t\right) \tag{4}$$

The variables are defined as follows:

q Real exchange rate RER (defined as the ratio of the price of non-tradables to tradables, where an increase in the value of RER means an appreciation).

F Vector of four trade balance fundamentals:

- TOT - Terms of trade
- GCON - Government consumption as a ratio of GDP
- OPEN - Trade openness defined as total exports plus imports as a ratio of GDP
- PROD - Productivity proxied by productivity differential between manufacturing and services industries.

NFI Ratio of net income from abroad to GDP

DRNK The difference between the change in RES and *NKI* (i.e., *DRNK* = $\Delta RES - NKI$), where, *DRES*-The ratio of change in reserves to GDP

NKI Ratio of net foreign capital inflows to GDP

CNER Rate of change in nominal exchange rate where exchange rate is defined in terms of foreign currency (USD) per unit of domestic currency.

MACRO Indicator of monetary policy measured as a ratio of change in domestic credit and lagged broad money supply.

The equation also includes the following short run determinants of the RER: changes in nominal exchange rates (CNER) and a measure of monetary policy (MACRO). The short run impact of changes in nominal exchange rate is expected to be positive. That is, devaluation in a currency would lead to RER depreciation, while a monetary expansion is expected to lead to a real currency appreciation. According to Edwards (1989) these two variables (nominal variables) have no long run impacts and that only the fundamental variables (the real variables) affect the RER in the long run.

The inclusion of capital account variables in the model, in addition to the usual trade balance fundamentals permits interesting interpretations of the effects of capital account stock determinants on the RER in the long run. When a country achieves a higher sustainable level of net foreign income in the very long run, this will lead to a more appreciated ERER. However, in the medium to long run, when the stock of net foreign assets is less than the desired level, the country has to depreciate its real currency value (i.e. run a current account surplus which is the counterpart of accumulating reserves) to allow building of assets to desired levels.

In order to estimate equation (4), a test of stationarity of the fundamental variables is carried out using the Phillip- Perron (1988) unit root test. The unit root tests indicated that most of the variables used in this study were non-stationary (integrated of order 1, denoted as $I(1)$). Thus, the model in (4) was estimated using the Unrestricted Error Correction Model (UECM) model proposed in Pesaran *et al.* (2001). The bounds test for cointegration derived from the UECM was used to test if the variables are co-moving. Pesaran et al.'s UECM model and the bounds test have two important advantages over the traditional error-correction models and cointegration tests (Engle and Granger (1987), Johansen (1988) and Johansen and Juselius (1990)). First, in the UECM model, the order of integration of the explanatory variables can be a mixture of $I(0)$ or $I(1)$. Second, the bounds test for cointegration was found to be reliable for small samples.

Next, the UECM framework used for modelling the ERER is outlined. The dependent variable is the RER ($\log q_t$) and the matrix x_t denotes the vector of all the independent variables. The UECM characterization of the RER is given by the following specification:

$$\Delta \log q_t = \alpha_0 + \varphi \log q_{t-1} + \psi x_{t-1} + \sum_{j=1}^{p-1} \beta_{yj} \Delta \log q_{t-j} + \sum_{j=1}^{q-1} \beta_{xj} \Delta x_{t-j} + w\Delta x_t + u_t \qquad (5)$$

where φ and ψ captures the long-run effects, while the βs capture the short-run effects of the determinants on RER. The UECM model in (5) can be estimated using the OLS method.

The bounds test was used to test the long-run relationship between RER and its determinants. The bounds test is equivalent to conducting a restricted F-test (or Wald test), where the null and alternative hypotheses are as follows:

$H_0 : \varphi = \psi = 0$ (no long-run relationship between $\log q_t$ and x_t)

$H_1 : \varphi \neq y \neq 0$ (there is long-run relationship between $\log q_t$ and x_t)

The asymptotic distribution of the test statistics of the bounds test is non-standard under the null hypothesis.

The bounds test is conducted as follows: if the computed F-statistic falls outside the critical value bounds, a conclusive inference can be drawn without needing to know the order of integration of regressors. For example, if the F-statistics is higher than the upper critical bound (UCB), then the null hypothesis of no cointegration is rejected. If the F-statistics is smaller than the lower critical bound (LCB), then the null hypothesis of no cointegration is not rejected. However, if the computed F-statistic falls between the LCB and UCB, the inference is inconclusive, and knowledge of the order of integration is required before conclusive inference can be made.

The rejection of the no cointegration relationship implies that there exists a stable long-run relationship between $\log q_t$ and x_t which can be described as follows:

$$\log q_t = \theta_0 + \theta_1 x_t + v_t \qquad (6)$$

where $\theta_0 = -\frac{\alpha_0}{\varphi}$, $\theta_1 = -\frac{\psi}{\varphi}$ and v_t is a mean zero stationary process. Note that θ_1 is the long run multiplier. The estimated model in (6), that is $\log \hat{q}_t$ is the estimated ERER.

The test and estimation procedure for the UECM model was conducted using the MICROFIT 4.0. Due to the limited number of sample observations and the loss of degrees of freedom, we used a maximum lag order of one. For all the countries, all the potential variables of LTOT, LPROD, LOPEN, LGCON, DRNK, NFI, CNER, MACRO and LRER(-1) are tested for long run relationship.

The long run coefficients obtained can then be used to generate the long-term path of RER. This long-term path of RER represents the ERER that is defined as the RER that is consistent with the internal and the external balance. Once the path for the ERER is generated, the values are then compared with the actual RER. The difference between actual RER and the estimated ERER is the misalignment in the exchange rates. The misalignment in exchange rate was expressed as a percentage.

Due to data constraints on the price of the tradables and non-tradables, many studies have used the relative price indices between the two countries for the calculation of the RER. The data for the RER in this paper was obtained from the World Bank. The RER is a trade-weighted index of foreign wholesale prices (WPI) to home country's price index (CPI), converted at relevant bilateral official exchange rates. The World Bank database defined RER as the price of tradables to non-tradables (Pt/Pn) and makes use of the ratio of wholesale price index of foreign country to consumer price index of domestic country. To suit the way RER was defined in our model, the data from the World Bank database was inversed. The rest of the data were computed from the following data sources: *World Bank World Development Indicator (2000)* and *IMF International Financial Statistics (2000)*. Table 1 gives the expected signs for the parameters used in the model.

The countries chosen for this study were Indonesia, Malaysia, Singapore and Thailand. These ASEAN economies have experienced similar development trajectories for the past three decades. The economic developments of these economies were built upon dramatic expansion in exports, particularly manufacturing (World Bank 1993). The sample period (1965-1998) was chosen to incorporate the earliest common data available as well as a deliberate intention to focus on pre-1997 Asian Financial Crisis exchange rate policies. This is to examine if exchange rate policies in these countries were important factor for triggering the 1997 Asian Financial Crisis.

THE EMPIRICAL ANALYSIS

Based on the Bounds test in Table 2, the computed F-statistics exceeds the UCB for Malaysia and Indonesia with the 8 regressors at the 5% significance level. This implies that there exists a long run relationship between the RER and the 8 regressors in these economies. In the case of Thailand, the rejection of the null hypothesis of no cointegration can be established if LPROD and LOPEN were dropped from the model. This implies that RER and LGCON, LTOT, NFI and DRNK are co-moving at the 5% significance level. For Singapore, cointegration relationship can be established if TOT is excluded from the model, implying that the RER in Singapore is cointegrated with all the predictor variables with the exception of TOT.

Table 3 gives the final specification for the most parsimonious models for the estimated ERER for each of the countries. All the estimated models pass the following diagnostic tests: serial correlation test of the residuals (Lagrange multiplier test), heteroskedasticity test of the residuals (White's test), normality test of the residuals (Jarque-Bera test) and model specification test (Ramsey's RESET test for functional form).

Table 1
Expected Signs of Parameters

Variables	*Expected signs*
Terms of Trade (LTOT)	+ve/-ve but mainly positive
Government Consumption (LGCON)	+ve/-ve but mainly positive
Productivity (LPROD)	Positive
Openness (LOPEN)	-ve
Change in Reserves (DRES)	-ve
Net Capital Inflow (NKI)	+ve
Change in Reserves minus Net Capital inflow (DRNK)	-ve
CNER	+ve
MACRO	+ve

Table 2
Cointegration Test–The Bounds Test

Country	*Computed F-Statistics*	*Lower Critical Bound (LCB)*	*Upper Critical Bound (UCB)*
Indonesia (8 regressors)	12.072	2.272	3.447
Malaysia(8 regressors)	5.872	2.272	3.447
Singapore(7 regressors)	4.544	2.365	3.553
Thailand(6 regressors)	3.537	2.141	3.250

Note: The 5% critical values were taken from Pesaran and Pesaran (1997: 478) Table F Case II: Intercept and No Trend.

Table 3
Long Run Parameter Estimates for Selected ASEAN Countries

	Indonesia	*Malaysia*	*Singapore*	*Thailand*
Constant	1.4878**	4.8838***	6.1342***	3.2528***
	(2.16)	(6.5)	(7.82)	(2.55)
Log(TOT)	0.5793***	0.4035**		0.2098
	(3.08)	(2.4)		(1.01)
Log(GCON)	-0.3309		-0.0859	0.2845*
	(-0.93)		(-0.44)	(1.83)
Log(PROD)	-1.6739***	-0.2385***	0.2776**	
	(-8.01)	(-5.22)	(2.02)	
Log(OPEN)		-0.4669***	-0.1914**	
		(-8.58)	(-2.22)	
NFI			0.0223*	0.0812*
			(2.78)	(1.73)
DRNK	0.0031	-0.0125***	0.0060**	0.0047
	(0.3)	(-5.29)	(2.11)	0.76)
Adjusted R^2	0.94	0.97	0.88	0.87

Notes: The numbers in parentheses are t-ratios. The dependent variable is log (RER). *,**,*** denote 10%, 5% and 1% levels of significance.

The long run coefficients of the model were obtained from the final specification and these values were used to derive the ERER. Instead of using the actual values of the fundamentals to derive the ERER, the five years moving averages of the fundamentals were used. The misalignment indices (denoted as RERMIS) are then computed as the difference between actual RER and ERER as a percentage of the ERER. Figure 2 shows the trends in the computed RER, ERER and RERMIS. Table 4 shows the magnitude of the RERMIS in percentages.

The actual RER movement in Malaysia, Indonesia and Thailand follow a depreciating trend with implications of increasing international competitiveness. In the case of Singapore, the depreciating trend seems to have haltered by the middle of the 1980s. From the middle of 1980s onwards, the Singaporean RER has been on an appreciating trend.

Figure 2: Actual RER, Estimated ERER and RER Misalignment

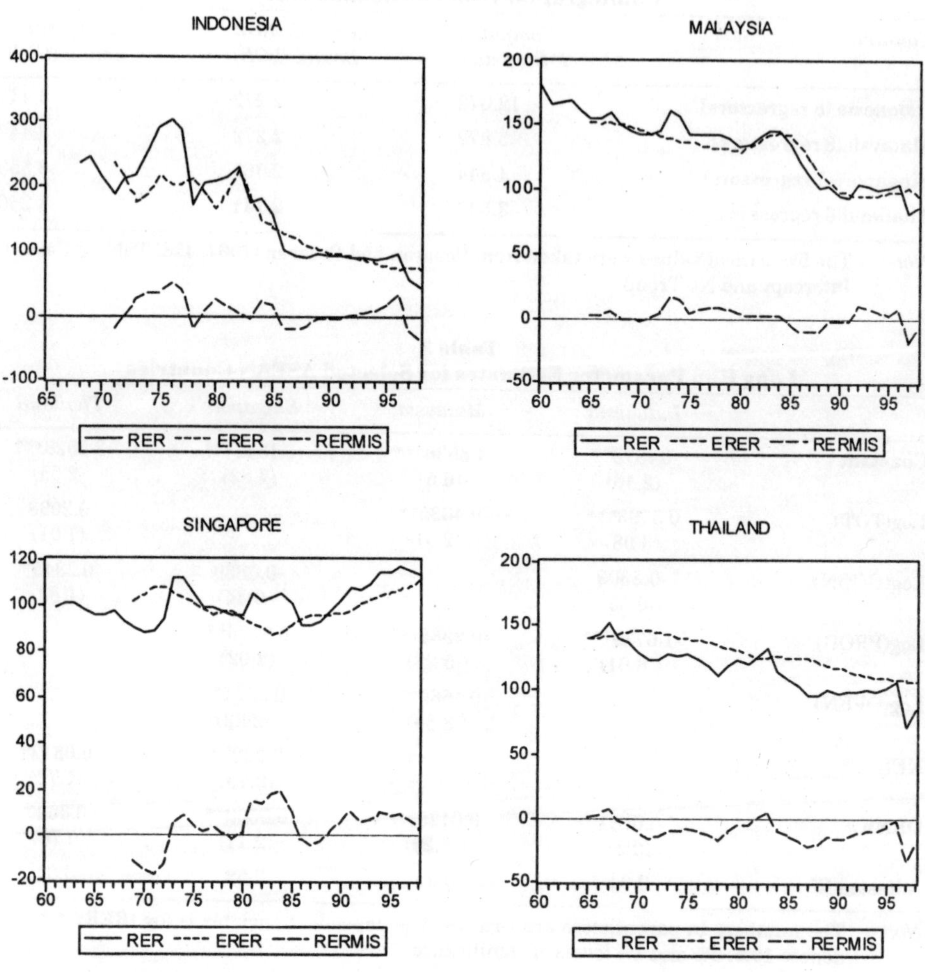

Table 4
Real Exchange Rate Misalignment -RERMIS (%)

Year	*Indonesia*	*Malaysia*	*Singapore*	*Thailand*
1965	NA	2.147046	NA	0.405256
1966	NA	2.343870	NA	1.798811
1967	NA	4.972974	NA	7.642010
1968	NA	-0.136898	NA	-1.776395
1969	NA	-1.549527	-10.88203	-5.254745
1970	NA	-2.319910	-15.28358	-11.22335
1971	-21.53582	0.053358	-17.14647	-15.99667
1972	-0.547301	3.727691	-12.81491	-14.49130
1973	24.95504	15.93871	5.671279	-10.65420
1974	34.17947	14.64851	8.667111	-9.879951
1975	34.94665	3.838899	4.366507	-8.273732
1976	50.65458	6.830400	1.324499	-11.05992
1977	42.20903	7.731433	3.176550	-13.69947
1978	-19.44209	8.031147	0.636884	-17.18833
1979	7.986588	6.163275	-1.431418	-10.58638
1980	26.55677	3.086971	1.003995	-6.035975
1981	12.73987	1.809769	14.30539	-5.368431
1982	2.793704	2.092504	13.28281	1.026726
1983	-4.329741	1.806043	18.11179	5.174594
1984	21.54012	1.690776	18.75385	-10.16262
1985	16.41818	-5.553879	9.994462	-13.56042
1986	-19.34585	-9.788509	-2.168913	-17.60646
1987	-20.14198	-9.828113	-4.479454	-22.79771
1988	-15.68812	-9.491248	-2.289793	-20.52117
1989	-5.189561	-2.588970	1.355632	-15.07106
1990	-5.509866	-2.944078	6.082490	-16.44545
1991	-4.383689	-2.355839	10.19832	-14.72368
1992	0.305713	9.332905	5.921156	-12.15686
1993	4.978946	8.349233	6.438103	-9.164215
1994	8.427084	4.846081	9.792729	-9.966416
1995	16.91082	2.599268	8.493253	-6.289692
1996	34.52227	7.150944	8.980943	-1.566320
1997	-23.20986	-19.45138	6.760194	-33.46977
1998	-39.51221	-9.249701	2.630080	-20.33061

The empirical results of this study support more recent research work that indicates that the equilibrium exchange rate is not a time invariant variable. The computed ERER using the framework in this study showed that the equilibrium itself changes overtime. Indonesia, Malaysia and Thailand's ERER generally exhibit a depreciating trend throughout the sample period. On the other hand, Singapore's ERER exhibits an appreciating trend since 1984.

The countries differ in terms of the magnitude of the real exchange rate misalignment (RERMIS). The RERMIS for the selected countries are given in Figure 2 and Table 4. The Indonesian Rupiah seems to be very volatile–experiencing double-digit RERMIS for most of the sample period. The Malaysian Ringgit experienced two episodes of double-digit RERMIS. They were in 1973-1974 (appreciation of the Ringgit) and during the 1997 Asian Financial Crisis (depreciation of the Ringgit). The Singapore Dollar also experienced two periods of double-digit RERMIS. The first episode was during the early years (1969-1972) after independence from Malaysia and the second episode was from 1981 to 1984. Note also that even though the actual NER and RER of Singapore dollar was on an upward trend since 1989, the positive misalignment (overvaluation) had started much earlier i.e. since 1973. The Thai Bhat seems to have experienced double-digit negative RERMIS for most of the sample period, implying that the Thai Bhat has been persistently undervalued from 1968 onwards (with the exceptions in 1982 and 1983).

The empirical analysis shows that prior to the 1997 Asian Financial Crisis, the Indonesian Rupiah, Malaysian Ringgit and Singapore Dollar were overvalued. On the other hand, the Thai Bhat was undervalued. The persistent exchange rate misalignment in Thailand seems to suggest a deliberate policy to keep the exchange rate undervalued not justified by economic fundamentals. The persistent exchange rate misalignment might have been an important contributory factor for the underlying instabilities in the Thai economy leading up to the 1997 Asian Financial Crisis. Thus, it was not surprising that Thailand was the first country in the region to be engulfed by the 1997 Asian Financial Crisis.

Further, the empirical findings also suggest that countries with higher levels of RERMIS such as Indonesia and Thailand seem to exhibit longer years of misalignment. These two countries also suffered more severe economic downturn during the 1997 Asian Financial Crisis.

CONCLUSIONS

This paper examined the hypothesis that selected ASEAN countries have kept their currencies undervalued during the period 1965-1998 to enhance export competitiveness. Using the UECM framework, the ERER was estimated and the misalignment between the actual RER and the ERER were measured. From the empirical analysis, three key findings can be inferred. First, Malaysia, Indonesia and Thailand experienced a downward trend in the RER. The depreciation of the RER is a result of the RER tracking the ERER in these countries.

Second, of the four ASEAN countries, Thailand seems to be the only country that had its currency persistently undervalued over the sample period. The serious undervaluation of the Thai Bhat may suggest the possibility of a deliberate exchange rate policy not supported by economic fundamentals of the country.

Third, countries with higher levels of RERMIS such as Indonesia and Thailand were more severely affected by the 1997 Asian Financial Crisis.

Fourth, unlike other ASEAN economies, Singapore showed an upward trend (appreciation in the currency) in both the actual RER and estimated ERER from the middle of 1980's. The appreciating currency with a mild positive misalignment has helped Singapore to become the most technology- and knowledge-intensive country in the ASEAN region.

In summary, the empirical evidence seems to suggest that there was no deliberate policy to keep the exchange rate undervalued in Indonesia, Malaysia and Singapore prior to the 1997 Financial Crisis. On the other hand, there is sufficient empirical evidence to suggest that there was a deliberate policy in Thailand to keep the currency undervalued from 1965 to 1997.

References

Benaroya, F. and Janci, D. (1999), Measuring Exchange Rate Misalignments with Purchasing Power Parity Estimates. In Collignon, S. & Pisani-Ferri, J. (eds) *Exchange Rate Policies in Asian Emerging Countries*. Routledge Press, London.

Baffes, J., Elbadawi, I., and O' Connell, S. (1999), Single-equation Estimation of the Equilibrium Real Exchange Rate, in Hinkle, L. and Montiel, P., *Exchange Rate Misalignment*, Oxford University Press, 405-464.

Edwards, S. (1989), *Real Exchange Rates, Devaluation, and Adjustment*. Cambridge, Mass.: MIT Press.

Elbadawi, I. and Soto, R. (1997), Capital Flows and Long Term Equilibrium Real Exchange Rate in Chile, *Revista de Analisis Economico,* 12 (1), 251-276.

Engle, R.F. and Granger, C.W.J. (1987), Cointegrating and Error Correction: Representation, Estimation and Testing. *Econometrica*, 55, pp. 251-276.

International Monetary Fund (IMF) (2000), International Financial Statistics (IFS). (CD-ROM).

Johansen, S. (1988), Statistical Analysis of Cointegration Vectors. *Journal of Economic Dynamics and Control*, 12, pp. 231-254.

Johansen, S. & Juselius, K. (1990), Maximum Likelihood Estimation and Inference on Cointegration with Applications to the Demand of Money. *Oxford Buletin of Economics and Statistics*, 52, pp. 169-210.

Montiel, P.J. (1997), Exchange Rate Policy and Macroeconomic Management in ASEAN Countries. In Hicklin. J.; Robinson D. and Singh, A. (eds) *Macroeconomic Issues Facing ASEAN Countries.* Washington: International Monetary Fund.

Phillips, P.C., & Perron, P. (1988), Testing for a Unit–root in Time Series Regression. *Biometrika*, 75: 335-346.

Pesaran, H. and Pesaran B. (1997), *Working with Microfit 4.0: Interactive Econometric Analysis*, Oxford University Press.

Pesaran, H., Shin,Y., and Smith R.J. (2001), Bounds Testing Approaches to the Analysis of Level Relationships. *Journal of Applied Econometrics*, 16, pp. 289-326.

Sekkat, K. & Varoudakis, A. (2000), Exchange Rate Management and Manufactured Export in Sub-Saharan Africa. *Journal of Development Economics* 61: 237-253.

World Bank (1993), The East Asian Miracle. Washington DC: Oxford University Press.

World Bank (2000), World Development Indicator (WDI). (CD-ROM).

SHARING THE BURDEN OF ADJUSTMENT:
What are the Institutional Factors Critical to Emerging Economies?

Hillar Neumann
Department of Economics, Northern State University South Dakota

John Meyer
Department of Accounting and Law, Northern State University South Dakota

This article uses regressions following the Koyck distributed lag model to estimate burden of adjustment coefficients which reflect the pace of desirable institutional and economic progress in terms of economic freedoms and opportunities as measured by the Heritage Foundation Index of Economic Freedom and the Transparency International Corruption Perceptions Index. Using the United States as a benchmark, current account balance, GDP growth, inflation and exchange rate economic coefficients are tabulated to facilitate pace of adjustment comparisons among 34 trading nations. In general, less corruption suggests faster adjustment progress, greater flexibility, and therefore less adjustment burden relative to the U.S. Economic freedoms do not consistently suggest faster adjustment, greater flexibility and less adjustment burden relative to the U.S. Labor market freedom shows very high significance in relation to GDP growth; however, labor market freedom shows negatively to current account balances in these respects.

INTRODUCTION

Paradoxically, the world's richest nation has become the world's largest debtor nation and continues to borrow at historically advantageous rates as U.S. consumption and economic power serve as the predominant purchasing engine driving globalized trade. Moreover, in 2006 foreigners invested approximately \$500 billion more in the U.S. than U.S. investments offshore. In 2005, the increase of foreign investments in the U.S. totaled \$1.4 trillion, more than the GDP of all except the seven largest industrialized nations. According to the latest Economic Report of the President of the United States net foreign direct investment in the U.S. caused 19% of U.S. exports, 10% of physical capital expenditures, and 13% of R&D spending. Presumably, improved investment flows could produce similar desirable results among less developed and emerging economies. This paper measures rebalancing needs among global trading

Corresponding Author: *hnj@northern.edu; meyerj@northern.edu* nations; e.g., whether they are competing effectively for global investment funds in terms of economic freedoms and labor market freedoms; and it illustrates that domestic progress should reflect these needs and their domestic flexibility to bear the burdens of adjustment.

It is obvious that reducing global investment imbalances is complicated by the fixed exchange rate systems of Southeast Asia and the flexibility of the U.S. dollar and the euro. It is also clear that U.S. deficit spending must be slowed. So too must the transition of China and Japan's emergence from the deflationary period of the 1990's be taken into account. The controversy engendered by these factors has resulted in a polarized debate about the causes and consequences of global trade and financial imbalances. One side blames the U.S., citing huge consumption, deficit spending, and a paucity of U.S. savings (Mann, 2000) (Orzag, Rubin & Sinai, 2005). The other side blames mercantilist policies in Southeast Asia and praises the accessible markets and investment friendly environment in the U.S. (Griswold, 2001) (Levey & Brown, 2005). The fact is that foreign capital account surpluses predominantly flow into the U.S. offsetting unprecedented U.S. current account deficits. Eventually, these imbalances need to be adjusted for a multiplicity of well known reasons (but see Krishnan & Sukar, 2006).

The U.S. current account deficit has persisted and deepened since the mid 1980's. Recently it has peaked at over 7% of U.S. GDP. Emerging market economies in Southeast Asia, China, and Japan are the major beneficiaries of U.S. import demand. Mann (2005) has called for a disaggregated approach to U.S. trade deficit analysis. Benassy-Quere, Duran-Vigneron, Lahreche-Revil and Mignon (2004) and Bergsten (2004) have noted that the diversification of U.S. current account deficit financing out of industrial countries towards emerging ones makes the G-20 an appropriate set for burden sharing and exchange rate realignments. We extend the G-20 approach to include 14 additional trading economies.

In previous work we have estimated that 85% of the U.S. current account deficit is a structural component unlikely to respond to U.S. monetary policy and 15% is transitory and thus susceptible to monetary policy influence (Meyer, Neumann & Wegleitner, 2006). We thus address herein that other side (85%) of the imbalance which is allegedly facilitated by East Asian central bank currency related trade strategies but also due to fundamental comparative advantage economic forces. The thrust of our emphasis on the institutional factors, therefore, is not to ignore the fundamental competitiveness issues but rather to shed some light on the fairness of adjustment sacrifice among emerging trading and the G-20 groupings in terms of the impact of institutional factors and thus ultimately having an investment impact upon their quality of life and longer term economic progress.

The estimations herein will follow the Koyck approach to distributed lag models. Not only do trade flows lag exchange rate adjustments by up to two years, but the institutional factors we want to emphasize as independent variables are obviously tied to longer term effects. As more fully explained in the empirical section, we will first estimate various economic adjustment coefficients, using data from the World Bank Development Indicators, and secondly relate these changes to institutional factors drawn from the Heritage Foundation Index of Economic Freedom and the Transparency International Corruption Perceptions Index. The policy implications of our results will suggest which among these countries should move faster, not only to effectuate a smooth multilateral adjustment process, but generally what institutional changes are also suggested to improve their investment competitiveness and relieve the pressures for resort to manipulated exchange rate adjustments.

BACKGROUND

The press informs us that approximately 85% of all global savings invested outside the country of origin ($47,612 billions) is in one way or another invested in the U.S. About 60% of this amount ($28,724 billions) comes from Japan, emerging Asia, Hong Kong, and Singapore, (Wall Street Journal, January 10, 2007). These amounts include an estimated $820 billion-plus global capital account surplus in dollars or dollar denominated securities held by foreign central banks (Roubini & Setser, 2005). The central bank reserve holdings of U.S. treasury securities and other dollar-denominated portions of global savings have already received considerable attention in the literature (see bibliography). The concern herein is about who can best bear the burdens of adjustment; the U.S. can't expect foreign central bankers to risk their domestic well-being to help resolve the so-called "global co-dependency" problem. We shall summarize below some of the main themes and challenges bearing upon these issues.

Global savings glut/U.S. private savings decline: This controversial issue is like the proverbial question about whether the chicken or the egg came first. Bernanke (2005) attributes the funding of U.S. current account deficits to the post-Asian crisis availability of savings there and elsewhere. He argues that foreign "savings glut conditions" have depressed U.S. savings and boosted the current account deficit. On the other hand, Catherine Mann (2004) says the U.S. has a "structural tendency toward consumption and a savings-investment imbalance" and this compliments reciprocal foreign central bank purchases of U.S. Treasury debt and the associated funding of the U.S. current account deficit. Coughlin and Pollard (2001) found that investments had a "large role" in determining current account deficits but domestic saving behavior could not be significantly linked.

There is some evidence that savings are increasingly likely to move offshore from other countries into U.S. investments than has previously been the case, and this may have contributed to growing U.S. current account deficits (Blanchard, Giavazzi, and Sa, 2005) (Edwards, 2005). Greenspan (2003) has attributed these trends to "improvements in international financial intermediation". Mann has consistently warned that global investors will eventually tire of the oversupply of U.S. assets in their portfolios, and when this happens, deeply troublesome "dollar depreciation and higher interest rates" will result (2003-4, 2005). Thus far, however, her suggested proportionate "mirror test" level of maxed-out private holdings of U.S. debt securities (as a percentage of global debt held privately) has not kept pace with the growth of U.S. debt securities as a proportion of global debt market values (from 10% of global value in 1995 to 30% in 2001). Moreover, in 2001 William Poole also found evidence that increasingly large proportions of foreign investments were being concentrated in U.S. "equities and other illiquid assets" that were not redeemable for cash on demand.

Although it is undisputed that the U.S. personal savings rate has dropped from about 5 percent of disposable income to under 2 percent in the last ten years, this could be attributed to many factors such as the growth of credit card usage, innovative home equity loans, etc. Nearly everyone agrees that U.S. Treasury securities and U.S. securities markets offer superior transparency and relative stability. Despite recent building slumps, booming U.S. real estate asset values have largely offset trends of falling savings rates. For instance, the assessed value of Los Angeles real estate is estimated to exceed the entire U.S. national debt. Additionally, U.S. corporations have refinanced and paid down their debts during recent low interest periods while corporate shareholder wealth has reached all-time highs. In 2004 the ratio of the net international investment position (NIIP) to NYSE listed stock market capitalization was 18.52%; and to (U.S.) household net worth was 5.24% (Krishnan & Suker, 2006).

"Bretton Woods 2": This term has been applied to emphasize the global implications of capital flows related to U.S. current account deficits and Asian exchange rate intervention. It is widely recognized that China, Japan, and other East Asian countries have heavily intervened to lend exchange rate advantage to their export market promotions. However, Michael Dooley, David Folkerts-Landau, and Peter Graber claim in a string of papers (2003-4) that these Asian governments are trapped by their own "mercantilist" development strategies. Since they have targeted the U.S. market to support export driven growth, they must continue to finance U.S. imports of their goods with U.S. Treasury and dollar purchases. Thus, "overvalued dollars dominate inward direct investment" and paradoxically they must support the dollar to keep their own currencies undervalued. Accordingly, these authors expect this interdependence to continue "for another generation".

"Global co-dependency": Catherine Mann (2004) says that "global co-dependency" is due to lagging global demand which has caused inordinate dependency on exports to the U.S. She thinks that as long as the "co-dependency of (U.S.) structural characteristics and (Asian) policy choices (continues) (t)here is a real possibility that (it) cannot be undone by anything short of global economic crisis." She says the widening trade imbalance is most serious with respect to Japan, China, and Asia, but "it is broad-based (among all U.S.) trading partners." Mann thinks that their exchange rate strategy is "a bargain with the devil" in the sense that when their own currencies eventually do appreciate, not only will their exports fall and imports rise, but so too will the value of the U.S. financial assets in their portfolios fall.

"Houthakker-Magee asymmetry": Consistent with the traditional view of balance of payments accounts, this is a well documented empirical pattern that has prevailed since the post-WWII adjustment period. U.S. imports have grown faster when U.S. income grows faster than its trading partners due to relatively cheaper imports vis-a-vis domestic goods and services. Conversely, when its foreign trading partners' income grows faster their goods and services become relatively more costly, and U.S. exports to destination markets tend to grow. Because of elasticity of demand for U.S. imports and the size of the U.S. market, if U.S. structural patterns of consumption and budget deficits continue unchecked, it is contended that the U.S. current account will still tend towards deficit growth even if the U.S. and its trading partners grow their income at a comparable rate (Mann, 2003) (Alda & Gannon, 2001).

"Conflicted virtue syndrome": Schnabl (2005) warns of additional recurrence of the zero-interest-rate liquidity trap associated with deflationary pressures on Japan as the yen appreciated from 360 to the dollar in 1971 to 80 per dollar in 1995. Because Japan's trade and capital account surpluses reflected relatively high domestic savings rates, and its dependence upon consumption-biased U.S. markets for its exports, these massive exchange rate adjustments failed to eliminate its trade surpluses during this era. Instead, the persistent appreciation of the yen and the paucity of domestic consumption imposed relentless deflationary pressures on Japan. As Japanese holders of dollars logically converted into yen in defensive reaction to its appreciation, needed policy options were seriously constrained by threatened U.S. trade sanctions and central bank purchases of increasingly costly dollar holdings. Although Japanese interest rates fell to zero and even negative returns, its virtuous savings rate conflicted with the need to ramp up domestic consumption, thus exacerbating a vicious cycle of yen appreciation and falling interest rates.

Of course, the current concern is that these phenomena could revisit both Japan and China since they must lend in dollars to support heavy U.S. consumption of their exports. In effect, their policy options are hampered by their own mercantilist trade policies and associated dollar denominated asset accumulations. When Japan finally raised its short term central bank rate to 0.5% (compared to 5.25% in the U.S. and 3.5% in the euro zone) in February 2007, this caused massive unwinding of the "carry trade" and contributed to temporarily destabilized markets in March 2007 and thereafter.

The "moral hazards" of mercantilist policy: The aforementioned themes, "global co-dependency," "Bretton Woods 2," and "conflicted virtue" illustrate the common factors driving the global trade adjustment dilemma. Savings in emerging and export dependent economies that often are not channeled through appropriate institutional environments into needed domestic and private sector investment tend to be driven by government policy and ultimately supported by inappropriate interest rates, government guarantees, and/or bailouts. This "moral hazard" situation tends to cause over-borrowing for speculative domestic projects and overinvestment in export sectors that, in turn, encourage the aforementioned mercantilist export and monetary policies. For Chinese companies, e.g., this phenomena and their tendency to plow back earnings into productive capacity becomes a vicious cycle that has benevolent results initially, but has the potential to ultimately trigger disruptive corrections domestically and internationally. On the other hand, the consumption-biased U.S. economy also suffers from a structural hazard that drives government and consumer over-borrowing and associated deficit spending. These excessive borrowing, production, consumption, spending, and savings distortions are nonetheless easily intermediated in the international financial markets; and the system spins on in increasingly greater volumes and velocity. Moreover, the development of easy access to offshore investments due to globalized financial liberalization tends to make it relatively more difficult and costly for smaller companies to compete for domestic investment funds.

THE THEORETICAL MODEL AND EMPIRICAL RESULTS:

As previously stated, we focus upon the pace of progressive domestic adjustments needed to help rebalance global trade and consumption patterns and associated savings, investment and spending stimuli. We measure the need for functional domestic consumption and market structure using the Heritage Foundation's Index of Economic Freedom and the need for institutional maturity and fastidiousness to foster these developments using the Transparency International Corruption Perceptions Index. Our regressions on these factors aim to suggest which countries have relative flexibility (in comparison to the U.S.) to shoulder the burdens of adjustment in terms of domestic refinements of sustainable development institutions and market structure versus those who are perhaps more justified in manipulative resort to exchange rate adjustments. We base our estimates on the model developed by L.M. Koyck (1954) and extended by M. Nerlove (1958) in the "stock adjustment" or "partial adjustment" model. This model assumes there is an equilibrium or desired long run level of some economic variable, Y_t^*. We assume this equilibrium long run level of Y_t takes on the following linear form. X_j represents a set of explanatory variables.

$$Y_t^* = \beta_o + \beta_1 X_t + u_t \quad (1)$$

The partial adjustment model assumes:

$$(Y_t - Y_{t-1}) = \delta\,(Y_t^* - Y_{t-1}) \quad (2)$$

Where δ is known as the partial adjustment coefficient ($0 \leq \delta \leq 1$).

Further we assume:

The actual change in $Y_t = Y_t - Y_{t-1}$

The desired change in $Y_t = Y_t^* - Y_{t-1}$

Given equation (2) we can re-arrange terms and solve for Y

$$Y_t = \delta Y_t^* + (1 - \delta)\, Y_{t-1} \quad (3)$$

Since

$$Y_t^* = \beta_o + \beta_1 X_t + u_t \quad (1)$$

We can substitute (1) into (3)

$$Y_t = \delta(\beta_o + \beta_1 X_t + u_t) + (1 - \delta)\, Y_{t-1}$$

$$Y_t = \delta\beta_o + \delta\beta_1 X_t + \delta u_t + (1 - \delta)\, Y_{t-1}$$

$$Y_t = \delta\beta_o + \delta\beta_1 X_t + (1 - \delta)\, Y_{t-1} + \delta u_t \quad (4)$$

Equation (4) is the partial adjustment model used to estimate the adjustment coefficient δ. We can estimate equation (4) and derive the adjustment coefficient

δ from the estimated coefficient on Y_{t-1}. We estimate the following form of the partial adjustment model:

$$Y_t = \gamma_o + \gamma_1 X_t + \gamma_2 Y_{t-1} + V_t$$

where

$$\gamma_2 = 1 - \delta$$

thus

$$\delta = 1 - \gamma_2$$

Adjustment Coefficient Estimation

In the following section we estimate the coefficient of adjustment, δ, for 34 economies including developed, emerging, and less developed countries. The estimation period is from 1983 to 2005 using annual data from the World Bank Development Indicator Database. We are concerned with estimating the pace of adjustment (δ) for four economic variables: the current account to gross domestic product (CAB), the growth of gross domestic product (GDPGr), inflation (INF), and the nominal exchange rate (ER).

The following models for each country are estimated:

A. $CAB_t = \beta_o + \delta\, CAB_{t-1} + \beta_k X_t + V_{t,1}$

B. $GDPGr_t = \alpha_o + \delta\, GDPGr_{t-1} + \alpha_k X_t + V_{t,2}$

C. $INF_t = \gamma_o + \delta\, INF_{t-1} + \gamma_k X_t + V_{t,3}$

D. $ER_t = \theta_o + \delta\, ER_{t-1} + \theta_k X_t + V_{t,4}$

Where X_t in each equation consists of the following:

A: $X_t \equiv$ GDP Growth, Nominal Exchange Rate, Gross Capital Formation Growth.

B: $X_t \equiv$ Gross Capital Formation Growth, Interest Rate, Consumption Growth, Budget Deficit/Surplus.

C: $X_t \equiv$ GDP Growth, Exchange Rate, Current Account Balance

D: $X_t \equiv$ Gross Capital Formation Growth, Interest Rate, Current Account Balance.

Table I (page 222) reports the estimated adjustment coefficients for each country. Table II (page 223) reports the adjustment coefficient for each country relative to the U.S. coefficient (1.000). In Table II if a relative adjustment coefficient exceeds 1.000, that nation's pace of adjustment exceeds that of the U.S. Relative coefficients less than 1.000 indicate the adjustment is slower. The adjustment coefficient is reported for each variable in the appropriate column.

The Role of Economic Freedom and Corruption in the Pace of Adjustment

In order to ascertain whether the degree to which a nation's ability to contribute to the global adjustment process is enhanced or retarded by the degree of economic freedom and/or the level of corruption a second set of regressions is required.

In this section we regress the estimated adjustment coefficient of each country against the Heritage Foundation's Freedom Index (FI) and Transparency

International's Corruption Perception Index (CPI). The following linear equation is estimated for each country set of adjustment coefficients (δ). The following equation is estimated:

$$\delta_{ij} = \beta_o + \beta_1(CPI_{ij}) + \beta_2(FI_{ij})$$

where:
i = country
j = variable

Tables III through VI (page 224) report the results from the second set of regressions. The Freedom Index (FI) and the Corruption Perception Index (CPI) are used as measures of economic freedom and corruption in each nation. The freedom index is constructed so that higher values correspond to greater freedoms and higher values of the corruption index correspond with less corruption.

In Tables III through VI the pace of adjustment coefficient, δ, is the dependent variable for each of the economic variables, while the CPI and FI are the explanatory variables. Also reported are the individual t-statistics and the R^2.

Table III, reports that in each equation the CPI is positively and significantly related to the pace of adjustment. Empirical evidence is shown that less corruption enhances the pace of the adjustment process. In the exchange rate equation, the negative FI suggests the higher the freedom index the slower the pace of adjustment of the nominal exchange rate. This could reflect, however, that these nations are relying less upon exchange rate manipulations.

Table IV reports regressions of the relative current account balance, the relative exchange rate, and relative inflation to the freedom and corruption indices. The results are not markedly different from those in Table III. Again, the CPI coefficients are positive and significant with respect to the relative CAB and relative inflation. However, the CPI coefficient is negative and significant with respect to the relative exchange rate. The freedom index is only significant with respect to the relative exchange rate and again has a negative sign. Thus, greater economic freedom and less corruption correspond with a slower adjustment of the nominal exchange rate, perhaps suggesting these nations rely less upon exchange rate manipulation.

Table V reports the regression results when the relative economic variables are regressed against the relative FI and CPI. These results are again similar to Tables IV and V. Relative freedom is only significant with respect to the relative exchange rate. In Table V, however, the positive REL FI coefficient implies those nations with greater freedom relative to the U.S. have an exchange rate that adjusts faster than the U.S. (RELER) The relative CPI is significant at the 2.5% level and negative with respect to both relative inflation and relative exchange rates. Nations with less corruption relative to the U.S. show slower inflation and exchange rate adjustment.

Table VI reports a variation of the freedom index. The Heritage Foundation freedom index was reconstructed in 2007 using new sub-indices. One of the sub-indices measures the degree of labor market freedom. Interestingly, the labor market FI was positive and significant when run against GDP growth and relative GDP growth. This lends empirical credence to the proposition that labor mobility speeds the growth of gross domestic product. Labor market freedom was also found to be significant but negative in the CAB to GDP and relative CAB equations. Labor market freedom thus tends to slow the adjustment of the current account balance, as suggested by the negative sign.

SUMMARY AND CONCLUSIONS

As indicated above, in this paper we presume that since that U.S. dollar is the principal global trading and financial currency, adjustment burdens must be measured against this benchmark. This doesn't mean we presume the U.S. doesn't need to make any changes. Instead, we attempt to measure the pace of relative adjustment among the tabulated economies so that the reader may form an impression from the given data. First, we tabulated adjustment coefficients to facilitate comparisons to the U.S. Thus, factor coefficients less than (1.000) indicate a slower pace of adjustment than the U.S. and factor coefficients greater than (1.000) indicate a faster pace of adjustment. Second, we regress these results to suggest the significance of coefficients for the various economic factors among these 34 economies.

The tables generated by the application of the Koyck and Nerlove adjustment models to World Bank Development Indicators and regressions on the economic freedom and transparency indices herein are intended to be informative on two levels:

First, Table II demonstrates those among the 34 sample nations that are adjusting on a faster or slower basis than the U.S. (1.0 coefficients) in terms of four economic variables: current account to GDP, GDP growth, inflation, and the exchange rate. The reader may examine Table II, e.g., and easily confirm that China, Japan, and Korea have greater indicated burdens of adjustment (coefficients < 1.0) relative to exchange rates and inflation than does the U.S. and that their GDP growth and current account balance coefficients support these conclusions (coefficients > 1.0). In contrast, e.g., considering India and the Philippines relative to the U.S., exchange rate and inflation adjustment burdens are not indicated (coefficients < 1.0) and are not supported by their GDP growth and current account balance coefficients (<1.0 GDP growth, > 1.0 Relative CAB). Indonesia, on the other hand, shows a need to adjust faster in terms of exchange rates (Relative ER < 1.0), but this is not supported in terms of inflation (equal to U.S.), GDP growth (>1.0) and the current account balance coefficients (>1.0).

Second, Tables III, IV, and V demonstrate the significant relationships between current account balances, exchange rates and inflation with respect to economic freedom and corruption indices, first as absolutes in Table III, and also relative to the U.S. in Table IV, and again relative to the economic freedom and corruption indices in Table V. Table VI additionally shows the consistent significance of labor market freedoms to GDP growth as indicated by the sub-indices of labor market freedom that have recently been added to the economic freedom index.

In general, one can conclude that higher values on the corruption index (less corruption) as indicated by Tables IV and V relate to faster adjustment and less burden of adjustment relative to the U.S. Moreover, higher corruption rates indicated by the negative sign of relative exchange rates to the CPI on Table IV also suggests that more corruption relates to greater burdens of adjustment. Somewhat counter-intuitively, however, the generally inconsistent results relating to economic freedoms suggest that these factors have less significance (except as suggested by the strong results relating to labor market freedoms in Table VI).

Table I
Adjustment Coefficients

	CAB	*GDP Growth*	*Inflation*	*Exchange Rate*
Argentina	0.1170	1.0000	1.0000	0.1160
Australia	1.0000	0.6150	0.0720	0.2560
Bolivia	0.5320	1.0000	1.0000	0.0480
Brazil	1.0000	1.0000	0.4220	0.4120
Canada	0.1980	0.7400	1.0000	1.0000
Chile	0.3670	1.0000	0.3390	0.1890
China	0.6560	1.0000	0.3980	0.2040
Egypt	0.4990	1.0000	0.1290	0.0500
France	0.1510	1.4700	0.3070	1.0000
Germany	0.0000	0.5090	0.3900	0.2300
Guatemala	1.0000	0.4180	0.6230	0.0650
India	0.2190	0.5920	1.0000	0.0000
Indonesia	0.2330	1.0000	1.0000	0.6010
Italy	0.1940	0.4060	0.3280	0.1760
Japan	0.2850	0.8350	0.3020	0.2390
Korea	0.3310	1.0000	0.5310	0.2010
Mexico	0.2260	0.3800	0.4020	0.4000
Nigeria	1.0000	1.0000	1.0000	0.0000
Pakistan	0.2060	1.0000	0.4790	0.0000
Paraguay	0.4200	1.0000	0.2460	0.0000
Peru	0.1360	1.0000	1.0000	0.1490
Philippines	0.2840	0.4830	1.0000	0.0000
Russia	1.0000	0.6030	0.6850	0.3520
Saudi Arabia	0.0000	1.0000	0.4910	1.0000
South Africa	0.4250	1.0000	1.0000	0.1380
Switzerland	0.1070	1.0000	0.0270	1.0000
Tanzania	1.0000	0.0900	0.1580	0.0000
Thailand	0.3130	1.0000	1.0000	0.0850
Turkey	1.0000	0.7420	0.2180	1.0000
United Kingdom	0.2740	0.7390	0.2070	0.2240
Uruguay	0.3310	1.0000	0.1060	0.0000
USA	0.0570	0.7940	1.0000	NA
Venezuela	1.0000	1.0000	0.3860	0.0000
Zimbabwe	1.0000	1.0000	1.0000	0.0000

Table II
Adjustment Coefficients Relative to U.S.

	Relative CAB	*Relative GDP Growth*	*Relative Inflation*	*Relative ER*
Argentina	2.0526	1.2594	1.0000	0.1160
Australia	17.5439	0.7746	0.0720	0.2560
Bolivia	9.3333	1.2594	1.0000	0.0480
Brazil	17.5439	1.2594	0.4220	0.4120
Canada	3.4737	0.9320	1.0000	1.0000
Chile	6.4386	1.2594	0.3390	0.1890
China	11.5088	1.2594	0.3980	0.2040
Egypt	8.7544	1.2594	0.1290	0.0500
France	2.6491	1.8514	0.3070	1.0000
Germany	0.0000	0.6411	0.3900	0.2300
Guatemala	17.5439	0.5264	0.6230	0.0650
India	3.8421	0.7456	1.0000	0.0000
Indonesia	4.0877	1.2594	1.0000	0.6010
Italy	3.4035	0.5113	0.3280	0.1760
Japan	5.0000	1.0516	0.3020	0.2390
Korea	5.8070	1.2594	0.5310	0.2010
Mexico	3.9649	0.4786	0.4020	0.4000
Nigeria	17.5439	1.2594	1.0000	0.0000
Pakistan	3.6140	1.2594	0.4790	0.0000
Paraguay	7.3684	1.2594	0.2460	0.0000
Peru	2.3860	1.2594	1.0000	0.1490
Philippines	4.9825	0.6083	1.0000	0.0000
Russia	17.5439	0.7594	0.6850	0.3520
Saudi Arabia	0.0000	1.2594	0.4910	1.0000
South Africa	7.4561	1.2594	1.0000	0.1380
Switzerland	1.8772	1.2594	0.0270	1.0000
Tanzania	17.5439	0.1134	0.1580	0.0000
Thailand	5.4912	1.2594	1.0000	0.0850
Turkey	17.5439	0.9345	0.2180	1.0000
United Kingdom	4.8070	0.9307	0.2070	0.2240
Uruguay	5.8070	1.2594	0.1060	0.0000
USA	1.0000	1.0000	1.0000	0.0000
Venezuela	17.5439	1.2594	0.3860	0.0000
Zimbabwe	17.5439	1.2594	1.0000	0.0000

Table III

	CAB		*Exchange Rate*		*Inflation*	
C	.2854**	.6732	.9967***	1.5032***	.1865	.0049
	(2.0895)	(1.6021)	(8.9667)	(5.1014)	(1.4569)	(.0144)
CPI	.0577**	.0645***	.0628***		.0556**	.0451*
	(2.2116)	(2.6815)	(2.4124)		(2.0927)	(1.6906)
FI		-.0066		-,0127***		.0039
		(.9906)		(2.5124)		(.6529)
R^2	.1418	.1611	.1797	.1575	.1346	.1329

* 10% level of significance
** 5% level of significance
*** 2.5% level of significance.

Table IV

	Relative CAB		*Relative ER*		*Relative Inflation*	
C	.3026**	.7138**	1.5032***	.9967***	49.4502	1864.95
	(2.269)	(1.995)	(5.1014)	(8.9667)	(.0136)	(1.6370)
FI		-.0070	-.0127***		38.828	
		(1.1279)	(2.5124)		(.6092)	
CPI	.0612**	.0684***		-.0628***	450.99*	556.0121***
	(2.300)	(2.3886)		(2.4124)	(1.7083)	(2.4317)
R^2	.1418	.1611	.1575	.1797	.1329	.1346

* 10% level of significance
** 5% level of significance
*** 2.5% level of significance.

Table V

	RELER	*RELER*	*RELER*	*RELINF*	*RELINF*
C	-.5289	-.1197	-.1084	.8784***	.5658*
	(1.884)	(.4568)	(1.2049)	(7.8516)	(1.6933)
REL FI	+1.0427***	.0193			-.5316
	(2.6769)	(.4343)			(.9880)
REL CPI		-.6372***	-.6431***	-.5435***	-.7074***
		(2.5203)	(3.4065)	(3.5411)	(3.6082)
R^2	.1731	.3430	.3431	.2321	.2536

* 10% level of significance
** 5% level of significance
*** 2.5% level of significance.

Table VI

	GDP Grow	*GDP Grow*	*CABGDP*	*RELCAB*	*REL Grow*
C	-.3469**	-.3112***	.7514***	.7968***	-1.5105***
	(2.0816)	(2.8346)	(3.4198)		(2.8346)
CPI		-.0190	.0752***	+.0797***	-.09213
		(.9939)	(3.7057)	(3.0957)	(.9939)
Labor FI	.0079***	.0087***	-.0084***	-.0089***	-.0422***
	(3.1670)	(3.3940)	(2.7638)	(2.5021)	(3.3940)
R^2	.2386	.2628	.2860	.2860	.2860

* 10% level of significance
** 5% level of significance
*** 2.5% level of significance.

References and Bibliography

Alda, M. & Gannon, J. (2001), "The U.S. Current Account Deficit: Causes and Consequences," JBIC Working Paper, No. 2. Research Institute for Development and Finance.

Bernanke, Ben S. (2005), The Global Saving Glut and the U.S. Current Account Deficit, Honer Jones Lecture, St. Louis, Missouri, April 14.

http://www.federalreserve.gov/boarddocs/speechs/2005/20050414/defualt.htm

Benassy-Quere, Agnes, Duran–Vigneron, Pascale, Lahreche-Revil, Amira and Valerie Mignon (2004), Burden Sharing and Exchange Rate Misalignments within the Group of Twenty. *In Dollar Adjustment: How Far? Against What?* eds. C. Fred Bergsten & John Williamson. Washington: Institute for International Economics.

Blanchard, Olivier, Francesco Giavazzi, and Filipa Sa (2005), The U.S. Current Account and the Dollar, NBER Working Paper No. 11137, February.

Bergsten, C. Fred & John Williamson (2004), Overview: Designing a Dollar Policy. In *Dollar Adjustment: How Far? Against What?*, eds. C. Fred Bergsten & John Williamson. Washington: Institute for International Ecomincs.

Chin, Menzie D. (2005), Getting Serious about the Twin Deficits, Council on Foreign Relations Special Report.

Chin, Menzie D. and Hiro Ito (2005), Current Account Balances, Financial Development and Institutions: Assaying the World 'Saving Glut', LaFollette School Working Paper No. 2005-023, October.

Chin, Menzie D. and Enswar S. Prasad (2003), Medium-term Determinents of Current Accounts in Industrial and Developing Countries: An Empirical Exploration, *Journal of International Economics* Vol. 59, 47-76.

Cline, William R. (2005), *United States as a Debtor Nation: Risks and Policy Reform*, Washington, Institute for International Economics and the Center for Global Development.

Coughlin, Cletus C. & Patricia S. Pollard (2001), What Drives Large Current Account Deficits? *International Economic Trends,* The Federal Reserve Bank of St. Louis, St. Louis, May.

Dooley, Michael, David Fokkerts-Landau and Peter Graber (2003), An Essay on the Revived Bretton Woods System. NBER Working Paper 9971. Cambridge, National Bureau of Economic Research.

Edwards, Sebastian (2005), Is the U.S. Current Account Deficit Sustainable? And If Not, How Costly is Adjustment Likely to Be? NBER Working Paper 11541, August.

Erceg, Christopher J., Luca Guerrieri and Christopher Gust (2005), Expansionary Fiscal Shocks and the Current Account, Board of Governors of the Federal Reserve System, International Finance Discussion Papers No. 825, January.

Ferguson, Roger W. (2005), U.S. Current Account Deficit: Causes and Consequences, speech to Economics Club of the University of North Carolina, Chapel Hill, North Carolina, April 20. http://www.federalreserve.gov/boarddocs/speeches/2005/20050420?default.htm.

Gramlich, Edward M. (2004), Budget and Trade Deficits: Linked, Both Worriesome in the Long Run, but not Twins. Remarks at the Los Angeles Chapter of the National Association of Business Economists.

Greenspan, Alan (2003), Current Account, speech to 21st Annual Monetary Polciy Conference, Cato Institute, Washington D.C., November 20. *www.federalreserve.gov/boarddocs/speeches/2003/200311230?default.htm.*

Griswold, Daniel T. (2002), America's Misunderstood Trade Deficit. U.S. Senate Committee on Finance. August 27.

Griswold, Daniel T. (2001), "American's Record Trade Deficit: A Symbol of Economic Strength." Cato Institute: Center for Trade Policy Studies, February.

Gruber, Joseph W. and Steven B. Kamin (2005), Explaining the Global Pattern of Current Account Imbalances, Board of Governors of the Federal Reserve System, International Finance Discussion Papers, Number 846, November.

http://www.federalreserve.gov/pubs/ifdp/2005/846/ifdp846.pdf

Kane, Tim (2005), The Brutal Price of a Dollar. *Backgrounder*, No. 1855, May 31, 2005. Washington: The Heritage Foundation.

Koyck, L.M. (1954), Distributed Lags and Investment Analysis, North Holland Publishing Company, Amsterdam.

Levey, David, and Stuart S. Brown (2005), The Overstretch Myth: Can the Indispensable Nation Be a Debtor Nation? *Foreign Affairs* 84 No. 2 (March/April): 2-7.

Mann, C. (1999-2000), *Is the U.S. Trade Deficit Sustainable?* Institute for International Economics, Washington, September. *Finance and Development*, Vol. 37 No 1, March.

Mann, C. (2003), *The U.S. Current Account, New Economy Services, and Implications for Sustainability*, Institute for International Economics, Washington, August.

Mann, C. (2004), *Managing Exchange Rates: Achievement of Global Re-balancing or Evidence of Global Co-dependency?* Institute for International Economics, Washington, July.

Meyer, John, Hillar Neumann Jr. and Jennifer Wegleitner (2006), Global Current Account Imbalances and the Opportunity for Monetary Correction, *Journal of Business and Behavioral Sciences*, Vol. 14 No.1, 209-222.

Mussa, Michael (2005), Sustaining Global Growth while Reducing External Imbalances. In *The United States and the World Economy: Sustaining Global Growth*, ed. C. Fred Bergsten. Washington: Institute for International Economics.

Nerlove, Marc (1958), Distributed Lags and Demand Analysis for Agricultural and Other Commodities, Agricultural Handbook No. 141, U.S. Department of Agriculture.

Orszag, Peter R., Robert E. Rukin, and Arlan Sinai (2005), "Sustained Budget Deficit: Long-Run U.S. Economic Performance and the Risk of Financial and Fiscal Disarray," The Brookings Institution.

Poole, William, Cletus Coughlin and Patricia Pollard (2001), Does the United States Have a Current Account Deficit Disorder? Federal Reserve Bank of St. Louis. *www.stlouisfed.org/news/speeches/2001/04_10_01.html.*

Roubini, Nouriel, and Brad Setser (2005), How Scary Is the Deficit? *Foreign Affairs* 84 No. 4 (July/August) 194-200.

Schnabl, Gunther (2005), "China, A Stabilizing or Deflationary Influence in East Asia? The Problem of Conflicted Virtue," In *Exchange Rates Under The East Asian Dollar Standard: Living with Conflicted Virtue,* Ronald I. McKinney, ed. Cambridge: MIT Press.

Truman, Edwin M. (2001), The International Implications of Paying Down the Debt. International Economics Policy Briefs PB01-7. Washington: Institute for International Economics.

Truman, Edwin M. (2003), The Limits of Exchange Market Intervention. In *Dollar Overvaluation and the World Economy*, eds. C. Fred Bergsten and John Williamson. Washington: Institute for International Economics.

Truman, Edwin M. (2005), Postponing Global Adjustment: An Analysis of the Pending Adjustment of Global Imbalances, Working Paper Series, Number WP 05-6, Washington: Institute for International Economics.

Zvi, Griliches (1967), "Distributed Lags: A Survey," *Econometrica*, vol. 36, No. 1, January.

A COMPARATIVE ANALYSIS OF TECHNICAL EFFICIENCY: A Study of the Formal and the Informal Sectors Manufacturing Industries in Bangladesh

Hedayet Chowdhury
Assistant Professor, Department of Economics
Kazakhstan Institute of Management

In the globalised economy competitiveness implies the ability to occupy the most advantageous position in a constantly changing market environment. Technical efficiency is considered to be central to the growth of productivity and international competitiveness in any economy. The study estimates technical efficiency in both formal and informal manufacturing industries of Bangladesh to shed light on the degree of efficiency of their resource use and potential for economic efficiency and growth. The results of the study will assist the Government and the policy makers in formulating policies for developing an efficient and competitive industrial sector vitally needed for long-term sustained growth of the economy.

I. INTRODUCTION

In Bangladesh, the formal sector operates in the organized capital and labor markets and the informal sector operates mostly in the unorganized factor markets. As large and medium firms operate in the organized input markets they have better access to capital-intensive technologies, skilled labor and better information. Consequently the formal sector has access to capital at a lower price and pays higher wages to labor than what the informal sector pays for such factors. On the other hand, small firms operate mostly in the unorganized input markets and operate with older and labor-intensive technologies. Due to superior technology and easy access to capital, large firms may determine the most efficient frontier and be technically more efficient than small firms. In addition, poor transportation system, periodic nation wide strikes, labor disputes, frequent power failures, limited and poor telecommunication facilities increases the transaction costs of doing business in Bangladesh. As such, it is argued that high market transaction costs and capital market imperfections act as a source of long-run market power to large firms but as entry and mobility barriers to small firms and under these conditions, even if small-scale firms are more efficient in production they can not grow very well.

In an economy where product and factor markets are perfectly competitive differences in technical efficiency between the formal and informal sectors could be due to organizational factors. But in less developed countries where markets are not perfect observed differences in technical efficiency between formal and informal sectors could be due to not only organizational factors but also the technological gap across the sector as well as economies of scale. In sum, the higher efficiency could be due to greater utilization of plant capacity, the realization of economies of scale, a declining incremental capital-output ratio, the gains of X-efficiency, higher marginal productivities, greater total factor productivity, and the overcoming of organizational dualism.

According to Frantz, Roger S. (1988)[1] technical efficiency and x-efficiency is not identical, because the differences in measuring one doesn't necessarily imply the other. Technical efficiency is caused by technical factors such as different skills among managers or workers, or because the particular technology being used, while being used to its capacity, is inferior to that being used by other firms in the industry. The issue is that at any point in time various vintages of capital are likely to be used, not because of a lack of attention on the part of managers, but because the diffusion of technology, is not an instantaneous process, or because investment funds available to different firms vary, or it may take time for the productivity of capital to reach its potential. Thus a faster rate of embodied technical progress will give the appearance of a greater degree of technical inefficiency. X-inefficiency, however, would be caused, not because skills vary or because diffusion of technology takes time, but because the use of skills varies, work norms can vary, effort has a certain discretionary element to it, and hence, motivation for cost and productivity consciousness is not always as present as it can be. Thus the existence of technical inefficiency as measured by an industry production frontier doesn't necessarily imply the existence of X-inefficiency.

The structure of the labor market could be one of the important factors in determining the relative technical efficiency of large and small firms. While capital market imperfections favor large firms, labor market segmentation may hinder them in realizing optimum technical efficiency and they have to pay higher wages compared to small firms. Moreover, labor unions sometime restrict large firms from getting rid off excess labor or replacing inefficient labor as they exercise power under the umbrella of 'trade union' which is largely motivated by political ideology. In this respect, small and household firms operated mostly within an unorganized labor market could minimize the cost of labor by employing a few permanent skilled laborers and mostly temporary semi-skilled or unskilled and unpaid family labor. Most small firms tended to make laborers work long hours by paying low wage rates. The large firms are fully subject to labor laws and unionization with little flexibility in labor replacement and working hours.

On the other hand, if organizational inefficiency of large and medium firms were more dominant than their relative advantage in access to superior technology and information, large firms would exhibit lower technical efficiency in production compared to small and household firms. Moreover, diversification into multi products and higher levels of vertical integration by large firms is more towards exercising market power than realizing higher levels of production efficiency. This, in turn, causes higher organizational complexity and consequently lowers levels of technical efficiency in production. Large firms could have maintenance of excess capacity as an entry deterrence strategy

(Leiberman, 1987)[2] and in such cases, the excess capacity of large firms results in lower technical efficiency in production.

Moreover, in Bangladesh most of the large enterprises in different sectors are still within the public sectors, which face unduly 'soft' (Khan and Hossain, 1989[3] and Ahmad, 1993[4]) financial constraints, where firm managers are not financially accountable, avoid risks and have weak interest in realizing full production capacity. On the other hand, large enterprises in different sectors within the public sectors enjoy a seller's market. In this market, enterprises increase productive capacity as much as possible in order to earn extra rents by obtaining scarce foreign exchange and concessionary imports, but in the absence of competition huge production capacity remains unrealized. Also, there is no exit threat or bankruptcy law for such enterprises. In fact as argued by Khan and Hossain (1989) and Ahmed (1993), financial constraints of industrial enterprises are soft. The production environment encourages them to produce output by using inputs lavishly. Consequently the enterprise manager has little incentive to use inputs effectively in the production process to increase productivity and is reluctant to respond to price signals. Both phenomena led to underutilization of existing production capacity.

Section 2 represents a literature review and section 3 presents the theoretical discussion. Section 4 discusses the sources of data used in this study. Section 5 shows the results of the stochastic frontier production function. And finally section 6 is the concluding section.

II. LITERATURE REVIEW

Seitz (1971)[5] concluded that technical efficiency depends mainly on vintage effects-the ability of plants constructed later to utilize more advanced technology. Jondrow *et al.* (1982)[6] concluded that efficient plants are large and of recent vintage but do not employ large quantities of capital relative to fuel or labor. Pitt and Lee (1981)[7] and Chen and Tang (1987)[8] reached the same conclusion based on their studies of manufacturing industries in developing countries. Todd (1971)[9] calculated the Farell efficiency frontiers for (rather aggregated) British manufacturing industries, observing that small firms account for some of the points on each estimated frontier, invariably because they use efficient input combinations that are more labor intensive than those of large firms. Yotopoulos and Lau (1973)[10] concluded that small firms in India are more economic-efficient. According to their finding the relative economic efficiency of the small firms, however, is not due to superior price efficiency. In fact they have found both large and small firms are price-efficient but the technical efficiency of small firms is more superior than large firms. Meller (1976)[11] estimated separate efficiency frontiers for five-size-classes of twenty-one Chilean industries and found that as usual the larger plants did not show efficiency frontiers superior to those of their smaller competitors, but he did not conclude that the extent of technical inefficiency of small plants with respect to their own efficiency frontiers was much greater than for large plants. He did find that efficient plants pay relatively high wages, which could indicate either an affinity of skill for efficiency or a transfer to the work force of the efficiency rents flowing to the better plants.

Meeusen and van den Broeck (1977a)[12] observed higher efficiency levels in the larger French manufacturing companies. Chen and Tang (1987)[13] found that larger firms were more efficient, but the difference was not significantly higher. Førsund and Jansen (1977)[14] found that the capital-labor ratios of best-practice plants are markedly higher than those of other plants, consistent with best practice involving more capital and newer vintages of equipment. Lee and Tyler (1978)[15] estimated frontier production function for Brazilian manufacturing firms, concluding that output elasticity of capital is higher on the frontier than in the average practice. Meeusen and van den Broeck (1977b)[16] also found the same indication that industries with higher efficiency levels exhibit higher output elasticities of capital. Downie (1958)[17] concluded that the less efficient British manufacturing industries displayed a conjunction of high seller concentration with collusive market agreements (such as price fixing). Carlsson (1972)[18] investigated a number of determinants of technical inefficiency in Swedish manufacturing industries, concluding that inefficiency is positively related to seller concentration (possibly because of the common underlying influence of scale economies, which are more important in the more efficient industries). He also found that industries producing more heterogeneous lines of products appear less efficient, a result expected when products are differentiated and some producers have happened upon more profitable varieties than have others.

Dhawan Rajeeb (2001)[19] carried out research on firm size and productivity differential based on a panel of US firms where he found that small firms are on the average more efficient than their large counterparts when size is defined according to the value of a firms assets. His hypothesis is that that the higher productivity or efficiency of smaller firms is the result of their leaner organizational structure that allows them to take strategic actions to exploit emerging market opportunities and to create a niche market position for themselves. Tornatzky and Fleischer (1990)[20] and Utterback (1994)[21] have argued that small firms utilizing their greater organizational responsiveness are better at adapting to environmental changes than large firms. Given their flexibility smaller firms are better organized to respond to the changing market structure and consumer tastes that have shifted production away from standardized mass-produced goods and towards stylized and personalized products (Carlsson, 1989)[22]. It is argued that recent advances in technology, increased competition and deregulation have reduced the minimum efficient scale of technology thereby making smaller sized firms more viable (Shephard, 1982; Carlsson, 1984)[23]. On the basis of analysis of input substitution possibilities and economies of scale in the US manufacturing sector Nguyen and Reznek (1991, 1993)[24] found that large size is not a necessary condition for efficient production. According to Philips (1991)[25] small firms are more efficient than large firms and small firms have played a dominant role in the growth of high technology industries, those which are by definition relatively new or use new techniques of production.

III. THEORETICAL FRAMEWORK: FRONTIER PRODUCTION FUNCTION

The study estimates the frontier production function by using parametric methods. Frontier production function is the outer-boundary in output space for a given set of input combinations. Technical inefficiency is defined as the amount by which the actual output falls short of the maximum possible output on the frontier.

The estimation of a parametric frontier requires the functional form to be pre-specified such as Cobb-Douglas, CES, Translog, etc. and within this set, frontier production functions can be estimated by the *deterministic* and the *stochastic* approach.

Deterministic frontiers confine all observations to be on or below the frontier and any deviation from the frontier is described as inefficiency, which means that the error term, random variables, covers the technical inefficiency, on the assumption that all factors are under the control of the firm and consequently, it does not allow for random shocks, which are beyond the control of an individual firm. Further it ignores the existence of measurement of error and any other source of random variation in observed output.

The stochastic approach assumes that the error term i.e., the deviation from frontier into two components: a white noise which is distributed symmetrically with zero mean reflecting random effects on production outside the control of the decision unit or exogenous shocks, e.g., political instability or strike, volatility due to labor union activity, power shortages, raw materials supply breakdowns, and statistical errors, etc., and an asymmetrical component reflecting technical inefficiency. This last component that measures technical inefficiency by the distance remaining in order to reach the optimum value is assumed to be the result of behavior factors which come under the control of the decision unit.

1. Deterministic Frontier

Aigner and Chu (1968) considered the estimation of a parametric frontier production function of the Cobb-Douglas form, using data on a sample of N firms. The model is defined by

$$\ln(y_i) = x_i\beta - u_i \ ; \qquad i = 1, 2, \ldots\ldots\ldots\ldots, N \qquad (1)$$

Where $\ln(y_i)$ is the logarithm of the (scalar) output for the i-th firm; x_i is a $1\times(K+1)$ -row vector, whose first element is "1" and the remaining elements are the logarithms of the K-input quantities used by the i-th firm; $\beta = (\beta_0, \beta_1, \ldots\ldots\ldots\ldots \beta_K)'$ is a $(K+1) \times 1$-column vector of unknown parameters to be estimated; and u_i is a non-negative random variable, related with technical inefficiency in production of firms in the industry involved.

The technical efficiency of the i-th firm may be defined as:

$$TE_i = \frac{y_i}{\exp(x_i\beta)} = \frac{\exp(x_i\beta - u_i)}{\exp(x_i\beta)} = \exp(-u_i) \qquad (2)$$

This output-oriented Farell measure of technical efficiency takes a value between zero and one. It shows the magnitude of the output of the i-th firm relative to the output that could be produced by a fully efficient firm using the same input set.

According to Greene (1980), consistent estimates can be obtained from the frontier production function using corrected ordinary least squares (COLS).

According to him if the ordinary least squares (OLS) technique is applied, we obtain the best linear unbiased and consistent estimates of the slope parameters, but we obtain a non-consistent estimate of the constant term. To solve this problem the residuals obtained by OLS are used to amend the constant term by the adding the maximum positive residual to it, and in this way a consistent estimate of constant is obtained. In this process all the residuals have the correct sign; they are non-positive and at least one is zero. After estimation of the parameter of the frontier production function, the technical efficiency level of each observation will be obtained by equation (2).

The important limitation of this approach is that since it doesn't allow for random errors, all the residual is considered as inefficiency.

2. Stochastic Frontier

Battasee and Coelli (1992) propose a stochastic frontier production function for panel data which has firm effects, and is assumed to be distributed as truncated normal random variables that may vary systematically with time. The model may be expressed as:

$$Y_{it} = X_{it}\beta + \left(v_{it} - u_{it}\right); \qquad i = 1,2,............,N; \quad t = 1,2,..........,T \tag{3}$$

Where Y_{it} is (the logarithm of) production of the i-th firm in the t-th time period; x_{it} is a 1 × (K+1) vector, whose first element is "1" and the remaining elements are the logarithms of the K-input quantities used by the i-th firm in the t-th time period; β is a (K+1) × 1 vector of unknown parameters to be estimated; v_{it} are random variables, assumed to be i.i.d $N(0, \sigma^2_v)$ and independent of the $u_{it} = u_i \exp(-\eta(t-T))$. u_i are non-negative random variables associated with technical efficiency in production. They are assumed to be i.i.d. truncated at zero of the $N(m, \sigma^2_u)$ distribution. h is a parameter to be estimated, and the panel of data need not be complete. (i.e. unbalanced panel data).

This model formulation includes a number of the special cases that have appeared in the literature. Setting h to be zero provides the time invariant model set out in Battasse, Coelli and Colby (1989). The additional restriction of m equal to zero reduces the model in Pitt and Lee (1981). Setting T = 1, one returns to the original cross-sectional, half-normal formulation of Aigner, Lovell and Schmidt (1977).

Maximum-Likelihood Estimation

Assume that v_is are i.i.d. truncations at zero of a $N(\mu, \sigma^2)$ random variable, i.e., its distribution $p+(x) = 2p(x)$ for $x \geq 0$ and $p+(x) = 0$ for $x < 0$, where

$$p(x) = \frac{1}{\sqrt{2\pi\sigma}}\exp\left[-\frac{(x-\mu)^2}{2\sigma^2}\right] \tag{4}$$

is the normal distribution Then in the case of v_i being i.i.d. $N(0, \sigma^2_v)$ Battese and Corra (1977) showed that the log-likelihood function ln (L) is evaluated as

$$\ln(L) = -\frac{N}{2}\left(\frac{\pi}{2}\right) - \frac{N}{2}\ln\left(\sigma^2\right) + \sum_{i=1}^{N}\ln\left[(1-\Phi(z_i)\right] - \frac{1}{2\sigma^2}\sum_{i=1}^{N}\left(\ln(y_i) - x_i\beta\right)^2 \tag{5}$$

Where, $z_i = \frac{(\ln(y_i) - x_i\beta)}{\sigma}\sqrt{\frac{\gamma}{1-\gamma}}$, $\gamma = \frac{\sigma_u^2}{\sigma^2}$, $\sigma^2 = \sigma_u^2 + \sigma_v^2$, and $\Phi(\cdot)$ is the cumulative distribution function of the standard normal random variable.

The ML estimates of β, σ^2 and g are obtained by finding the maximum of the ln (L) defined in equation 5.

The computer program, Frontier version 4.1, is used to obtain the ML estimates for the parameters of this model. This program uses a three-step estimation procedure (Coelli , Rao, Battasee, 1998, p. 188):

1. The first step involves calculation of the OLS estimators of β σ^2. These are unbiased estimators of the parameters in the ln(L), with the exception of the intercept β_0, and σ^2.
2. In the second step, the likelihood function is evaluated for a number of values of g between zero and one. In these calculations, the OLS estimates of σ^2 and β_0 are adjusted by $\sigma^2 = \frac{\sigma^2_{u(OLS)}\left[\pi(T-K)\right]}{\left[T(\pi - 2\hat{\gamma})\right]}$ and $\hat{\beta}_0 = \hat{\beta}_{0(OLS)} + \sqrt{\frac{2\hat{\gamma}\hat{\sigma}^2}{\pi}}$ respectively. The OLS estimates are used for the remaining parameters in β.
3. The final step uses the best estimates (that is those corresponding to the largest log-likelihood value) from the second step as starting values in a Davidson-Fletcher-Powell (DFP) iterative maximization routine, which obtains the ML estimates when the likelihood function attains global maximum.

Estimation of Mean Technical Efficiency

The mathematical expectation (mean) of the technical efficiency, $TE_i = \exp(-u_i)$ can be calculated, for given distributional assumptions for the technical inefficiency effects. It can be shown that, if the u_is are i.i.d half-normal random variables, as assumed above, then

$$E\left[\exp(-u_i)\right] = 2\left[1 - \Phi\left(\sqrt{\gamma\sigma}\right)\right]\exp\left(-\frac{\gamma\sigma^2}{2}\right) \tag{6}$$

The ML estimator of the mean technical efficiency is obtained by substituting the ML estimators for the relevant parameters in the above equation.

Prediction of Firm level-level Technical Efficiencies

The technical efficiency of the i-th firm is defined by $TE_i = \exp(-u_i)$. This involves the technical inefficiency effect, u_i, which is unobservable. Even if the true value of the parameter vector β, in the stochastic frontier model, $\ln(y_i) = X_i\beta + v_i - u_i$, was known, only the difference, $e_i \equiv v_i - u_i$, could be observed. The best predictor of u_i is the conditional expectation of u_i, given the value of v_i-u_i. The result was first recognized and applied in the stochastic frontier model by Jondrow, Lovell, Materov and Schmidt (1982) as

$$E\left[\exp(-u_i)\middle|e_i\right] = -\gamma e_i + \sigma_{uA}\left\{\frac{\phi\left(\frac{\gamma e_i}{\sigma_{uA}}\right)}{1-\Phi\left(\frac{\gamma e_i}{\sigma_{uA}}\right)}\right\} \quad (7)$$

where $\sigma_{UA} = \sqrt{\gamma(1-\gamma)\sigma}$ and f is the density function of the standard normal variable.

Battese and Coelli (1988) point out that the best predictor of $\exp(-u_i)$ is obtained by using

$$E\left[\exp(-u_i)\middle|e_i\right] = \frac{1-\Phi\left(\sigma_{uA}^2 + \gamma e_i/\sigma_{uA}^2\right)}{1-\Phi\left(\gamma e_i/\sigma_{uA}^2\right)}\exp\left(\gamma e_i + \frac{\sigma_{uA}^2}{2}\right) \quad (8)$$

The technical efficiency predictor implemented in the FRONTIER computer program is obtained by replacing the unknown parameters in the above equation with their ML estimates.

Tests of Hypothesis

The generalized likelihood ratio test requires the estimation of the model under both the null and alternate hypothesis. Under the null hypothesis, $H_0: \gamma = 0$, the model is equivalent of average response function, without the technical inefficiency effect, u_i. The test statistic is calculated as

$$LR = -2\{\ln[L(H_0)/L(H_1)]\} = -2\{\ln[L(H_0)] - \ln[L(H_1)]\} \quad (9)$$

Where $L(H_0)$ and $L(H_1)$are the values of likelihood function under the null and alternative hypothesis, H_0 and H_1, respectively. If H_0 is true, this test statistic is usually assumed to be asymptotically distributed as a chi-square random variable with degrees of freedom equal to the number of restrictions involved (Coelli (1995)).

IV. DATA SOURCES

The study uses the secondary data published by the Bangladesh Bureau of Statistics, which is the main official source of statistical data for Bangladesh. For the formal sector, the study uses the report "Census of Manufacturing industries" (CMI) for the year 1989-90 and 1992-93 and for the informal sector, the study uses the "Report on Integrated Annual Survey of Non-Farm economic Activities 1989-90" and the "Report on Annual Establishment & Institution Survey 1992-93". The study selected the years 1989-90 and 1992-93 for comparison in terms of efficiency and total factor productivity between the formal and informal sector manufacturing industries because the data on the informal sector is available only for these two years. The other limitation of the study is that the data on fixed capital is not available for informal sector for the year 1989-90. That's why to make comparison with respect to performance between the formal and informal sector manufacturing industry, the study uses inputs labor and raw materials only. Labor is defined as the total number of person engaged. Output is measured in terms of Gross output. The study uses 4-digit level data that is classified according to the 'International Standard Industrial Classification' (ISIC).

Industry division:(2-digit industry)

31 Food, Beverages & Tobacco
32 Textiles, Apparel, Leather
33 Wood, Wood Prods., Furniture
34 Paper, Printing & Publishing
35 Chemicals, Rubber, Plastic
36 Nonmetallic Mineral Products
38 Metal Prods., Machinery, Equip.

V. EMPIRICAL RESULTS AND DISCUSSION: TECHNICAL EFFICIENCY ESTIMATED BY STOCHASTIC FRONTIER PRODUCTION FUNCTION

Using two inputs i.e., labor and raw materials we try to estimate the technical efficiency of the formal and informal sectors in the manufacturing industry in Bangladesh for the period of 1998-90 and 1992-93. As the data on "fixed capital" for the informal sector is not available for the period 1989-90, we finally use labor and raw materials as inputs in our analysis in order to compare technical efficiency between the formal and informal sectors in both periods.

Figure 2.1

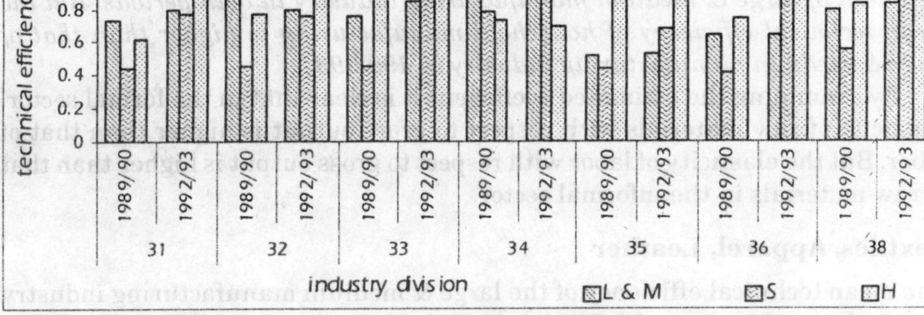

The study found that the mean technical efficiency of the small manufacturing industry increased over time. During 1989-90 the mean technical efficiency of the small manufacturing industry in all divisions was lower than that of the large & medium manufacturing industry. But during 1992-93 in industry divisions 33, 35, 36 and 38 the technical efficiency of the small manufacturing industry was higher than that of the large & medium manufacturing industry. In this respect the performance of the household manufacturing industry was better compared to the small manufacturing industry in Bangladesh. In industry divisions 33, 35, 36 and 38 technical efficiency in the household manufacturing industry was higher in both periods than that of large & medium manufacturing industry, whereas in industry divisions 31 and 32 mean technical efficiency of household manufacturing industry was higher only for the year 1992-93. Stochastic regression based on labor productivity as a dependent variable for the year 1992-93 shows the informal sector to be more efficient than the formal sector.

Let us now see the difference in the estimated mean technical efficiency of the formal and informal sectors in each industry division.

Food, Beverages & Tobacco

The mean technical efficiency of the large & medium manufacturing industry for the year 1989-90 is 0.734 and for the year 1992-93 is 0.796, which means that mean technical efficiency increased by 8.45 percent during the two reference periods. The mean technical efficiency of the small manufacturing industry was 0.445 in 1989-90 and 0.771 in 1992-93. In the small manufacturing industry the mean technical efficiency increased by 73.12 percent during the two reference periods. In both periods the mean technical efficiency of the small manufacturing industry is lower than that of the large & medium manufacturing industry. In the case of the household manufacturing industry the mean technical efficiency was 0.623 in 1989-90 and 0.950 in 1992-93. Mean technical efficiency increased between the two reference periods by 52.58 percent in the household manufacturing industry. But the interesting point is that the mean technical efficiency of the household manufacturing industry was lower in 1989-90 but higher in 1992-93 than that of the large & medium manufacturing industry.

The mean technical efficiency of the small manufacturing industry is lower than that of large & medium manufacturing industry in both periods. But the mean technical efficiency of household manufacturing is higher than that of large & medium manufacturing industry in 1992-93.

By examining the estimated coefficient it is clear that in the formal sector, elasticity of raw materials with respect to gross output is higher than that of labor. But the elasticity of labor with respect to gross output is higher than that of raw materials in the informal sector.

Textiles, Apparel, Leather

The mean technical efficiency of the large & medium manufacturing industry was 0.961 in 1989-90 and 0.794 in 1992-93. In the textiles, apparel & leather sub-sector the mean technical efficiency of the large & medium manufacturing industry declined by 17.43 percent between 1989-90 and 1992-93. For the small manufacturing industry in this sub-sector the computed mean technical efficiency was 0.454 in 1989-90 and 0.765 in 1992-93, which indicates that mean technical efficiency increased by 68.47 per cent from 1989-90 to 1992-93. The estimated mean technical efficiency of household manufacturing was 0.771 in 1989-90 and 0.954 in 1992-93. In the household manufacturing industry mean technical efficiency between these two periods increased by 23.73 per cent.

The mean technical efficiency of the large & medium manufacturing industry is higher than that of the small manufacturing industry in both periods. Though the mean technical efficiency of the "household manufacturing" industry in 1989-90 was lower, in 1992-93 it was higher than that of large and medium manufacturing industry.

The estimated coefficient of labor is lower in the large & medium manufacturing industry but it is higher in the small manufacturing industry.

Wood, Wood Prods., Furniture

The mean technical efficiency of large & medium manufacturing industry was 0.764 in 1989-90 and 0.853 in 1992-93, indicating an 11.65 percent increase in mean technical efficiency between these two periods of time. In the small manufacturing industry of wood, wood products and furniture sub-sector, the mean technical efficiency was 0.453 in 1989-90 and 0.939 in 1992-93. The mean technical efficiency of small manufacturing industry increased by 107.51 percent between these two periods. In case of household manufacturing, the mean technical efficiency was 0.871 in 1989-90 and 0.948 in 1992-93 indicating an 8.93 percent increase of mean technical efficiency from 1989-90 to 1992-93.

The mean technical efficiency of household manufacturing is higher than that of large & medium manufacturing industry in both periods. The mean technical efficiency of small manufacturing industry is higher than that of the large & medium manufacturing industry only in 1992-93.

Paper, Printing & Publishing

In 1989-90 the mean technical efficiency of large & medium manufacturing industry was 0.922, which increased to 0.969 in 1992-93. The rate of increase was 5.13 percent during the two periods. In the case of the small manufacturing industry the mean technical efficiency was 0.786 in 1989-90, which increased to 0.946 in 1992-93. For the small manufacturing industry the rate of increase in mean technical efficiency between the two periods was 20.28 percent. The mean technical efficiency of household manufacturing industry was 0.736 and 0.687 in 1989-90 and 1992-93 respectively. Within these two years the mean technical efficiency of household manufacturing industry decreased by 6.60 percent.

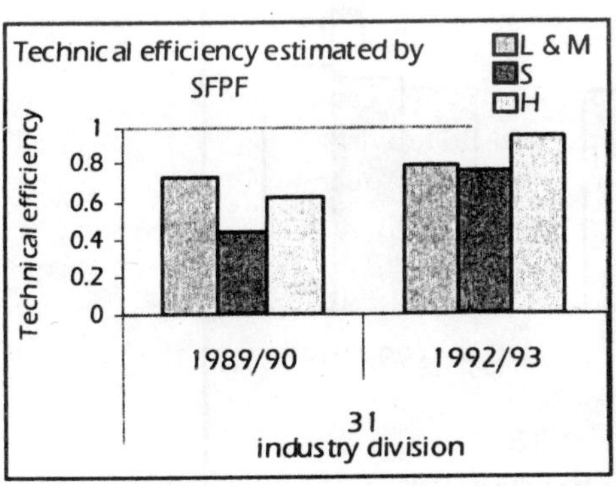

(a)

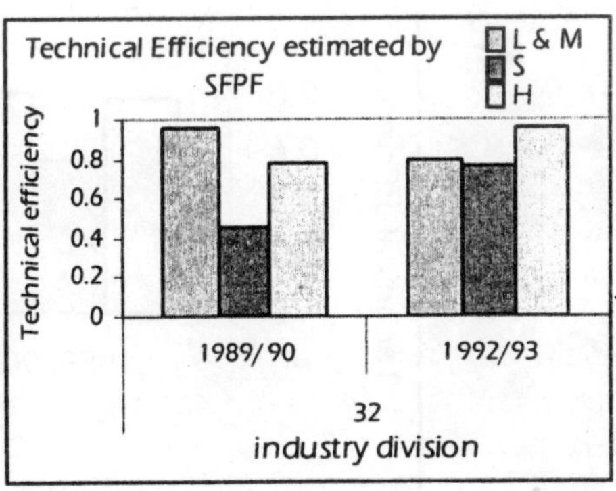

(b)

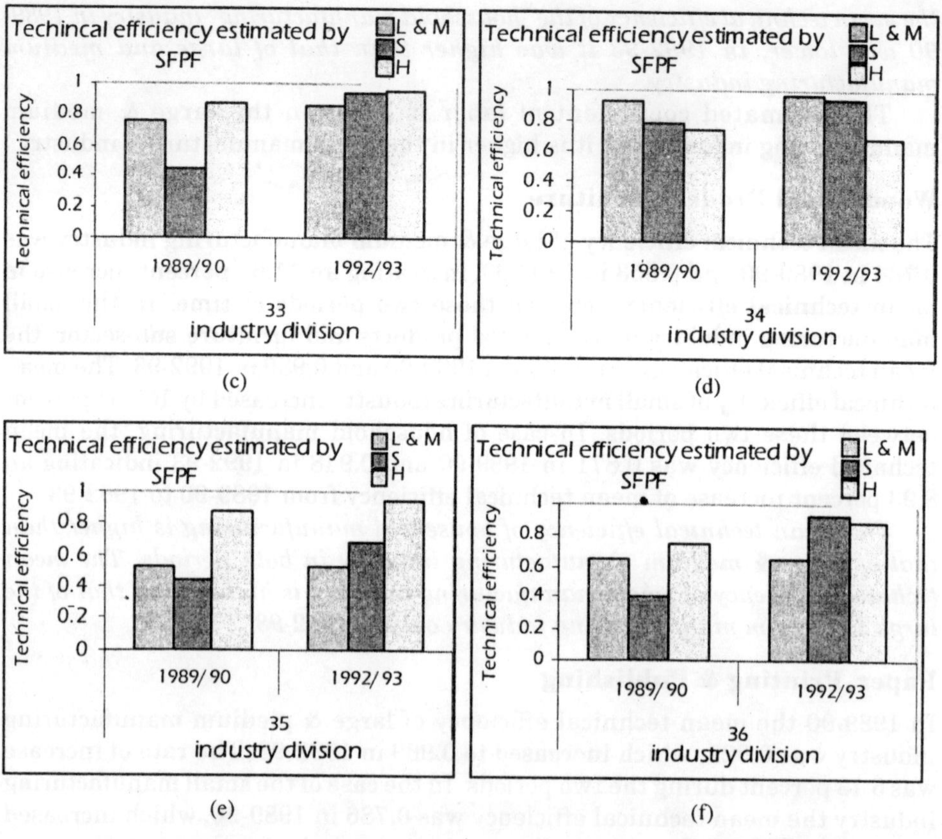

(c) (d)

(e) (f)

Figure 2

Technical Efficiency Estimated by Stochastic Frontier Production Function (SFPF)

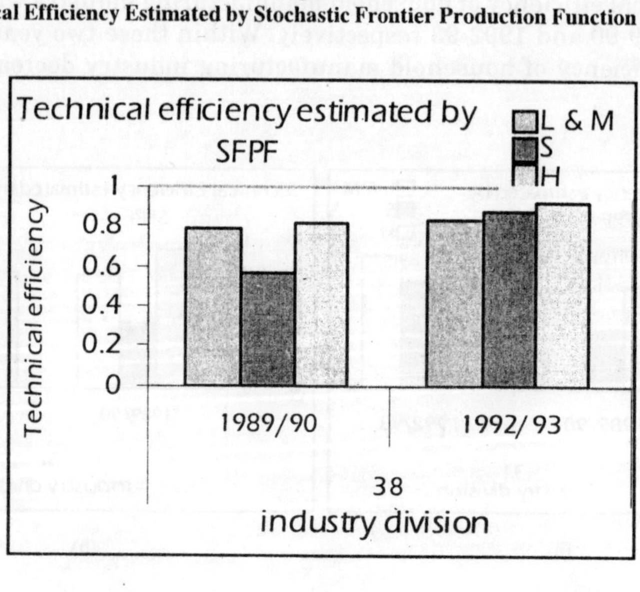

The estimated mean technical efficiency of the paper, printing and publishing sub-sector shows that in both periods it is higher in large & medium manufacturing industry than that of the small and household manufacturing industries.

Chemicals, Rubber, Plastic

In this sub-sector, household manufacturing achieved a higher technical efficiency in both periods than that of the small and large & medium manufacturing industries. For the large & medium manufacturing industry the mean technical efficiency was 0.512 in 1989-90 and 0.528 in 1992-93. For small manufacturing it was 0.436 in 19989-90, which increased to 0.675 in 1992-93. The increase in mean technical efficiency for the small manufacturing industry was 54.83 percent between the two periods. The mean technical efficiency of household manufacturing, was 0.873 in 1989-90 and 0.939 in 1992-93.

Nonmetallic Mineral Products

For both periods the mean technical efficiency of large & medium manufacturing industry in this category, is the same i. e., 0.645. For small manufacturing industries of Non metallic mineral products the mean technical efficiency increased from 0.419 to 0.927 from 1989-90 to 1992-93, indicating a rate of increase by 121 per cent between these two periods. In 1992-93 the mean technical efficiency of small manufacturing industry was higher than that of the large and medium manufacturing industry. *In the household manufacturing industry, the estimated mean technical efficiency was higher than that of large & medium manufacturing industry in both periods*, which was 0.747 in 1989-90 and 0.898 in 1992-93.

Metal Prods., Machinery, Equip.

The mean technical efficiency of large & medium manufacturing industry was 0.791 in 1989-90 and 0.829 in 1992-93. *The mean technical efficiency of household manufacturing industry was higher, than that of large & medium manufacturing industry for both periods.* For the household manufacturing industry, the mean technical efficiency was 0.828 in 1989-90 and 0.927 in 1992-93. *The mean technical efficiency of small manufacturing industry was lower, than that of large & medium manufacturing industry in 1989-90, but was higher in 1992-93.*

From the above analysis, it is clear that in divisions 33, 35 and 36, mean technical efficiency of small manufacturing industry was higher than that of large & medium manufacturing industry in 1992-93 only. In divisions 33 and 35 mean technical efficiency of household manufacturing industry was higher than that of large and medium manufacturing industry for both periods. Except for division 34 mean technical efficiency of household manufacturing industry was higher than that of large & medium manufacturing industry in all divisions in the period 1992-93.

Labor Productivity

By using the Cobb-Douglas production function for the Bangladesh Manufacturing industries, the study has made an attempt to explain the differences in labor productivity.

By dividing both sides of the Cobb-Douglas production function by L, we get

$$\frac{Q}{L} = A\left(\frac{K}{L}\right)^{\alpha} L^{\alpha+\beta-1}\, e^{V} \tag{10}$$

It is assumed that gross output per worker not only depends on capital per worker and total employment but also some other factors that could contribute to an increase in labor productivity. To identify other sources of productivity change, the study introduces efficiency index (EF) and dummy variable, DInf, taking a value of 1 if the industry belongs to the informal sector and 0 otherwise, to the Cobb-Douglas production function, we get,

$$\frac{Q}{L} = A\left(\frac{K}{L}\right)^{\alpha} L^{\alpha+\beta-1} \left(EF\right)^{\varphi} e^{\zeta DInf}\, e^{V} \tag{10.1}$$

Where Q/L is the labor productivity and K/L is the capital intensity. Assuming the largest plants (regardless of ownership) in an industry exhaust available economies of scale, we use the size of the average plant (measured in Gross production) in the size class containing the largest plants within each four-digit industry as a proxy for minimum efficient scale (MES). The EF index is the ratio of total production of the industry to the production of an economically efficient scale of production. The above equation may be rewritten as below:

$$\frac{Q}{L} = A\left(\frac{K}{L}\right)^{\alpha} L^{\Phi} \left(EF\right)^{\varphi} e^{\zeta DInf}\, e^{V} \tag{10.1.1}$$

Taking log of both sides we have,

$$\ln\left(\frac{Q}{L}\right) = \ln A + \alpha \ln\left(\frac{K}{L}\right) + \Phi \ln(L) + \varphi \ln(EF) + \xi\, DInf + V \tag{10.1.2}$$

Where, $\Phi = \alpha + \beta - 1$. If $\Phi > 0$, there is increasing returns to scale; $\Phi = 0$, indicates constant returns to scale; and $\Phi < 0$, indicates decreasing returns to scale. A positive value of j will indicate higher efficiency in larger industry. Similarly, a positive value of "ζ" is interpreted as an indication of greater technical efficiency of the informal sector's industry than that of formal sector's industry.

At this point the stochastic frontier production function has been estimated on the basis of equation 10.1.2 for the year 1992-93. Stochastic regression is rejected in the case of industry divisions 33 and 36. It is found that the DInf variable is significant in all other industry divisions implying that technical efficiency of the informal sector, is higher than that of the formal sector.

VI. CONCLUSION

On the basis of stochastic analysis using two inputs labor and raw materials the study found that the mean technical efficiency in small manufacturing industry increased between the two periods. During 1989-90 mean technical efficiency in the small manufacturing industries for all divisions was lower than in the large & medium manufacturing industries. But during 1992-93 for industry divisions 33, 35, 36 and 38 mean technical efficiency in the small manufacturing industry was higher than in the large & medium manufacturing industry. In this respect the performance of the household manufacturing industry was better than the small manufacturing industry in Bangladesh. In industry divisions 33, 35 and 38 technical efficiency in household manufacturing industry was higher in both periods than in the large and medium manufacturing industry whereas in industry divisions 31, 32 and 36 mean technical efficiency in household manufacturing industry was higher for the year 1992-93 only. Stochastic regression based on labor productivity as a dependent variable for the year 1992-93 shows that the informal sector is more technically efficient than the formal sector.

APPENDIX-I
REGRESSION RESULTS

Table 1 A-1
Results of Stochastic Frontier for Food, Beverages & Tobacco industry

Variables	*Formal Sector*		*Informal Sector*	
	Large and Medium MFG.	*Small manufacturing*	*Household manufacturing*	*Small and Household MFG.*
Constant	1.6720945	3.0700351	0.29491463	3.0953188
	(4.0252234)	(4.1405355)	(8.2875020)	(10.702201)
Labor	0.35713056	0.92131957	0.58497415	0.78839521
	(5.4113129)	(2.7938340)	(1.5271228)	(2.8106029)
Raw materials	0.75577282	0.32493604	0.36293539	0.31313144
	(19.312481)	(3.0852670)	(7.8405606)	(6.8760838)
σ^2	0.12396403	0.23790631	0.20511439	0.31746439
γ	0.10326621	0.68938818	0.12466218	0.34221322
μ	0.22628562	0.25613262	-0.31981248	-0.65921320
η	0.31302102	0.11852769	0.25122426	0.17387654
Log Likelihood Function	-18.278477	-17.246511	-20.971070	-41.436791
LR test	1.6204092	5.4804640	6.2611262	10.480106
1989-90	0.73381850	0.44510322	0.62279955	0.58996488
1992-93	0.79585982	0.77058116	0.95023927	0.89646312
N	50	24	24	48

Table 1 A-2
Results of Stochastic Frontier for Textiles, Apparel, Leather industry

Variables		*Formal Sector*		*Informal Sector*	
		Large and Medium MFG.	*Small manufacturing*	*Household manufacturing*	*Small and Household MFG.*
Constant		1.1313505 (5.7933030)	2.2747460 (4.9445969)	0.21857990 (10.581333)	2.5720886 (10.680493)
Labor		0.25284335 (5.0993727)	1.2583287 (6.7901797)	0.51143466 (3.4340211)	1.0371798 (5.3657846)
Raw materials		0.82223430 (26.350693)	0.35237416 (3.8005371)	0.54901738 (9.3486395)	0.35046017 (7.3047056)
σ^2		0.76381720	0.09673939	0.08390841	0.16024618
γ		0.90307835	0.16362999	0.00609771	0.67775229
μ		-1.6610681	0.25163041	0.045239355	0.20842957
η		-1.9400316	1.1188349	1.7351088	0.12049684
Log Likelihood Function		-16.269668	-18.733496	-5.1965493	-26.854983
LR test		9.9887019	9.0004891	3.5743370	21.814872
Mean	1989-90	0.96139335	0.45431095	0.77119026	0.50348181
efficiency	1992-93	0.79379759	0.76537283	0.95419427	0.80658454
N		40	34	20	54

Tablel A-3
Results of Stochastic Frontier for Wood, Wood Prods., Furniture industry

		Formal Sector		*Informal Sector*	
		Large Medium MFG.	*Small manufacturing*	*Household and manufacturing*	*Small and Household MFG.*
Constant		1.1821162 (2.5318194)	3.4781539 (12.594367)	2.2356738 (31.666392)	3.0949780 (8.6241663)
Labor		0.20328113 (1.7455395)	0.77730592 (2.6790083)	0.59892456 (4.6487996)	0.13199090 (4.8099362)
Raw materials		0.88078822 (9.9555639)	0.25254403 (3.9996758)	0.48113355 (20.893000)	0.18601961 (2.5766045))
σ^2		0.07980242	0.51381032	0.030657092 (2.1080208)	0.11092312
γ		0.07578732	0.01826566	0.022597375 (0.17802082)	0.10135140
μ		0.15553794	0.06127018	0.052641041 (1.5452503)	0.21205861
η		0.54002569	2.6208968	0.92723590 (2.1421403)	1.1251715
Log Likelihood Function		-3.2051884	-60.637572	4.2291704	-14.117057
LR test		1.3229041	9.9821028	1.5802505	9.7995495
	1989-90	0.76438341	0.45261574	0.87066016	0.53258322
	1992-93	0.85344960	0.93923221	0.94843640	0.80690669
N	18	20	14	32	

Tablel A-4
Results of Stochastic Frontier for Paper, Printing & Publishing industry

		Formal Sector	Informal Sector		
		Large and Medium MFG.	*Small manufacturing*	*Household manufacturing*	*Small and Household MFG.*
Constant		2.2103712	3.5991768	0.66986986	3.0095681
		(20.82161)	(4.004251)	(0.7188291)	(7.790180)
Labor		0.7646187	0.6718150	0.65497276	0.6812885
		(12.98666)	(1.407463)	(0.4604491)	(2.400787)
Raw materials		0.4630445	0.1471334	1.0739660	0.3299496
		(13.82010)	(1.535597)	(4.2577746)	(4.737676)
σ^2		0.0149983	0.0891434	0.18537118	0.0848388
		(3.343636)	(2.397068)	(0.7896033)	(2.291693)
γ		0.0151425	0.8197524	0.99999999	0.1672965
		(0.104688)	(0.759766)	(199559.73)	(5.136538)
μ		0.3014053	0.5406498	-0.1437388	0.0753478
		(0.981569)	(0.390834)	(-0.301060)	(2.865395)
η		0.9623378	0.1477608	0.27404110	2.1809193
		(0.971427)	(1.219674)	(0.3794571)	(8.385003)
Log Likelihood Function		11.169286	-2.841085	0.09547820	-4.496422
LR test		0.6926764	2.1846924	0.35623118	15.221363
Mean	1989-90	0.9223206	0.7862047	0.73617370	0.4784753
efficiency	1992-93	0.9696452	0.9456395	0.68758725	0.9171197
N		18	16	8	20

Table A-5
Results of Stochastic Frontier for Chemicals, Rubber, Plastic industry

Variables		Formal Sector	Informal Sector		
		Large and Medium MFG.	*Small manufacturing*	*Household manufacturing*	*Small and Household MFG.*
Constant		0.96978506	3.3554441	1.4254449	3.1077980
		(2.1667476)	(13.908182)	(4.1612477)	(8.3578383)
Labor		1.3326581	1.1932505	0.089372126	0.77989930
		(19.5593)	(15.353334)	(0.56809743)	(3.1802694)
Raw materials		0.5046894	0.22210436	0.80172013	0.38160758
		(11.85154)	(7.8032953)	(12.351816)	(5.7149180)
σ^2		5.4817482	0.25852683	0.077694973	0.17581729
		(1.301906)	(2.2245300)	(2.3070739)	(2.4316823)
γ		0.9772324	0.14473453	0.012732358	0.18671638
		(49.88069)	(0.8905167)	(0.21695734)	(2.3484515)
μ		-4.6290137	0.38687341	0.062904378	0.36236979
		(-1.036466)	(0.5226910)	(0.40002078)	(1.6111929)
η		0.0589634	0.79415857	0.74262247	1.1370346
		(0.788736)	(1.1193361)	(0.69863922)	(3.2265655)
Log Likelihood Function		-47.21591	-14.357142	-2.3065348	-19.280669
LR test		23.82070	4.4752251	0.55691511	14.012921
Mean	1989-90	0.512469	0.43629128	0.87336287	0.32812211
efficiency	1992-93	0.52775529	0.67551209	0.93879980	0.68573759
N		52	18	14	28

Table A-6
Results of Stochastic Frontier for Nonmetallic Mineral Products industry

Variables		*Formal Sector*		*Informal Sector*	
		Large and Medium MFG.	*Small manufacturing*	*Household manufacturing*	*Small and Household MFG.*
Constant		2.0989974	1.1752290	2.4112945	1.8275081
		(5.1425113)	(2.470019)	(63.50706)	(2.504991)
Labor		0.31335013	2.6893138	0.5506323	0.14790368
		(2.7406866)	(3.162631)	(36.32985)	(2.1800626)
Raw materials		0.78497848	0.2432161	0.4731377	0.40632274
		(11.911625)	(1.443500)	(38.09410)	(2.3510838)
σ^2		0.10061733	0.5572063	0.0141178	0.55232167
		(1.5064508)	(0.883072)	(0.595896)	(1.3676347)
γ		0.47930161	0.0026145	0.9885582	0.18412248
		(1.6098175)	(0.149837)	(46.11889)	(0.6077154)
μ		0.43920861	0.0763378	0.0387355	-0.6377925
		(1.6972952)	(1.836093)	(0.193425)	(-0.624418)
η		0.00553443	2.4598747	0.1058899	2.0073120
		(0.0233812)	(5.838403)	(13.19516)	(1.5641061)
Log Likelihood Function		-43.196667	-11.38838	12.207791	-16.302961
LR test		2.3198655	4.6602979	12.969349	2.4917448
Mean	1989-90	0.64489511	0.4194727	0.74708711	0.5099276
efficiency	1992-93	0.64638245	0.9270315	0.8987557	0.8991932
N		22	10	8	14

Table A-7
Results of Stochastic Frontier for Metal Prods., Machinery, Equip., industry

Variables		*Formal Sector*		*Informal Sector*	
		Large and Medium MFG.	*Small manufacturing*	*Household manufacturing*	*Small and Household MFG.*
Constant		1.0105934	4.0242876	1.9160786	0.33786821
		(4.8184678)	(5.9555681)	(7.6171688)	(11.327707)
Labor		0.46132947	0.72502519	0.26185145	0.76831743
		(7.6736036)	(1.3463760)	(1.3410925)	(4.0810298)
Raw materials		0.77473873	0.17638987	0.71163642	0.27954670
		(23.664293)	(3.4756378)	(14.511504)	(22.713060)
σ^2		0.04593164	0.30016127	0.13120175	0.33928101
		(3.1806686)	(2.9354439)	(3.0962580)	(8.9500599)
γ		0.18503370	0.014013716	0.01089319	0.03072124
		(0.8594051)	(2.1876110)	(0.6095350)	(0.7808612)
μ		0.18437898	0.12971314	0.07560970	0.20418750
		(1.0831908)	(1.8261962)	(1.0619383)	(2.0688832)
η		0.23086544	0.15243265	0.89536182	0.96586187
		(0.9495116)	(3.9598170)	(2.7983257)	(2.6809328)
Log Likelihood Function		8.9782687	-39.176474	-10.215547	-69.618341
LR test		3.6904678	4.7197836	1.6565691	8.8077065
Mean	1989-90	0.79107409	0.56037797	0.82805883	0.58879876
efficiency	1992-93	0.82942765	0.87600856	0.92714841	0.81802785
N		74	42	24	74

Table A-8
Results of Stochastic Frontier for Labor Productivity differences: 1992-93

Variable	*31*	*32*	*33*	*34*	*35*	*36*	*38*
Constant	5.28615	4.781873	3.053361	4.72319	7.74521	4.876791	5.419196
	(17.049)	(18.741)	(15.590)	(29.836)	(5.1994)	(2.52526)	(28.4407)
ln(K/L)	8.5633	0.037318	0.078875	0.05030	0.02904	0.133038	-
	(2.0997)	(0.6007)	(1.8714)	(1.3351)	(2.4317)	(1.15719)	0.134405
							(4.06419)
ln(Lab)	0.0177	-	0.003816	-0.02367	-0.21154	-	0.009102
	(0.5455)	0.031797	(0.1098)	(2.7009)	(-3.265)	0.114038	(0.03368)
		(-1.2359)				(-2.4970)	
ln(EF)	0.58006	0.496629	0.435591	0.39563	0.71470	0.388305	0.630353
	(10.351)	(6.8250)	(7.3462)	(3.2794)	(9.3862)	(4.28440)	(21.336)
DInf	1.06757	0.908731	0.725466	0.48720	1.06609	0.927168	0.784101
	(5.0222)	(3.4195)	(3.2305)	(1.4334)	(4.6418)	(3.61907)	(6.11365)
s^2	2.62251	2.551172	0.102614	0.15655	0.727331	0.098369	1.079011
	(1.4944)	(1.7750)	(3.5635)	(4.6970)	(2.43936)	(1.11662)	(1.57043)
g	0.98126	0.974424	0.00086	0.99999	0.986196	0.004411	0.965788
	(49.748)	(39.072)	(0.0399)	(163.81)	(3.96830)	(0.00421)	(52.3859)
m	-3.2083	-3.15336	-0.01878	0.17325	0.160811	-0.04166	-2.04166
	(-1.178)	(-1.477)	(-0.0185)	(1.4967)	(0.19513)	(-0.0209)	(1.16175)
Log Likelihood Function	-37.449	-33.4741	-6.44329	0.31701	-31.9064	-4.63423	-28.8252
LR test	8.50228	6.467352	?	4.51377	3.177022	?	9.595914
Mean efficiency	0.6294	0.63293	0.996505	0.70606	0.528184	0.992279	0.722424
N	49	42	23	19	40	18	70